CONFIGURING CISCO ROUTERS FOR ISDN

McGraw-Hill Cisco Technical Expert Titles

ARS   *Troubleshooting Cisco Internetworks*   *0-07-047235-1*
Fischer   *Configuring Cisco Routers for ISDN*   *0-07-02273-5*
Gai   *Internetworking IPv6 with Cisco Routers*   *0-07-022836-1*
Lewis   *Cisco TCP/IP Professional Reference*   *0-07-041140-1*
Parkhurst   *Cisco Router OSPF Design and Implementation*   *0-07-048626-3*
Sackett   *Cisco Router Handbook*   *0-07-058097-9*
Slattery/Burton   *Advanced IP Routing in Cisco Networks*   *0-07-058144-4*

To order or receive additional information on these or any other McGraw-Hill titles, in the United States please call 1-800-722-4726, or visit us at www.computing.mcgraw-hill.com. In other countries, contact your McGraw-Hill representative.

Configuring Cisco Routers for ISDN

Paul Fischer

McGraw-Hill

New York   San Francisco   Washington, D.C.   Auckland   Bogotá
Caracas   Lisbon   London   Madrid   Mexico City   Milan   Montreal
New Delhi   San Juan   Singapore   Sydney   Tokyo   Toronto

McGraw-Hill

A Division of The **McGraw·Hill** *Companies*

1 2 3 4 5 6 7 8 9 0 AGM/AGM 9 0 3 2 1 0 9 8

ISBN 0-07-022073-5

The sponsoring editor for this book was Steven Elliot, and the production supervisor was Clare Stanley. It was set in Vendome by **TIPS** Technical Publishing.

Printed and bound by Quebecor/Martinsburg.

McGraw-Hill books are available at special quantity discounts to use as premiums and sales promotions, or for use in corporate training programs. For more information, please write to the Director of Special Sales, McGraw-Hill, 11 West 19th Street, New York, NY 10011. Or contact your local bookstore.

This book is printed on recycled, acid-free paper containing a minimum of 50% recycled, de-inked fiber.

CONTENTS

Dedication

To my wonderful wife Martha, without whom this book would not have been possible.

Special thanks to: Anita Szostak for doing most of the illustrations in this book. Though her Macintosh was crashing multiple times a day she still met my deadlines. David Drutz for editing the text before anyone else saw it. John Kincaide, author of *"UNIX Computer Telephony—The Complete Guide,"* for the most awesome book review I have ever seen. Without him this book would not be as good as it is. Larry DeWaard, Margaret Turek, and Dr. Ed Bershoff of BTG, Inc. (NASDAQ: BTGI). Without their loan of Cisco routers this book would not exist.

Additional thanks to book reviewers Bill Davidsen, Hilary Silvert, Chip Bumgardner, Lou Perna, John Yesford, and one kind soul whose name never reached me even though their comments did.

My most heartfelt thanks to the most amazing production crew I have ever worked with—Paulette Miley for copy editing, Connie Hosa for composition, Jessica Ryan for proof reading, Jan Wright for the index, and Robert Kern for project management. Writing a book is a team effort and I feel blessed to have had so many good people helping me.

Foreword

In the Beginning ...

The first router I configured was a Telebit Netblazer. It was the precursor to many of today's dial-in servers. This particular model had eight serial ports connected to five Telebit T3000 rack-mounted modems. It was the most professional wide-area network system I had designed in my career. It provided dial-on-demand access to and from four remote sites equipped with smaller routers from Telebit (Personal Netblazers). The fifth modem was used for a dial-on-demand connection to the Internet.

Over several days, I managed to implement a basic packet-filtering firewall to prevent attacks on the remote sites from the Internet. All told, I spent an entire week setting up the dial-in network and testing access with the smaller routers. Although the WAN was a success, I was not happy with the solution. True, it saved my client thousands of dollars when compared with the cost of 56Kbps leased lines to the same locations. As a bonus, the customer was happy and continued to send work my way.

However, there seemed to be an inherent problem centered on the language used to program the Telebit routers. There were more than 300 lines of router code at the main site. Many lines seemed redundant, and I could never get the hang of it. It was needlessly complex, and it involved too much work for occasional administration. Minor changes could require a whole day and several calls to Telebit for technical support. Although I used the product for other customers' needs, I would never gain confidence with the Telebit router command language. Eventually they would merge with ITK, a German telecommunications company, in August of 1997.

Enter Cisco

A year later (for a different customer), I got the job of installing the Internet connection for the company. The whole thing was a mess. The site systems administrator had quit and no one knew the password for the Cisco router. I had never seen a Cisco router before, but I figured it could not be much worse than Telebit. I rolled up my sleeves and jumped in feet first.

Within an hour, I had gotten a fax from Cisco telling me how to wipe out the router configuration and, by doing so, remove the access and enable passwords. Once that was complete, I obtained the TCP/IP configuration information from the Internet service provider (ISP) and configured the router from the initial configuration dialog. The simplicity and elegance of the Cisco router language awed me. It was intuitive, easy to learn, and—more importantly—easy to read. I was in heaven. I started designing my entire client WAN and Internet connections with Cisco routers and never looked back.

I hope you enjoy learning about Cisco routers as much as I have.

Paul A. Fischer
Vienna, VA
July 1998

Introduction

This book is a hands-on guide to installing and maintaining Cisco routers. It focuses primarily on Cisco routers that use ISDN and modems because they are more complex in configuration than those that use leased lines. It also covers leased-line configurations, including point-to-point lines and Frame Relay connections. In addition, there is extensive information on more advanced topics, such as using your Cisco router as a firewall and setting up DHCP.

This is not a book on TCP/IP (the primary networking protocol used on the Internet). Some basic information is provided here, but you should seek another book, such as *TCP/IP Network Administration* by Craig Hunt (O'Reilly and Associates, 1997), if you need more in-depth information on TCP/IP.

Who Should Read This Book?

These days anyone can find that he or she has accidentally become a network administrator. Accountants and programmers are often singled out for this honor because they are the most technical people in their organizations. I know of at least one case where the person sitting next to the router became the router administrator because his or hers was the only phone that would reach! People who have no background or training in networking and become network administrators are called "accidental" administrators. Accidental administrators are programmers, accountants, managers, and others who (by necessity) have had the responsibility of router maintenance foisted upon them. These people spend their days doing other tasks and only attend to the router when there is a problem. Not steeped in networking knowledge and lore, they usually find network tasks frustrating (especially because most texts are written on the level of networking professionals). Whether you fit this classification or not, this book will be useful if you work with Cisco routers. It's designed to allow you to quickly set up network connections without extensive network training. This is accomplished though the use of actual Cisco router code and detailed explanations of how the code affects the network.

If you are an accidental administrator, this book could be your lifeline when working with your router. If you aren't an AA (Accidental Administrator) and you just want to learn more about configuring routers and designing networks, this book is a good place to start.

Acronyms

As with any technical text, this book relies heavily on acronyms. Wherever possible, the first use of an acronym is expanded to the whole phrase. For your convenience, all acronyms are also referenced in the Glossary at the back of the book.

How Does It Teach?

In this book, we show specific cases of Cisco router connections and describe actual products in detail. Wherever possible, we use the exact IOS (Internetworking Operating System) version and router designation and configuration. A variety of products and scenarios are covered for the greatest possible range of configurations.

The basic approach for networking is to work from the inside of the connection out. A typical connection looks like that in Figure I-1, with one or more telephone companies at the center of the connection (Layer 1). All the telephone companies are collectively known as the Public Switched Telephone Network, or PSTN.

Each end of the network contains a type of digital modem, whether it is an ISDN NT-1 or a CSU/DSU (Channel Service Unit/Data Service Unit) for a leased line (Layer 2). Layer 3, on the outside of the connection, is the router itself. It makes no sense to try to get two routers talking if there is a problem with a cable, data line, or modem between them.

Figure I-1
A basic network design with the PSTN in the center and CSU/DSUs and routers at each end.

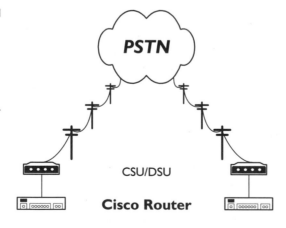

PSTN

CSU/DSU

Cisco Router

In each layer, we will discuss troubleshooting methods designed to help you isolate faults and determine how to correct them. We will also discuss dealing with the telco (telephone company), modem manufacturers, and Cisco Systems, Inc., while attempting to correct problems.

Caveat Router

As router products and versions of IOS change, some of the actual commands change. This is the natural evolution of technical products. We live in a fast-paced world of computer and network products, where new pieces of hardware and software are being released daily. Cisco Systems is no different from any other company in this field.

Because of this, neither the publisher, the author, nor Cisco Systems, Inc., will be held responsible if something in this book does not match your router configuration. We have taken steps wherever possible to provide detailed information on the equipment used to create the configurations used in this book, so that you may emulate them as closely as possible.

In this book, IOS version 11.2(8) and higher is used for IOS router configurations. The 700 series router OS used was version 4.2(1).

Conventions

In the text of the book there are several sections where actual router configuration dialog has been recorded. In these sections you might notice notations such as ^Z, ^D, ^C, and so forth. These notations denote control characters typed into the command line interface of the router. Holding down the Ctrl key on your keyboard while typing a letter produces control characters. For example, if you wanted to enter the control character "Z", you would hold down Ctrl and press "Z". Control characters can also be described with the letters "ctrl-" in front of them, for example, "ctrl-Z."

The Goals of This Book

The goals of this book are to give you a complete set of basic skills for data networking. Although you might not be able to leap a tall network in a single bound when you complete this book, you should understand how to set up and troubleshoot basic data connections. This includes leased-line connections (such as T1, 56K, and Frame Relay) and dial-up connections, such as modems and ISDN.

You will also have an excellent reference for getting into more advanced topics with your Cisco router, including security and network monitoring. Keep this book on your shelf as a reference. All your friends will envy you, not only because it proves you know more about the exciting and fast-paced world of Cisco routers, but also because it is witty beyond all technical books that have come before it.

Finally, this book seeks to make you part of the growing world of Cisco router administrators. Through it, you will uncover references and resources for Cisco routers that you never knew existed. This, in turn, will lead to as many educational opportunities as you wish to have.

If you only want to be a part-time Cisco router manager and not travel the dark mystical paths of the networking guru, use the book sparingly—mostly as a reference. If, however, you seek the higher salaries and nearly infinite tranquility possessed by such network gurus, this book will not get you there.

It just might be the best possible starting point money can buy, though!

CONFIGURING CISCO ROUTERS FOR ISDN

CHAPTER

The History of Cisco

In this chapter we'll discuss some of the major reasons why Cisco products are so successful. This includes management, accounting, and technical reasons. We also discuss some of Cisco's acquisition strategy and study one acquisition in particular.

Why Buy Cisco?

The OSI reference model for networking is a ten-layer model, and the TCP/IP protocol model has eight layers. Most of you know about the standard seven layers in the OSI model listed in Table 1-1:

Table 1-1

The seven-layer OSI networking model

Layer Number	Layer Name
7	Application
6	Presentation
5	Session
4	Transport
3	Network
2	Data Link
1	Physical

Table 1-2 lists the standard five layers in the TCP/IP protocol model.

Table 1-2

The five-layer TCP/IP model

Layer Number	Layer Name
5	Application
4	Transport
3	Network
2	Data Link
1	Physical

Users are mostly concerned with the applications layer, which governs what they see and how they do their work. Network administrators are typically concerned with the transport, network, data link, and physical layers. These network layers need management on a daily basis and provide the infrastructure the users rely on. Apparently, no one is concerned with layers 5 and 6 of the OSI model. Perhaps that is why TCP/IP is the dominant protocol on networks everywhere, because it has already dispensed with two whole layers no one cared about.

But where do the missing three layers come in? These are internal company political layers. Anyone who has been involved in making decisions about networks knows them intimately. They come into play around the conference table when management, accounting, and technical people try to decide which products to use to build their network. The hidden three layers are most appropriately known as the technical layer, the administration (or, more informally, the "boss") layer, and the accounting (or "bean counter") layer.

There are many practical reasons to buy Cisco products that meet the needs of all three hidden layers of the networking models. Technical people know Cisco products are solid and feature-rich. They also know that Cisco support and software distributions are excellent. Management can look at the long prestigious list of Cisco customers and the fact that 85 percent of the Internet backbone (the part of the Internet that links ISPs to each other over extremely high-speed connections) uses high-end Cisco routers. Accounting also likes the price. Although less flexible on pricing than some of their competitors, Cisco reasonably prices their products.

Cisco technical support is legendary in the networking industry. They do true 24x7 support, with support centers in enough time zones to be able to pass problems from engineer to engineer. Their internal trouble-call tracking system allows incoming engineers to track problems as the outgoing engineers go off duty. This allows customers to have continuity in support while they work on a single problem. The customer might not have the manpower to have someone else take up the task when they leave, but Cisco can keep rotating engineers through the problem so that the customer always has fresh technical help. In a real crisis, it is not unheard of for Cisco support engineers to build custom versions of IOS for the customer, thereby getting bug fixes in the hands of users immediately. Cisco tracks these changes to make sure they get back to the mainstream IOS code.

But Cisco support goes way beyond even this. There are multitudes of resources available on Cisco's WWW (World Wide Web) site at http://www.cisco.com. This includes IOS and other software updates, management information bases (MIB) for use with simple network management protocol (SNMP)-based tools (such as HP OpenView and Cisco Works), troubleshooting engines, and documentation. Users who have support contracts can log in to the Web site and gain access to pricing, more technical information, and the ability to open support calls without being forced to wait on hold until a support engineer is available.

Cisco also offers a tantalizing advantage in their training and education opportunities. Aside from the normal array of basic and advanced classes, they also offer certifications. Unlike other certifications such as MCSE (Microsoft Certified Systems Engineer) and CNE (Certified NetWare Engineer), which have tended to become almost ubiquitous in the employment market, the CIE (Cisco Internetworking Expert) is the cream of the crop. CIEs command salaries starting at more than $100,000 per year. It is not a simple course, and less than 7 percent of those who make it to the final exam pass. Those who do, however, can practically write their own ticket in today's job market.

Cisco management tends to focus on what the rest of the companies their size are doing. They also focus on what larger companies are doing, especially companies that are currently where Cisco would like to go in the future. With clear market leadership, Cisco is a manager's dream choice for a network equipment vendor. Companies of all shapes and sizes use Cisco networking equipment. They hold large parts of the market in telecommunications providers, ISPs, large corporate backbones, and wide area networks. Cisco's products scale to support the smallest networking needs (such as simply connecting two sites together) up to huge routers and switches for enterprise-wide networking. They provide products in a multitude of technologies, including ISDN, ADSL, Frame Relay, Ethernet, Fast Ethernet, ATM, and FDDI. Speed for these connections scale from 9600 bits per second and below to one gigabit per second and above. With such a huge range of products and technologies, it is easy to see why corporate management loves Cisco.

Accountants also like Cisco. While their products tend to cost slightly more than the competition, only the shortsighted look at the initial cost of hardware as the sole gauge of the total cost of ownership. Studies have shown for years that administrative and support costs in later years can significantly affect the cost of networking equipment. Some of the things that make Cisco less expensive to operate in the "out" years are low maintenance costs, access to a large pool of trained professionals, and excellent training. The fact that even accidental administrators can run small Cisco networks part time with little or no training also helps keep "out" year costs to a minimum.

Seldom can all three of the "hidden network layers" agree on a single vendor. Many times, votes are cast and recast until a single solution bubbles to the top. Cisco products are always a good compromise if all parties cannot agree outright that Cisco be their one and only network equipment provider.

"I am Cisco of Borg. Resistance is Futile, Prepare to be Assimilated."

Some Information about Cisco

Not into *Star Trek?* Well, the Borg are a half-biological, half-technological interplanetary species that forcefully assimilates other species to improve themselves. (Trust me, the analogy works.)

Cisco Systems, Inc., is the Borg of the networking world. Unlike some companies that might try to develop every new technology that comes along, Cisco assimilates smaller companies that have already developed the technology they want. They do this by purchasing large stakes in these companies or simply buying them outright. This strategy has helped them advance their product line and stock price at a fantastic rate year after year (see Figure 1-2 for a graph of Cisco's stock price). Figure 1-1 shows a timeline of Cisco acquisitions and buy-ins. Although you might not have heard of some of these companies, their products have become some of the products you know and love today.

Figure 1-1
Timeline of Cisco acquisitions and investments.

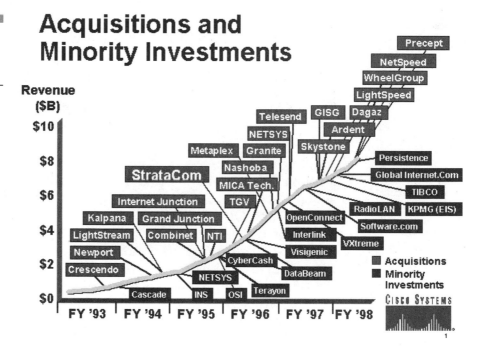

Figure 1-2

As you can see from this graph, a dollar invested in Cisco Systems, Inc., (CSCO on the NASDAQ stock exchange) in March of 1990 would have been worth $65.00 in March of 1998. By comparison, a dollar invested in the Dow Jones Industrial Average would only be worth $5.00.

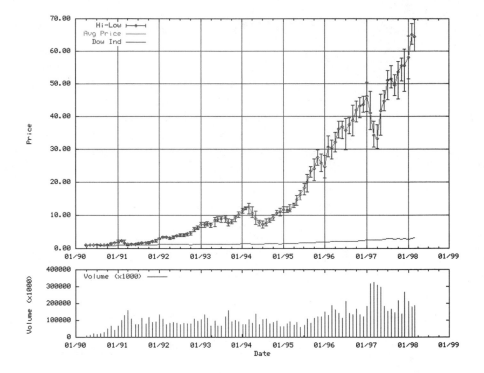

The Combinet Acquisition: A Case Study

Other companies have sometimes handled a strategy of acquisition badly, resulting in poor products, a large loss of technical knowledge through attrition, or poor support for old and new products resulting from apathy. When Cisco wanted to enter the rapidly growing ISDN SOHO (Small Office/Home Office) and RO (Remote Office) market, they purchased Combinet. If the Combinet acquisition is any measure of Cisco commitment to companies they assimilate, then clearly they do not suffer from these particular failings.

Combinet's main product was a small router with single ISDN and single Ethernet ports. It was slow to boot, cumbersome to work with, and hard to upgrade, and it did not support the Novell IPX/SPX networking protocol. However, it was stable and, once configured, ran for a long time without problems. Cisco initially repackaged the Combinet products as the Cisco 750 series of ISDN routers. They added support for the Novell protocol, added more IOS-like commands, and also added more command-line help.

Shortly after releasing the Cisco 750 router series, Cisco introduced the 760 series. These routers had a markedly different appearance. Their edges were smoother and rounder. They stacked well on top of each other, while still providing the necessary airflow to keep them from overheating, and they looked far more modern. Technically speaking, this was far more than a repackaging of Combinet's products. The Cisco 760 series boots in less than one quarter the time that it takes a 750 to boot. It also synchronized with the phone company (telco) lines faster, making the leap from power on to connection in record time. Further, the 760 series marked the first time Cisco ISDN routers had POTS (Plain Old Telephone Service) ports on the back, making them more than just a router. Now a small or home office could be supplied completely and flexibly with voice, fax, and data connections at a fraction of the previous cost. To top it all off, the initial cost on the 760 routers was less than the 750's cost.

Cisco has continually advanced their product line with the technical capabilities assimilated from Combinet ever since the acquisition. They have recently released the 770 series of routers, which replace the single Ethernet port in the 760 series with a four-port Ethernet hub. Cisco has likely used technology acquired from Combinet to introduce and expand the ISDN capabilities on the 1600, 2500, 2600, and 3600 router series. New features continue to make the products more useful to the SOHO and RO network user. These have included staggeringly useful capabilities like DHCP (Dynamic Host Configuration Protocol) and NAT (Network Address Translation).

The DHCP protocol allows the router to configure automatically client workstation network parameters. NAT allows a SOHO or RO network to hide behind a single network address issued by an ISP. NAT saves you money on your Internet connection (making many users look like one to the Internet) and acts as a virtually unbreakable security firewall, because no one can make a connection into your private network behind the router.

Although it is only one example in a long history, the Combinet acquisition illustrates the synergy attainable if "assimilation" is handled properly. By strengthening their product line through acquisition without suffering any of the downsides, Cisco has become an excellent case study for both managerial and technical techniques. Many large companies have earned bad reputations for improper handling of mergers and acquisitions, but so far, Cisco is not one of them.

Is the Author in Cisco's Pocket?

After reading this chapter some of my friends told me I sound as if I were in Cisco's pocket. Although this chapter might lead you to believe I am, that simply is not true. My friends are used to reading Microsoft books where the author has nothing but praise for the monolithic software giant. Having dealt with Microsoft for a long time, I can easily list 20 major problems with their products that they do not admit to. Fortunately for me, I can not do the same for Cisco, either for their products or for their technical support.

Although I cautiously praise Cisco in this chapter, I do so from personal experience. In my five-year association with Cisco, the good experiences have far outweighed the bad. I have always received competent and consistent technical support regardless of the cost of the maintenance contract I was using. I am still amazed that they treat a US$100 support contract the same as a US$10,000 support contract.

If forced to list my worst experiences, there are two that immediately come to mind. The first is the general turnover in their sales group, which sometimes has left me unable to get a quote for equipment. The second happened just before publication. My employer purchased on-site installation for a large network installation we were doing. Multiple Cisco representatives were constantly contacting me, asking if I needed help. This became quite an annoyance when I was unable to complete a simple configuration change because I was paged four times within a half hour's time. Each call was another helpful Cisco employee asking if I needed any help.

Sometimes this chapter is a bit too pro-Cisco even for me. This is simply a reflection of my personal experiences with the company. I hold no illusions of their being perfect; no large corporation is. They are simply a reflection of their policies and people, and what I have seen of them has been awesome.

PART

1

Cisco Products

## CHAPTER 2

Cisco Hardware

To say that Cisco Systems, Inc., has a few products is like saying McDonald's sells a few hamburgers. Since 1984, Cisco has improved their original routers, enhancing features both in hardware and in operating system software, mounting success upon success. Most of the *big iron* (that's industry-speak for large expensive pieces of equipment) Cisco sells will only be seen by a few highly trained network engineers. Folks who are full-time, part-time, and accidental network administrators will most likely only see Cisco's smaller offerings.

These smaller products have become commodities since the advent of the Internet (it's that World Wide Web thing, and if you don't know about it by now, I'm certainly not going to let you in on the secret). Routers used to be specialty items—seldom seen, and only sold as part of communications packages by network design and trouble-shooting companies, or by large telephone companies. Now every Mom-and-Pop ISP (Internet Service Provider), two-bit consultant, and mail-order catalog has routers, hubs, cabling, and other hard-core data communications gear available. All you need is a credit card, and a Cisco router can be at your door in a few short hours, sooner if you're in a major metropolitan area.

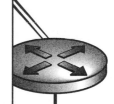

We will focus on a small cross section of Cisco routers, primarily, those available as commodity products and the series just above them. This will provide a broad overview of what products are available and suggest how to use them. Most of the commodity routers come in fixed configurations, although each router series has several variants available. The newer and higher-end routers are available in modular configurations. These tend to be more expensive and much harder to configure, although they're extremely flexible. Additionally, you will need to understand what external, non-Cisco products are required to make the router talk to phone company networks and, also, what highly specialized cables are necessary.

Hardware Platforms and How They Differ

In this book, we will cover seven different series of router and two different series of access server. The 700, 1000, 1600, 2500, 2600, 3600, and 4x00 family of routers will be covered, as well as the AS5200 and AS5300 access servers. Before we go any further, it's important to let you know that access servers are also routers, but specialized in the task of supporting dial-in users on modems, ISDN lines, or both.

Most of these routers run the Cisco IOS (Internetwork Operating System). This is one of the major advantages of Cisco routers in the marketplace. Once you learn to perform a task on one Cisco router, you can perform that task on any other router that runs the IOS. Only a few routers do not support IOS; among them are the Cisco 700 series of ISDN access routers, which came out of Cisco's acquisition of Combinet.

Choosing the Right Router

If you are in the unenviable position of having to choose a router for the first time, there are some basic things you need to understand first. Simply ordering a router does not mean that it will work in your environment. Cisco has more than 25 different versions of their highly successful 2500 series routers. How will you know which one is good for you?

First, you must have a clear understanding of what the current requirements for the router are. What will it do (that is, route, bridge, firewall)? What types of network media (for example, Ethernet, Token

Ring) will you connect to the router? What types of wide area network connections (for example, ISDN BRI, T1, Frame Relay) will it have? Once you know this, you must ask yourself what future demands will be made on it and plan your requirements accordingly.

Plan your network equipment with the future in mind. Although this is difficult and future needs can be vague, a little extra time spent up front can make for a more flexible network. Routers can see service in multiple locations years after their initial configuration and installation. Understanding that networks are usually totally different in implementation than when we first conceive them should help you see more possibilities for future uses of the equipment. Even if you never expect the router to have more tasks than what you first conceive, you should consider spending more money on it, because it might one day move on to another part of the network where a more robust router is needed.

Once you know your current and future network hardware needs, you need to look at other concerns. Different Cisco routers have different types of memory. Some have more than one type, including flash, boot flash, main RAM, shared RAM, and non-volatile RAM. Your network protocol and service needs will determine what version of IOS software will be necessary; that, in turn, will determine the minimum amounts of memory you need. It is strongly recommended that you purchase more memory than the strict minimum. More memory helps the router handle heavy loads better and allows it to buffer more packets.

Over time, your needs will change, and software will grow to consume more RAM. If, in the future, you need to upgrade memory (a physical component) to support new software, it will require taking the router out of service and physically upgrading it. Adding memory or any physical component requires physical access to the router and expertise to insure that the router is not damaged in the process. This is trivial for small networks, but in wide area networks can pose a much larger problem and involve greater cost (usually plane tickets and hotel rooms—or bus tickets and a sleeping bag if your company is cheap). You also need more time to take the router apart properly to reassemble and test it. Also, if by some small chance you have a bad component, you might not find out about it until much later, requiring several trips to complete the repairs. These things lengthen the down time, and add more risk. Best to try to avoid them by stocking up on RAM at the beginning, if you can.

Once you know what your needs are, you should look through this partial list of Cisco products. It's always best to make sure all models listed here are available, and to find out what new ones have been introduced to the market. It is also an excellent idea to stay in the same router family if you can when building a network. Networks have a tendency to grow beyond the size and scope of their initial design. If you spend a little more to stay in one family of routers, you get a deeper understanding of that family and save yourself from possibly having to learn multiple ways of doing the same thing. You will also find your parts exchanges and hardware upgrades easier to design, implement, and document.

In order to make it easier for you to select the right router for you, Table 2-1 condenses the important information you'll need to consider when choosing a router. Following the table, the text lists each router family in terms of general specifications; next, each member product of that family is listed, detailing its differences. In the case of completely modular routers, like the Cisco 4x00 family, many (but not all) of the available network modules are listed, including the maximum number of each module allowed in each type of chassis.

Table 2-1

List of routers and their basic differences; ISDN support can be added to a router wherever the word "Module" is used

Router	Processor	Main Memory	Modular	ISDN BRI	ISDN PRI	IOS
700 Series	Intel 80386 25MHz	1.5-2.0MB	N	Y	N	N
1000 Series	Motorola 68360	8-16MB	N	Some	N	Y
1600 Series	Motorola 68360 33MHz	2-18MB (2-24MB model 1605-R)	Y	Some and Module	N	Y
2500 Series	Motorola 68030 20MHz	8-16MB (4-16MB CFRAD)	2524 and 2525	Some and Module	N	Y
2600 Series	Motorola MPC860 40MHz	16-64MB	Y	Module	N	Y
3620	IDT R4700 80MHz	16-64MB	Y	Module	Module	Y
3640	IDT R4700 100MHz	16-128MB	Y	Module	Module	Y
4000-M	Motorola 68030 40MHz	8-32MB	Y	Module	Module	Y
4500-M	IDT Orion 100MHz	1632MB	Y	Module	Module	Y
4700-M	IDT Orion 133MHz	16-64MB	Y	Module	Module	Y
AS5200	Motorola 68030 20MHz	8-16MB	Y	N	Module	Y
AS5300	R4700 150MHz	32-64MB	Y	N	Module	Y

700 Series Routers

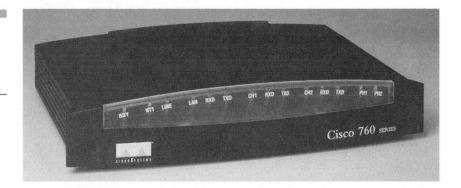

Figure 2-1
Cisco's 760 and 770
family of routers
share the same bold
look.

The Cisco 700 series of routers has three main families: the 750, 760, and 770. The 750 family has been discontinued; it was basically the acquired Combinet product repackaged with a Cisco logo. The 760 family was a major leap forward from the original 750s. It had much more aesthetic packaging and a whole slew of options and features (like address translation and POTS ports) not available on the 750s. The Cisco 770 family added the option of a built-in four-port hub instead of a single Ethernet port, giving SOHO (Small Office/Home Office) users a single piece of equipment to supply all their phone and networking needs.

Both the 760 and 770 family of routers are identical inside the box. They are powered by a 25MHz Intel 80386 microprocessor and have 1.5MB standard DRAM (upgradeable to 2.0MB), 1MB Flash memory, and 16KB NVRAM. All versions include many standard features, including:

■ Cisco Fast Step Windows-based GUI and Cisco Clickstart Web-based GUI for simplified configuration

■ Dynamic addressing of the Cisco 700 family and remote workstations, which eases configuration and network management issues

■ Port and address translation for creating private networks and an additional layer of network security

■ Dial-on-demand routing, which transparently dials the ISDN line only when it is needed and then automatically takes the connection down, saving money on per-minute connection costs

■ Multilink PPP for standards-based B-channel aggregation (RFC1717)

■ Snapshot routing for IP and IPX, which prevents the ISDN line from being dialed only to exchange periodic routing updates

■ Available STAC data compression for throughput of up to 512Kbps (for software versions supporting compression)

■ PAP, CHAP, PPP dial-back, caller ID, and access lists protect network resources from unauthorized access

■ Remote management and monitoring using SNMP, Telnet, and the console port

■ Support for all major ISDN central office switches worldwide

Those routers that include POTS ports also provide:

■ Analog telephone ports for sharing the ISDN BRI line with devices such as standard telephones, fax machines, and modems

■ DTMF support for basic network configuration of the Cisco 700 family with a push-button telephone, after which a network manager can dial into the Cisco 700 to complete the installation

In addition, some versions of 700 series routers have a built-in NT-1 device for North America and an external S/T port for support of additional ISDN devices, such as ISDN telephones.

The 760 and 770 family of ISDN BRI (Basic Rate Interface) routers are available in several variants. For a list of variants and part numbers, see Table A-1 in Appendix A.

Figures 2-2A and 2-2B

The rear view of a Cisco 766-M. Shown (from left to right) are the 9-pin serial port, Ethernet port, Ethernet crossover switch, ISDN S/T, ISDN U, POTS 1 and 2, power input, and power switch. The 776-M router is identical to the 766-M, except for three additional Ethernet ports in place of the Ethernet crossover switch.

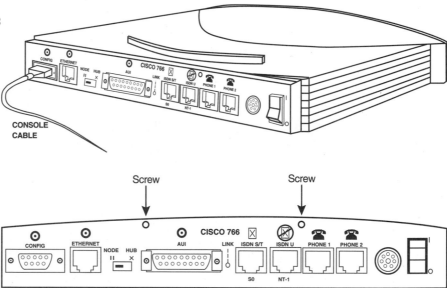

As you read through the book and learn more about Cisco routers and ISDN, you'll find it easier to determine which of these features you'll need. You should always check with your Cisco authorized contacts to make

sure you order the right router for your location. Several of these routers come in different "flavors" to support the different ISDN standards in Japan, Canada, Netherlands, Taiwan, Singapore, and so forth. Never believe that a router built for the United States will work in Australia without checking first!

The operating system software for all Cisco routers must be purchased separately, and the Cisco 700 series is no different. However, it is different from most Cisco routers because it does not run IOS. There are only two different packages available for the Cisco 760 and 770 family of routers: the Internet Ready Feature Set and the Remote Office Feature Set. The Internet Ready Feature Set is designed for a SOHO environment connecting to the Internet or a corporate WAN using only the TCP/IP protocol. It supports a maximum of four devices on the network (PCs, network printers connected to the Ethernet not to PCs, and so forth). Users who have more than four devices might experience problems with this feature set.

The Remote Office Feature Set is designed for remote offices. It adds the Novell IPX/SPX protocol, on-the-fly data compression, and support for 1,500 devices on the network. For users whose ISP or corporate WAN supports on-the-fly data compression, the additional $140 cost for purchasing the Remote Office Feature Set can be justified by the increased connection speed alone. On-the-fly compression can provide as much as four times the effective speed of your WAN connection, depending on the data you are transferring.

1000 Series Routers

Figure 2-3
The Cisco 1000, designed for remote office WAN connections using ISDN or leased lines, is the lowest cost IOS-based router.

The Cisco 1000 series routers were the lowest cost IOS-based routers available when they were available. They have been discontinued, but they are listed here because you might run into one in the field. There are only three variants available: the 1003, 1004, and 1005. This makes the 1000 series router one of the smallest in Cisco's product line. (See Table A-2 in Appendix A for a list of part numbers and features.)

The Motorola 68360 microprocessor powers all series 1000 routers. Each router ships with 8MB of main memory and no Flash memory. Standard features for all 1000 series routers include:

- One Ethernet 10BaseT port (RJ-45)
- One console port (RJ-45)
- One WAN port: either DB-60 for serial, or RJ-45 for ISDN BRI
- One slot for an optional PCMCIA Flash memory card
- Software boot using TFTP over an Ethernet LAN connection or using the optional Flash memory card
- IP, IPX, and AppleTalk routing
- Support for the following WAN encapsulations: HDLC, LAPB, Frame Relay, SMDS, X.25, PPP, and SLIP
- Router management through the console port or over the network using SNMP or Telnet
- AutoInstall for downloading configuration files automatically over a WAN
- LAN-to-LAN DDR routing over ISDN and modem lines

Figure 2-4
Rear view of Cisco 1003 and 1004 router shows (from left to right): an ISDN BRI port, a 10BaseT Ethernet port, the console serial port, the PCMCIA slot, and the power input.

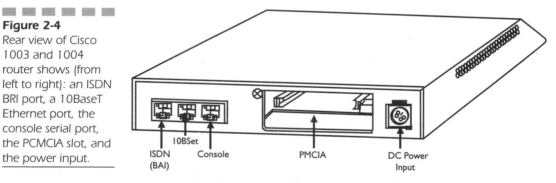

Figure 2-5
The rear view of the Cisco 1005 exchanges the ISDN port for a serial port.

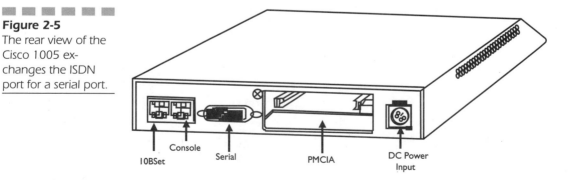

The 1003 and 1004 use ISDN BRI for their WAN connection; the 1005 uses a serial port capable of both synchronous and asynchronous communications. In order to make an ISDN connection, the 1003 requires an external NT-1; the 1004 has one built in. Targeted for the remote office market and not the SOHO market, neither has the POTS ports that are available on the 700 series routers. The ISDN service provider supplies the NT-1 connection worldwide (except in North America, where the NT-1 is supplied by the customer). Therefore, the Cisco 1004 router is for use in North America, and the Cisco 1003 router is applicable worldwide.

Designed for use with external serial-device WAN connections, the 1005's singular WAN port (DB-60) supports asynchronous serial communications at speeds up to 115.2Kbps. Also supported are synchronous connections (such as leased lines, Frame Relay, switched 56Kbps, SMDS, and X.25) at speeds up to 2.048Mbps. Asynchronous connections typically take place over a modem, although other equipment can be used. Synchronous communications use CSU/DSUs, which convert the digital signal used by the router to the one used across the phone company network. Many types of synchronous communications gear are available, and the type of connection you use will determine what type of external gear you'll need.

One of the most intriguing parts of this series of routers is a PCMCIA slot for a Flash memory card. In Cisco routers, the router operating system is generally stored in Flash memory, which is usually internal to the router only. You can readily swap the PCMCIA Flash memory card loaded with your IOS software in and out, making IOS upgrades amazingly easy.

With a small set of spare Flash memory cards, a WAN administrator could upgrade an entire WAN by loading the latest version of IOS on the spare cards and sending them out to the LAN administrators in the field. When they arrive, the LAN administrators could swap them out during a maintenance window, check the new code for proper operation, and return the old cards if the upgraded IOS is working properly. The WAN administrator can then load the latest version of IOS on the returned cards and send them out to other sites. The cycle would repeat itself until all sites had the same version of IOS. Should anything go wrong, all that is necessary is to place the old Flash card back in the router, and the site is immediately restored to operational status.

The series 1000 routers use Cisco IOS as their operating system. There are four basic versions available for routing and bridging with this series:

- IP Only
- IP/IPX
- IP/AT (Apple Talk)
- IP/IPX/AT

You can also get IOS versions designated PLUS, PLUS 40, or PLUS 56. The PLUS feature set contains additional features, such as NAT, data encryption, RADIUS, OSPF, and Network Timing Protocol (NTP). VPDN (L2F tunneling) and RADIUS are available on the PLUS feature sets starting with Cisco IOS Release 11.2(10)P. 11.3.PLUS 40 and PLUS 56 add 40-bit and 56-bit DES (Data Encryption Standard) encryption capabilities providing additional security by protecting network traffic over public networks (but you should be aware that 56-bit DES was thought to be secure until it was broken in July 1998). All these choices can make selection difficult. However, many feature sets cost the same, and therefore it is possible to upgrade your license in the future free of charge.

1600 Series Routers

Figure 2-6
The Cisco 1600 routers have a real space-age look. It would not look out of place sitting on the navigation console in a Star Trek episode.

The Cisco 1600 is at the low end of an extremely flexible class of routers that also includes the 2600 and 3600. The product is sleek, stylish, and very flexible. Most variants come with one Ethernet and one WAN interface, while the 1605-R has only two Ethernet ports. All come with one WAN interface card slot to add optional WAN interface cards (WICs). The WAN interface cards used in the 1600 series are interchangeable with 2600 and 3600 routers as well. This makes for extreme flexibility across a business. (See Table A-3 in Appendix A for a full list of 1600 series variations.)

As with the 700 and 1000 series, the 1600 series of Cisco routers is too narrow to fit in a standard 19″ communications rack. This makes it more suited to environments where it will sit on a shelf, probably on top of the Ethernet hubs that provide LAN services for small offices. In a situation where an ISDN BRI WAN connection serves a small office and two Ethernet segments need to have different security policies, the 1605-R with an ISDN BRI card is the perfect solution. It is the lowest-cost router Cisco makes that provides dual Ethernet and ISDN capabilities. The same configuration in a Cisco 2600 chassis would cost nearly twice the price. Network managers looking for the best price/performance ratio should take a good long look at the 1600 series.

A Motorola 68360 microprocessor running at 33MHz powers all 1600 series variants. Most ship with 2MB of main memory and 4MB of Flash memory. Main memory tops out at 18MB, and Flash tops out at 16MB. The exception is the 1605-R. It ships with 8MB of main memory and 2MB of Flash and tops out at 24MB of main memory and 16MB of Flash. While this might seem odd, there is a good reason for it. The Cisco 1601-1604 routers have a "Run from Flash" architecture. This means that operating system software is stored in Flash memory uncompressed and executed from Flash memory. The Cisco 1605-R router has a "Run from RAM" architecture. Software is stored in Flash memory compressed and executed from RAM. The **-R** suffix designates run from "RAM."

The 1600 series is a big step up from the entry-level 1000 series. Not only is the router more flexible, but the software offers features that are usually unheard of in routers of this price range. These software features include:

- Advanced security, including optional integrated firewall, encryption, and virtual private network (VPN) software
- Network Address Translation (NAT), which reduces the cost of Internet access
- End-to-end quality of service (QoS) and multimedia support
- Integrated data service unit/channel service unit (DSU/CSU) up to T1 speed and integrated Network Termination (NT-1)
- Multi-protocol routing and transparent bridging for IP, IPX, AppleTalk, and IBM/SNA protocols
- WAN optimization features, such as dial-on-demand routing (DDR), bandwidth-on-demand (BOD), Open Shortest Path First (OSPF) on-demand circuit, snapshot routing, compression, filtering, and spoofing to reduce WAN costs

Figure 2-7
The back of the well-designed 1600 series router makes configuration and maintenance easy. Also shown are examples of an expansion card and a PCMCIA card.

There is a dizzying array of software images available for the 1600 series. These include all possible mixes of IP, IPX, AppleTalk, and IBM protocols, with additional feature sets of FIREWALL, PLUS, PLUS 40, and PLUS 56. Remember, you only need to license the feature sets you are going to use from day one. You can always upgrade your IOS license later if your requirements change.

The 1600 series is an excellent small office and Internet router. In cases where a full-blown firewall is too expensive, a 1600 with IP and FIREWALL feature sets helps insure network security while keeping the total cost for access and security under $3,000.

2500 Series Routers

Figure 2-8
The Cisco 2500 series router might not be pretty, but it's the workhorse of many networks.

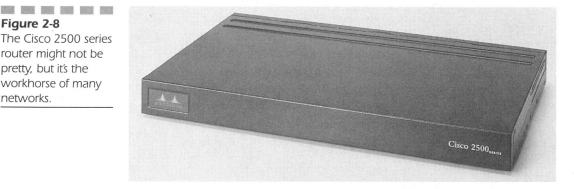

For the most part, the Cisco 2500 series routers are fixed-configuration routers. They are one of the oldest products in Cisco's product line, and the number of variants has grown because of low price and high popularity. They offer quite a variety of features, each filling its own niche in the marketplace. The 2500 series can be divided into several families based on these features: LAN/WAN, Access Server, Dual LAN/WAN, Hub, Frame Relay Access Devices (FRAD), and Modular.

The LAN/WAN family consists of the 2501 through 2504 routers. These offer one Ethernet or Token Ring port, two high-speed serial ports, and (in the 2503 and 2504) an ISDN BRI port. The Access Server family consists of the 2509 through 2512 routers. These offer one Ethernet or Token Ring port, two high-speed serial ports, and either 8 or 16 low-speed serial ports (typically for modems or dumb terminals). The Dual LAN/WAN family (consisting of the 2513 through 2515 routers) offers two Ethernet or Token Ring, or one of each and two high-speed serial ports. The Hub family consists of the 2505, 2507, and 2516 through 2519 routers. These offer dual high-speed serial and either 8, 14, 16, or 23 Ethernet, or 14 or 23 Token Ring ports.

The Frame Relay Access Devices (FRAD) family has only four variants: 2520 through 2523. Each of these can come configured normally or in one of two subvariants. The normal model has a single Ethernet or a Token Ring port and two high-speed serial ports, one ISDN BRI port, and two or eight low-speed asynchronous serial ports. The first subvariant is the CF or CFRAD. This subvariant disables the LAN and ISDN ports in software thereby supporting only serial communications connections in the local office and over a WAN. It is designed to allow customers to migrate their branch-to-SNA host access from dedicated Synchronous Data Link Control (SDLC) links to Frame Relay services with a cost-effective, reliable solution.

The second subvariant is the LF or LAN FRAD. This subvariant disables the ISDN port in software. It allows customers to purchase an ISDN hardware port now, but not pay the full price for it until they are ready to use it. The LAN/WAN family also comes in CFRAD-, LAN FRAD-, and ISDN-only subvariants. The ISDN subvariant disables the high-speed serial ports, allowing only the ISDN port to provide WAN connectivity.

This might seem strange, but you can buy network ports to meet future needs without paying full price. These ports come disabled and can be activated later. This cost reduction is not immediately evident, because FRAD and ISDN subvariant routers cost more than their fully enabled counterparts. You save when you purchase the IOS software. All Cisco 2500 series routers require an IOS software purchase as a separate item, except for FRAD and ISDN subvariants. These routers include IOS software in their list price, which saves you several hundred to several thousand dollars. A simple upgrade of your IOS license and the disabled router ports come alive, ready for you to expand their role in your network.

The Modular family consists of the 2524 and 2525 routers. These routers offer one Ethernet or Token Ring port and three optional WAN module slots. WAN modules are available in the following modules:

- 2-Wire Switched 56-Kbps DSU/CSU
- 4-Wire 56/64Kbps DSU/CSU
- Fractional/Full T1 DSU/CSU
- Synchronous serial five-in-one high-speed serial port
- ISDN BRI with ST bus connector
- ISDN BRI with NT-1 and U bus connector

These modules go beyond the normal Cisco fixed configuration routers by allowing you the choice to incorporate normally external devices into the router. All other 2500 series routers require external CSU/DSUs and ISDN NT-1s to complete their WAN port connections. However, the 2-wire 56Kbps, 4-wire 56/64Kbps, fractional/full T1, and ISDN U bus modules allow you to integrate them directly into the router. The five-in-one (which is, basically, a high-speed serial port) and ISDN S/T bus modules require external devices like all other series 2500 routers.

Purchasing a series 2500 modular router and WAN modules that integrate external devices like DSU/CSU's and NT-1s is not a clear-cut decision. Although the base cost difference can be negligible in some cases, the costs can quickly skyrocket past that of a fixed configuration router and external devices. However, you must consider more than just cost when you evaluate their overall worth in your network design. By bringing external devices into the router, you gain control over them through IOS. This can be a big plus if you have no technical people on-site. These cards give you the ability to configure, monitor, and test data lines from the router, rather than talking site personnel through the use of external versions of these devices.

Another consideration is the inability to create hardware configurations that do not exist in fixed configuration routers. The three WAN slots are not identical: Two are for serial WAN connections, and one is for ISDN. If Cisco had enabled the end user to create a triple ISDN BRI router, they would have added a real asset to the 2500 series. This would allow users to have a small entry-level ISDN hub at a main office to experiment with multiple ISDN line connections for remote offices and home users.

For a complete listing of 2500 series router variations, see Table A-4 in Appendix A.

A Motorola 20-MHz 68030 microprocessor powers all 2500 series routers. This is not enough power, however, to run certain high-end applications like BGP (Border Gateway Protocol, a memory-intensive dynamic routing protocol), packet filtering, and other firewalling and high-speed multi-protocol routing over LANs and WANs. Although the 2500 series is one of the most flexible low-end routers Cisco sells, keep in mind when selecting it for a particular application that it is also the oldest. In most cases, such as Internet access at speeds up to dual T1/E1, you will have no problem. Only once you add other applications to the 2500 will you begin encountering bottlenecks because of its older processor.

The 2500 series routers ship with a minimum of 8MB of Flash memory, except for the mission-specific routers, like CFRAD and LAN FRAD sub-variants, which require only 4MB of Flash memory. However, depending on the Cisco IOS release that you order, it might require more. You can install one or two Flash SIMMs, but never more than 16MB total. If you install dual Flash SIMMs, they must be the same size. Cisco installs DRAM as required by the IOS version ordered. Possible DRAM configurations are 4MB, 8MB, or 16MB. In each case, 2MB of DRAM is reserved for shared memory and the rest is used for main router memory. Refer to Cisco's IOS software configuration Web pages to determine your memory needs.

You should seriously consider purchasing extra DRAM and Flash memory for your router from the beginning. Series 2500 routers require you to open the router and add or replace memory SIMMs to perform memory upgrades. This might be a task too complex and delicate for accidental administrators and non-technical personnel. IOS versions will likely only get larger and consume more memory. By configuring your routers with extra memory initially, you will ease upgrades to future releases and enhanced feature sets.

All series 2500 routers come with a console and an auxiliary port. Both are low-speed asynchronous serial ports that have RJ-45 connectors. Both can be used for terminal connections, but only the console port is active during boot and the initial configuration dialog. In addition, logging is, by default, on for the console port and cannot be turned off. Many sites connect a modem to the auxiliary port. This can allow dial-in terminal connections for Telnet and rlogin sessions to host computers, as well as for remote router maintenance. You can also configure the port to support dial-in WAN connections using protocols like PPP (Point-to-Point Protocol). This could be used for many applications, including remote access to the LAN, remote router configuration, and dial-on-demand routing to back up a full-time WAN connection.

Figure 2-9
The back end of a
2500 series router is
all business. Shown
here are the access
servers 2509, 2509-
RJ, 2511, and 2511-
RJ. The RJ models
have female RJ-45
ports for serial
connections; the
non-RJ models use
one 50-pin high-
density connector for
serial connections.

A fan-out cable converts the high-density port into eight RJ-45 male cables. After the serial ports is an Ethernet port. On non-RJ models there are two high-speed serial ports; RJ models only have one. A console port and an auxiliary port complete the catalog of available connectors.

The 2500 series of routers has the first chassis that will fit in a standard 19″ or 24″ communications rack. You will need to purchase external brackets separately, but rack-mounting routers help to keep them organized and easily accessible. Communications racks are available in any height. Most smaller sites use the 19″ standard and mount the rack near the ceiling, with all the cabling terminated on the rack. This way the local site personnel or accidental administrator can configure individual connections at will.

The 2500 series supports a full range of routing and bridging protocols, including IP, IPX, AppleTalk, DEC Net, LAT, and IBM. It also supports a wide variety of feature sets, including Desktop, Enterprise, Firewall, APPN, PLUS, PLUS 40, PLUS 56, and RMON. Also available are mission-specific versions for FRAD and ISDN routers. These specific versions lower the cost of a router by disabling some of the network ports. Feature sets and protocols are defined in Chapter 3.

2600 Series Routers

Figure 2-10
The Cisco 2600 is the
mid-range member
of Cisco's new class of
modular router.

There are only two variants of the 2600 series available at this time, the 2610 with a single Ethernet port and the 2611 with dual Ethernet ports. These have given up the aesthetics seen in the 1600 series for pure functionality. Looking more like the workhorse 2500 series, the 2600 offers some new features, such as LED status indicators for power, RPS (redundant power supply) status, network activity, and network interface status. Also new are an easy-to-open chassis design, allowing fast and easy access for installation of memory or AIM (Advanced Integration Module) and a variable-speed fan for quiet operation in office environments.

Powered by a Motorola MPC860 RISC (Reduced Instruction Set Computing) microprocessor running at 40MHz, the 2600 series offers a new level of router performance for such a low cost. The RISC processor allows Cisco to deliver features unheard of previously in such a low-cost router. These include:

- Support for advanced QoS (Quality of Service) features, such as Resource Reservation Protocol (RSVP), Weighted Fair Queuing (WFQ), and IP Precedence
- Security features such as data encryption, tunneling, and user authentication and authorization
- Support for cost-effective, software-based data compression and data encryption
- Integration of legacy networks via data link switching plus (DLSW+) and Advanced Peer-to-Peer Networking (APPN)
- High-speed Ethernet-to-Ethernet routing (12,000-15,000 packets per second (pps)) for maximum scalability

Flash memory starts at 4MB in the base configuration and is expandable to 16MB. Some of the larger feature sets already require 8MB of Flash memory, so make sure you order enough. System memory (DRAM) starts at 16MB and is expandable to 64MB. More memory is always a plus, because it allows you to run more protocols, larger feature sets, and more services simultaneously. It also allows you to keep your packets-per-second rate as high as possible by not depriving the processor of memory it needs for packet buffers.

Each 2600 series router comes with two WAN interface card (WIC) slots, one network module (NM) slot, one advanced integration module (AIM) slot, and console/auxiliary ports capable of running at 115.2Kbps. With the addition of a voice interface card (VIC) conversion module (NM-1V or NM-2V), the Cisco 2600 adds support for two to four voice/fax ports. This allows you to route voice and fax traffic over a WAN link back to a central site. It also acts as a micro phone switch, allowing local users to dial extension numbers in order to call each other. The addition of voice and fax over IP adds a whole new dimension to Cisco router functionality. Cisco, always a leader in data networking, is poised to move into this voice/fax market with support for WAN technologies such as Frame Relay, leased lines, and ISDN.

The voice/fax network modules slide into the Cisco 2600 network module slot and contain either one or two voice interface card (VIC) slots. At less than twice the price of a single VIC slot, the dual VIC slot network module offers a price break to those who think they might one day need extra VIC capacity. The VICs are daughter cards that slide into the voice/fax network modules and provide the interface to the telephony equipment. Just as you can swap the Cisco WICs with other WICs, you can deploy the Cisco VICs interchangeably with other VICs in the voice/fax network modules.

Figure 2-11
The back of the series 2600 router. On the left is a NM-2V module with two VIC cards installed. The two WIC slots have an ISDN and dual serial board, respectively. On top is an example of a card for the internal AIM slot.

The NM-2V converts the single network module slot into dual voice interface card (VIC) slots. Adding a two-port VIC card expands the 2600 beyond mere data routing to servicing voice and fax over IP and acting as a small office phone switch.

The 2600 series supports a variety of WIC, VIC, and NM cards. These provide a "pay-as-you-go" approach to voice and data networking. Because most of these cards are compatible with the 1600 and 3600 series routers, you reduce your costs for maintaining inventory and gain greater flexibility in your network design and evolution. Currently available cards are listed in Tables A-5 and A-6 in Appendix A.

Both routers in the 2600 series can be ordered with RPS. This helps reliability by providing diverse power sources, making it a must for high reliability applications. Also available are rack-mount brackets for standard 19″ and 24″ communications racks.

IOS software for the 2600 series is limited in scope when compared to the 2500 and 3600 series. It supports only five protocol sets, and not all variations of them. The available IOS sets and their memory requirements are listed in Table 2-2.

Table 2-2

Memory requirements for Cisco 2600 available IOS software sets

IP	IP/IPX/AT/DEC	Remote Access Services	Enterprise	Enterprise/APPN	
Base feature sets	4MB Flash 16MB DRAM	8MB Flash 16MB DRAM	4MB Flash 16MB DRAM	—	—
Plus feature sets	8MB Flash 20MB DRAM	8MB Flash 20MB DRAM	—	8MB Flash 24MB DRAM	8MB Flash 32MB DRAM
Plus 40 feature sets with 40-bit encryption	8MB Flash 20MB DRAM	—	—	8MB Flash 24MB DRAM	8MB Flash 32MB DRAM
Plus 56 feature sets with 56-bit encryption	8MB Flash 20MB DRAM	—	—	8MB Flash 24MB DRAM	8MB Flash 32MB DRAM

It is disturbing that certain feature sets that seem essential to small offices, particularly the firewall feature set, are missing. This is an extremely new router, and hopefully Cisco will extend the IOS software available for this series in the near future.

3600 Series Routers

Figure 2-12
The 3620 and 3640 return to a more cultivated look. They are much more rounded and aesthetic than the severe-looking 2500 and 2600 series.

Unlike the 2600 series, the 3600s have no built-in LAN or WAN ports. The Cisco 3640 server is equipped with four network module slots; the Cisco 3620 has two. A plethora of NM, WIC, and VIC cards are available, making the 3600 the ultimate in configurable routers. Although only NM card slots are available, mixed-media cards allow you greater flexibility. They come in three varieties, all of which include two WIC slots. The varieties are configured with: single Ethernet, dual Ethernet, or one Ethernet plus one Token Ring interface. The NM-1V one-slot and NM-2V two-slot voice/fax network modules are also available, turning one NM slot into one or two VIC slots.

Cisco bills the 3600 router as a "power branch office" router. While this is definitely true, it can also run small-to-mid-sized main offices that have a variety of needs. The 3600 series can fulfill several roles, including LAN-to-LAN router, LAN-to-WAN router, Access Server, and Voice/Fax over IP router. LAN-to-LAN connectivity comes in three flavors: 10Mbps and 100Mbps Ethernet, and Token Ring media. WAN connections are available in just about every possible variation, including high-speed sync serial, ISDN BRI, Channelized T1/ISDN PRI (Primary Rate Interface), low-speed sync/async serial, low-speed async serial, 2- and 4-wire 56/64Kbps leased line, and full/fractional T1.

Access server configurations can support up to 60 digital modems. Configurations include:

- Dial-in modem access over single or dual T1 service for 24 to 48 users
- Dial-in modem access over single or dual E1 service for 30 to 60 users
- Dial-in modem or ISDN B-channel access over single or dual T1 PRI service for up to 46 users
- Dial-in modem or ISDN B-channel access over single or dual E1 PRI service for up to 58 users

A single or dual E1/T1 card uses one NM slot. Digital modem NM cards are available in 6, 12, 18, 24, and 30 port models. A fully loaded access server configuration requires only three NM slots on a 3640, leaving one slot for LAN and WAN connections. The channelized T1/E1 card routes calls to modems and ISDN B-channels, but provides no explicit WAN connections. A 3640 used as an access server could use ISDN to back-haul data to a main site. Cisco supports linking multiple B-channels together for increasing bandwidth in multiples of 64Kbps. This would provide enough bandwidth for a large number of modem and ISDN users, using bandwidth on demand to keep back-haul costs down. If leased lines are cheaper than ISDN dialup, then a better solution would be to add a fourth card to the router to support LAN and WAN connections. The LAN connection could be used to connect with other LAN equipment, such as servers, routers, and other access servers. The WAN connection would be the primary method of back hauling the data; ISDN could still provide a backup WAN connection in case the primary connection failed or provide additional bandwidth when needed.

Voice/Fax over IP configurations require at least one WAN port, using either an NM or a WIC card. For "power branches" that want LAN, WAN, and phone services, one mixed-media LAN card could be used to provide Ethernet or Token Ring service, while WIC cards provided the WAN connection back to the home office. You could handle this in a single NM slot, leaving room for four VIC ports on the 3620 and 12 VIC ports on the 3640. In this configuration, the 3640 acts as both a 12-port phone switch and a LAN-to-WAN router. By concentrating all these features in a single piece of hardware, you can reduce the complexity and cost of establishing a remote office.

It is even possible to configure a 3640 for LAN-to-LAN, LAN-to-WAN, Access Server, and Voice/Fax functionality. A single-port channelized T1 NM card and a 24-port digital modem NM card take two of the four slots. A two-slot VIC carrier card and two VIC cards provide four voice/fax ports in one NM slot. Finally, a dual Ethernet and Dual WIC slot card provides LAN-to-LAN services and a home for up to two WAN ports. A configuration like this might not be practical to many users, but it should give you a sense of the flexibility available in the 3600 series.

An IDT R4700 RISC processor powers the 3600 series routers. The 3620's processor runs at 80MHz and comes with 16MB of DRAM, which is expandable to 64MB. The 3640 has a 100MHz processor and 16MB of DRAM, expandable to 128MB. Both routers come with 4MB of Flash memory, expandable to 32MB. The 3620 is capable of routing 20—40 Kpps (or kilo packets per second); the faster processor in the 3640 allows it to route 50—70 Kpps. Both 3600 series routers come with the following features:

- Optional Redundant Power Supply (RPS)
- Console and auxiliary ports (up to 115.2Kbps) (back to kilobits per second)
- Wall-mounting and rack-mounting kits for standard 19″ and 24″ racks
- Dual Type II PC card slots
- Optional compression module

Of these options, the RPS, PCMCIA slots, encryption module, and compression module are the most interesting. The RPS unit allows you to provide dual power feeds to a router. This allows incredible flexibility in dealing with power issues, such as temporary outages, which might require moving the router's power source. Without RPS, a router would need to shut down in order to have its power source switched. Flash memory can be installed internally in two Flash SIMM slots or externally in two PCMCIA card slots. The external PCMCIA slots use Flash cards and provide a better place to store your IOS software because they allow you to upgrade simply by swapping cards. This makes installation and upgrades much easier, quicker, and virtually foolproof.

Hardware encryption and data compression used to be very specialized equipment seen only by intelligence and data communications professionals. They have long been available in IOS software, but place a heavy load on the router's main CPU. The encryption network and data compression modules have their own coprocessor to off-load these functions from the central router engine. This allows the main CPU to do what it does best: routing. Neither requires the identical hardware at the other end, allowing cheaper routers in the field to use software encryption and compression. The compression module can off-load processing as many as 128 simultaneous WAN, ISDN, and Frame Relay connections, but cannot increase compression ratios. If it were able to do so, it would either become incompatible with software compression, or require another hardware compression module on the other end of the connection.

There is a huge number of NM, WIC, and VIC cards available for the 3600 series, and more coming to market all the time. A partial list of the more important cards is in Appendix A, Tables A-7 and A-8. Included are the maximum number of each card that can be used and the minimum IOS version necessary.

Figure 2-13
The back of the 3620 with multiple expansion cards.

Figure 2-14
The back of the 3640 filled with expansion cards.

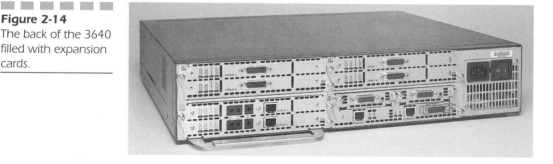

Figure 2-15
Some of the many
network modules
available for the
3600 series, includ-
ing voice, LAN, and
WAN.

The Cisco 3600 series supports run-from-RAM images only. Both the 3640 and 3620 support the following types of memory:

- Main processor memory—used to store the running configuration and routing tables. Cisco IOS software is executed from the main memory.
- Shared (packet) memory—used for packet buffering by the router's network interfaces.
- Flash memory—used to store the IOS software image. Can be stored on either the Flash SIMM or PCMCIA card.
- Nonvolatile random-access memory (NVRAM)—used to store the system configuration file and the virtual configuration register.
- EPROM-based memory—stores the ROM monitor, which allows booting an operating system software image from Flash or PCMCIA memory when Flash memory does not contain a valid boot helper image.

Both the 3640 and 3620 platforms partition their DRAM into main processor memory (pmem) and shared packet memory (iomem) areas. The IOS software is capable of making a distinction between the two with a fine granularity. For example, a 16MB DRAM configuration splits the memory by default into 12MB for pmem and 4MB for iomem. This 75/25 split occurs upon system initialization, and allows enough packet memory to bring up the most common interface combinations regardless of the total amount of DRAM present.

In addition, users have the ability to choose from several options to change this split when required. The new IOS command **memory-size iomem** allows DRAM split increases of 30, 40, and 50 percent, depending on the type and number of network modules configured.

The Cisco IOS supports an auto-adjusting feature upon startup. If the iomem percentage has been configured too high (leaving insufficient pmem available for bringing up the IOS image), the IOS automatically reduces the percentage to a lower value. If the lowest value (75 percent of DRAM) is insufficient for an image to boot, then the router does not have enough DRAM to run that particular IOS image, and the router will complain about it. Main and packet DRAM cannot share or borrow from each other as on the 25xx series routers. If the main DRAM memory is insufficient, then an increase in memory or a smaller IOS image is required.

Most average-size networks require at least 2.0MB of free processor memory and 1.2MB of free iomem. You can use the Cisco IOS command **show memory free** to view the amount of used and available system memory. Table A-9 in Appendix A shows the default division of DRAM, based on the amount present in the router.

There are many different IOS feature and protocol sets available for the 3600 series. To make matters more complex, the different chassis have different costs associated with the same features. Almost every combination of the protocol and feature sets is available. The protocol sets include IP, IPX, IBM, DECnet, AppleTalk, Desktop, Enterprise, and LAT Terminal. Feature sets include PLUS, PLUS 40, PLUS 56, and APPN. Most notably missing is the firewall feature set, which would enhance the router's security capabilities dramatically. Hopefully, Cisco is already working on adding this to the IOS capabilities of the 3600 series.

4000 Series Routers

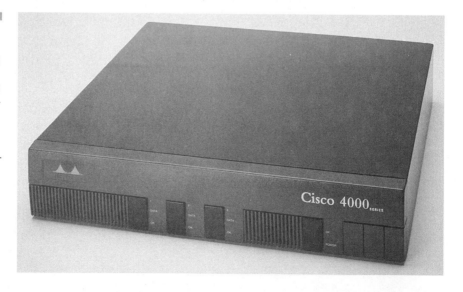

Figure 2-16

Utilitarian in appearance, the 4000 series routers confound those who would tell them apart from their family members merely by their good looks.

The Cisco 4000 series consists of the 4000-M, 4500-M, and 4700-M. They are completely modular routers and contain no LAN or WAN ports by default. All router chassis in this series look the same, right down to the label on the removable front panel, which says "Cisco 4000." In fact, the only way to tell them apart from the outside is by looking at the serial number label, usually located near the power switch. It will start with 4000, 4500, or 4700.

The major differences between different members of the 4000 series are the CPU and number of various types of Network Processor Modules (NMP) they can use. Cisco based the 4000-M on the older Motorola 68030 microprocessor running at 40MHz. From that somewhat meager starting point, the 4500-M jumps to an IDT Orion RISC CPU running at 100MHz. This gives the 4500-M three to five times the pps (packets per second) rate of the 4000-M. Like the 4500, the 4700 uses the IDT Orion RISC CPU, but it is clocked one-third faster at 133MHz.

The 4000 series routers use three separate and distinct types of memory SIMMs for Flash, main, and shared memory. All 4000 series routers start with 4MB of Flash memory and are expandable to 8MB or 16MB. The 4000-M ships with 8MB of main memory and is expandable to 16MB or 32MB. The 4500-M comes with 16MB standard and is expandable to 32MB. The 4700-M ships with 16MB and is expandable to 32MB or 64MB. For shared memory, all versions ship with 4MB and are expandable to 16MB. However, the 4500-M and 4700-M add the flexibility of upgrading to only 8MB, if desired.

4000 series routers have three Network Processor Module (NPM) slots. Because of their vast differences in age and CPU speed, some NPMs are only supported in certain chassis, while others are limited in number. Table A-10 in Appendix A lists the various NPMs and their configuration limitations by chassis. Table A-11 lists incompatible NPM configurations, which should help keep you accidental administrators from committing accidental misconfigurations.

The 4000 series has many of the same types of media available to it as the previous modular series, the 3600. However, there are some interesting additions and deletions. Notably, there are typically no external communications devices like DSU/CSUs, modems, and NT-1s available in this product series. All ISDN BRI ports requires external NT-1s. All serial ports require modems or DSU/CSUs, and the channelized T1/E1/PRI cards require external CSUs. Note that an external CSU is not the same as a CSU/DSU. The channelized T1 cards act as the DSU; therefore, you only need a CSU.

The notable additions are the extremely high-speed LAN and WAN interfaces supporting ATM (Asynchronous Transfer Mode), FDDI (Fiber Distributed Data Interface), DS-3, E3, and HSSI (High Speed Serial Interface) at speeds of 12, 45, 52, 100, and 155Mbps. These features make the 4000 series an entry-level backbone router. It does not have advanced features like firewall feature set or voice/fax modules; rather, its strengths lie in raw packet routing capabilities.

The back of the router provides much more real estate for network connectors and LEDs, making it easier to maintain cables and see network port status. As with almost all other Cisco routers, there is also a console and auxiliary port.

The 4000 series routers can be confusing when you first start working with them. The slots are numbered 1 through 3, from right to left when you are looking at the back. In addition, the ports on each card are numbered from zero up, although zero is sometimes in different locations. Because there are no fixed configurations, the IOS software must number the ports dynamically as it located them, starting with slot 1. In Figure 2-17, you can see a 4000 series router that has three dual serial port NPMs. Table 2-3 below that picture shows how the physical ports (which are only labeled zero and one) are mapped to the IOS serial ports you configure in software. In the case where a non-serial card, such as a dual Ethernet NPM, was in the middle, the slot-one serial ports would still be zero and one, but the slot three serial ports would become two and three.

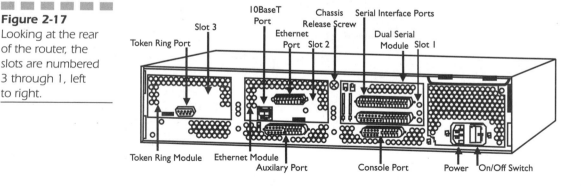

Figure 2-17
Looking at the rear of the router, the slots are numbered 3 through 1, left to right.

Matching interface numbers to physical ports can be confusing, because all interfaces of the same type are numbered consecutively, even though they might not be physically configured that way.

Figure 2-18

The configuration above demonstrates the port numbering scheme of the 4000 series router.

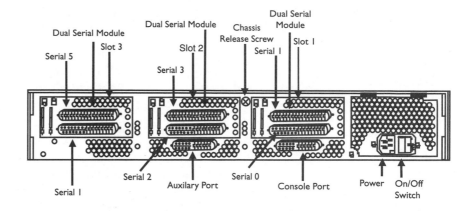

Table 2-3

Interface numbering scheme for three dual serial Network Processor Modules (NPMs) in a 4000 series router

Slot No.	Interface Type	IOS Serial Port Number
1	Serial Port (Top) Serial Port (Bottom)	1 0
2	Serial Port (Top) Serial Port (Bottom)	3 2
3	Serial Port (Top) Serial Port (Bottom)	5 4

There are many different IOS feature and protocol sets available for the 4000 series. To make matters more complex, the different chassis have different costs associated with the same features. Almost every combination of the protocol and feature sets is available. The protocol sets include IP, IPX, IBM, DECnet, AppleTalk, Desktop, Enterprise, and LAT Terminal. Feature sets include PLUS, PLUS 40, PLUS 56, DBConn, and APPN. (No, you are not having *déjà vu* all over again; you have read this paragraph before: The 3600 series has nearly the same complexity as the 4000 series.) Note that DBConn is available in the 4000 series, but not in the 3600, and that the firewall feature set also is missing from this series. Hopefully, Cisco will get the hint for the 4000s as well as the 3600s.

Access Servers

Access servers are a special classification of routers. Most Internet users don't realize it, but they use one every time they connect to their ISP. More and more companies are turning to access servers to fulfill their internal connectivity needs. In this section we discuss what access servers are, what they do, and how to size them for your environment. We also discuss some of the models available from Cisco.

What Are Access Servers?

Access servers are a specialized class of router that provides network access services to remote users over dialup connections. Users connect over digital phone lines and access standard modems or ISDN B-channel connections. Either type of connection uses the same link to the telephone company—a T1 or E1 leased line with or without ISDN PRI service layered over it. Most access servers are used for modem dial-in service only. Examples of this are ISPs and content providers, such as America Online.

The total number of dialup connections depends on the number of channels available from all digital leased lines connected to the access server. These leased lines will be either T1 or E1 lines, depending on which part of the world you are in. In North America they are T1, and in Europe, E1. T1 lines provide 24 and E1 lines provide 30 available channels for connections. By themselves, these lines can be used only for analog modem connections. However, by layering ISDN PRI service over them, the channels can be used for modem or ISDN B-channel connections. To gain this flexibility requires the sacrifice of one channel for ISDN signaling; therefore, ISDN T1s support 23 and ISDN E1s support 29 connections.

Each user connects to an access server over one channel on the digital leased line. There is a one-to-one correlation between the maximum number of users and the total number of available channels. Initiation of a connection reserves a channel exclusively for a user. When the user terminates his connection, the channel is again available for use. Therefore, if an ISP wants to support 100 simultaneous users in a single location, they must have at least 100 channels available. The two access servers discussed in this book are the AS5200 and AS5300, which support a maximum of 60 and 120 channels, respectively. The AS5800 is a huge access server that supports as many as 720 channels, making it beyond the scope of this book.

Sizing Access Servers

Sizing an access server to meet unknown future needs used to be extremely difficult. You needed to choose equipment that supported a fixed number of connections, analog or ISDN service only, and would not support multiple connections from a single user over multiple chassis. Users want this capability so that they can incrementally add bandwidth to their network connection if their operating system supports MPPP (Multilink Point-to-Point Protocol). It is now much easier to size an access server, because Cisco has the ability to support ISDN and analog connections in one chassis and connect a single dialup user across multiple access server chassis.

Allowing a single user to add bandwidth over multiple chassis makes it possible for ISPs to add additional Cisco access servers, without forcing the users to change their configurations. This can be used both for ISDN and modem dial-in connections, providing ever-increasing throughput. Cisco provides this capability with the Multichassis Multilink Point-to-Point Protocol (MMP) which manages bandwidth and routing during an MPPP user's connection to different chassis.

The Old Versus the New

Before access servers, terminal servers and modem banks supported large numbers of dial-in connections. Analog phone lines (POTS) would be wired for each modem connection supported and terminated at the back of a chassis that held rack-mounted modems. These modem racks usually supported 12 to 24 modems and took up eight inches or more in a standard 19-inch communications rack. Each modem would have its own 25-pin serial cable, which would snake down to the terminal server. The terminal server managed the modems and had the Ethernet connection to the network. It usually had 12 to 36 serial ports, but some were available with 60 serial ports. Because of the size of 25-pin serial ports, terminal servers took up 8 to 14 inches in the rack.

An older configuration of 12 modems per modem rack and a 36-port terminal server would take up four feet of rack space and need at least 77 individual cables. Today's access servers have integrated modems, ISDN support, and the terminal server in the same box. Because of this high level of integration, they need only four cables to support the same number of modems and are as small as 3.5" high.

Reducing the number of cables and components has made today's access servers many times more reliable than those of previous years. The tight level of integration allows network administrators to configure, monitor, and maintain all the various pieces of the access server quickly and easily. This reduces the administrative costs of providing dial-in access, as does a feature like MMP. By combining all these features and reducing administrative costs, the access server has taken its place as the product of choice in the dial-in server market and has helped make dialup networking much more reliable for its users.

Cisco Access Server Connections

All Cisco access servers can provide both modem and ISDN connections. Support for ISDN connections requires only a channelized T1 or E1/ISDN PRI card. This manages the ISDN PRI connections with the telephone company and the ISDN calls themselves. Modem support requires the addition of modem carrier cards and modem modules. The modem carrier cards exist solely to provide a home for modem modules. Modem modules contain six or twelve modems each. These modems are not the typical end-user product, but rather digital modems on a single chip. This technology allows access servers to reduce drastically the space needed for large numbers of modems.

Cisco uses Microcom and MICA modem technology in their access servers. Microcom modem modules are the older technology and hold 12 modems each. The AS5200 and AS5300 will take the Microcom modem modules, but the AS5800 will not. In both the AS5200 and AS5300, two Microcom modem modules can fit in a carrier card, with a maximum of two carrier cards per access server. Simple arithmetic shows a maximum of 48 Microcom modems, causing many people to wonder how you attain the maximum capacity of 60 modems in the AS5200. Because this maximum is only possible if you are using E1 connections, the channelized dual E1 card for the AS5200 adds an additional slot for a Microcom modem module. This is not true of the AS5300, which can only support 48 Microcom modems.

All three access servers can use the MICA modem modules. The carrier cards for the AS5200 support five modem modules; those for the AS5300 support ten. Both the AS5200 and AS5300 can hold two MICA carrier cards. An AS5200 using MICA modems has the same number of maximum connections as one using Microcom modems (60). However, the AS5300 is able to support 120 MICA modems, far outstripping 48 available with Microcom technology. If you are upgrading from an AS5200 to an AS5300, you can extend the useful life of existing equipment and keep your costs down by reusing your Microcom modems, thus avoiding the purchase of new equipment. Any new purchase of access servers should include the MICA cards, because they are supported in all three chassis.

Both the AS5200 and AS5300 are three-slot access servers. Modem carrier cards can occupy any two available slots. The third slot is for a channelized T1 or E1/ISDN PRI card. This terminates the digital leased lines from the phone company. The AS5200 card supports two digital leased lines; the AS5300 supports four. In countries that have T1 lines, the AS5200 supports a maximum of 48 modems and the AS5300 supports 96. Countries that have E1 service allow the AS5200 to support 60 modems and the AS5300 to support 120. ISDN service reduces these numbers by one for each digital leased line connected to the access server, but adds high-speed ISDN support. This means the AS5200 can support 46 modems or ISDN connections with T1 service and 58 with E1 service. The AS5300 can support 94 connections with T1 service and 116 with E1 service.

The choice between T1 and E1 is (unfortunately) not yours. It has already been determined for you by the phone standards in your country. You must make sure you order the equipment to match the line your local phone company provides, or your access server will not work.

Access Servers (5200)

Figure 2-19
The AS5200 is the entry-level access server. It is an excellent choice for corporate dial-in/out and small ISP POPs.

The AS5200 is scalable and configurable to meet the needs of diverse corporate and ISP customers. The AS5200 is a three-slot access server, with one slot reserved for a channelized T1/PRI or E1/PRI card. The other two slots hold carrier cards for modem cards.

The AS5200 ships with two high-speed serial ports, one Ethernet port and standard console ports. There are three slots available for modems and channelized T1/E1 cards. It is powered by a 20MHz Motorola 68030 microprocessor and ships with 4MB boot Flash, 8MB system Flash, 4MB shared DRAM, and 8MB main DRAM memory. Boot Flash memory is expandable to 8MB; all others are expandable to 16MB.

You can purchase a complete AS5200 one piece at a time or pre-bundled. If you order piecemeal, have a sales engineer look over the configuration to be sure you have not forgotten anything important. Bundles are purchased by connection type (T1 or E1) and number of modems. You will usually find it easier, and possibly cheaper, to order bundles.

Figure 2-20
The AS5200 shown
here has a dual T1
card on top and four
12-port Microcom
modem cards
installed in the two
slots below.

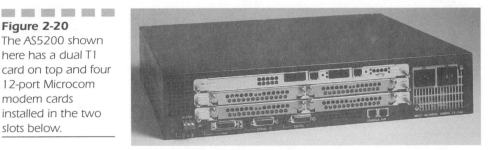

The AS5200 supports IP, IBM, AppleTalk, DEC, and IPX protocols. It also supports the Desktop, Plus, Enterprise, and RMON feature sets. Not all possible combinations are available, so check the latest documentation available to determine which feature sets you need.

Access Servers (5300)

Figure 2-21
The second genera-
tion access server, the
AS5300, supports as
many as 120
modems in the same
space as an AS5200.

The AS5300 is almost exactly like the AS5200, only denser. This is not to say that it is heavier (it is), but it more densely packs modem modules and leased-line connection cards to hold more in the same space. Where the AS5200 has dual connection cards, the AS5300 has quad channelized T1 and E1 cards. This allows up to 120 analog or 116 ISDN connections from the local phone company.

The AS5300 ships with standard console ports and two Ethernet LAN ports, one 10BaseT and the other configurable as either 10 or 100BaseT. There are three slots available for modems and channelized T1/E1 cards. It is powered by a 150MHz R4700 microprocessor and ships with 4MB boot Flash, 8MB system Flash, and 32MB main DRAM memory. Boot Flash memory is expandable to 8MB, system Flash to 16MB, and main DRAM to 64MB.

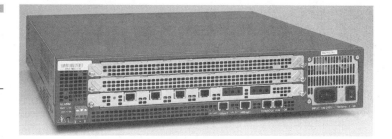

Figure 2-22
The more densely packed rear of the AS5300 is crammed with ports and slots.

The AS5300 supports IP, IBM, AppleTalk, DEC, and IPX protocols. It also supports the Desktop, Plus, Enterprise, and RMON feature sets. Not all possible combinations are available, so check the latest documentation to determine which feature sets you need.

AS5800 Access Server

Figure 2-23
AS5800 Carrier-Class Access Server is capable of handling 720 asynchronous/ISDN dial ports in a single box.

The AS5800 is beyond the scope of this book. It is a Carrier-Class access server. Cisco calls it this because it is about the size of an aircraft carrier. In fact, the United States Navy is looking to add several to the North Atlantic fleet. A New York City apartment costs less. Of course, it also has less room!

The Truth About Dial-in Speeds (or ISDN Versus Dial-in)

Many think that 56Kbps modem connections rival the speed of a single 64Kbps ISDN B-channel. Because both are measured in kilobits per second, they seem only 8Kbps apart. There appears to be little overall difference in speed, but looks are deceiving. The modem only seems one-eighth slower than an ISDN connection. However, you must also take into account asynchronous vs. synchronous communications protocols and the *real* attainable speeds of 56Kbps modems.

Asynchronous communications use start and stop bits to indicate where bytes begin and end. This adds two additional bits to each eight-bit byte; therefore, 10 bits are transmitted per byte of data. *Synchronous* communications use a clock outside of the data channel to indicate where bytes begin and end. Only 8 bits per byte are sent, making it 20 percent faster than asynchronous communications at the same data rate. So, a modem (which is asynchronous) operating at 56,000 bps is only able to send 44,800 bps of real data. The rest of its capacity is used for start and stop bits. So, in actuality, a 56Kbps modem is only 70 percent as fast as an ISDN B-channel.

This also assumes that you could get a 56Kbps connection in the first place. Most dial-in users never see the full 56Kbps due to line noise on their phones and distance from their house to the dial-in server. Most users see speeds of 52, 48, and 44Kbps. Because ISDN lines are all digital lines specially conditioned to support data connections, you will always be able to get the full 64Kbps.

The Idea of Interfaces

Cisco routers rely on the idea of interfaces. The *interface* is the physical, virtual, or pseudo connection to the network. The easiest to understand is the physical interface, because you can see and touch it. Virtual interfaces are a subset or superset of physical interfaces, such as sub-interfaces or group interfaces. Pseudo interfaces do not relate to physical interfaces at all, but rather act like an interface in relation to the network.

Physical interfaces are straightforward. Wherever you have a port on your router, you have a physical interface. There is a one-to-one correlation between the interfaces on your router and the interface command lines in your router configuration. Cisco IOS automatically discovers all physical interfaces on your router and puts entries for them in the configuration. By default, they are added in an inactive state. You must make changes to the router configuration, either through the initial setup dialog, or by editing the configuration manually.

Each time you want to make changes to how a certain interface behaves, you need to edit the configuration. If you want all interfaces to express that behavior, you must configure each one separately.

Types of Interfaces

There are three basic types of interfaces: LAN, WAN, and console. LAN interfaces are high-speed local connections and are available from 4Mbps to 155Mbps. WAN interfaces are for connecting networks across greater distances and scale from 9.6Kbps on up, using leased lines and dialup connections. Console ports are for local terminal users and router maintenance. The console port is strictly for local connections, but the auxiliary port, through an attached modem, can act as a WAN port.

Cabling Differences

Most LAN connections use well-known standards for cabling. WAN connections, on the other hand, have evolved over time. This means there is a larger requirement for backward compatibility. This is extremely important when you choose the cables you'll need to make WAN connections.

Cisco offers a wide variety of WAN cables in their catalog. You must know what pieces of equipment are being cabled together as well as what ports they have before you can determine what cable to buy. While this sounds simplistic (even silly), you should not proceed otherwise. The first time Murphy's Law catches you with piles of expensive equipment on hand and nothing works for lack of an inexpensive cable, you will remember these sage words of advice, bow your head in shame, and cry out, "Why didn't I listen to the author"

This has happened to me twice, much to my chagrin. Now I check everything before I place my purchase orders.

Most ISDN interfaces use RJ-45 connectors. The real exception is the
channelized T1 and E1/ISDN PRI cards for the Cisco 4000 series routers.
Unlike the 3600 series and the access servers, these cards do not have built-
in CSUs. Make sure you get a cable to convert their DB-15 connector to
whatever your external CSU needs (in the case of the Adtran T1 ESF CSU
ACE, an RJ-45 port).

Exercise caution with serial ports as well. There are many types of
serial ports and many types of connectors. Standard console, auxiliary,
and low-speed serial ports typically use RJ-45 connectors. These use standard RJ-45 cables, but require RJ-45 to DB-9 or DB-25 connectors to allow
you to attach them to PCs, modems, and terminals. Usually you get one
of each of these with every Cisco router. From them, you can determine
the proper configuration of the cable and connector to make your serial
device work. In dual-type serial cards that have high-speed and low-speed
serial connections, octopus cables are available with built-in connectors.
Again, make sure to check what you will be attaching it to, because some
low-speed serial ports can be used synchronous or asynchronous. Synch
devices usually use V.35 connectors, and async devices usually use EIA/
TIA-232 DB-25 connectors.

High-speed serial ports can come with 50-pin large connectors or 60-
pin high-density connectors. The only card that still uses the larger 50-pin
connector is the NP-2T for the Cisco 4000 series. All others use the high-
density 60-pin connector. Both terminate in X.21, V.35, EIA/TIA-232, EIA/
TIA-449, and EIA/530 connectors. There is also usually a choice of male or
female and DCE or DTE.

In addition to the low-speed and high-speed serial ports, Cisco offers a
high-speed serial interface (HSSI) card for the 4000 series routers. This should
not be confused with high-speed serial ports, which have a maximum
speed of 4Mbps (seen in Figure 2-18). HSSI ports are extremely fast, supporting speeds up to 54Mbps. A HSSI card has a 50-pin high density SCSI
(Small Computer Systems Interface) port for its data connection. If you are
setting one up for the first time, ask questions of your T3/E3 CSU/DSU
vendor and your Cisco sales engineer to make sure you get the right cables.

## CHAPTER 3

Software

Cisco is generally viewed as a hardware company noted for their many networking products. Often overlooked is the software (the operating system) necessary to make the hardware function. You would expect Cisco to use one or more types of operating system software (and they do), but the most commonly used one is the Cisco Internetworking Operating System, or IOS. Cisco also makes a large line of other software products for network management, router configuration, accounting, security, router functionality enhancement, and more.

In this book, we will focus on the software products that are either necessary (operating systems) or optional (configuration tools) for the routers described in the hardware section. The primary operating system discussed is Cisco IOS. IOS has many features and supports a wide variety of networking protocols, although not all of them are available on all platforms. The low-end access routers (Cisco 760 and 770 series) do not use IOS, but rather their own operating system, which was inherited from the acquisition of Combinet.

The optional software from Cisco we will focus on will be for router configuration and management and for enhanced functionality. There are six main products for configuring and managing routers: CiscoView, CiscoWorks, CiscoWorks for Windows, Cisco Resource Manager, Cisco ConfigMaker, and Fast Step.

Operating Systems

At the heart of every router is a good operating system. These bear little or no resemblence to the ones on your desktop computers, because they are built for the single specific function of routing packets between interfaces. Without one, a router is just a very expensive paperweight.

IOS

Cisco IOS is the operating system for the majority of Cisco routers. It's one of the core reasons for Cisco's success, because it maintains its user interface across multiple platforms. This makes knowledge of IOS portable across most of the Cisco product line. If a user can configure a low-end router like a Cisco 2500 for Frame Relay, they can do the same on larger routers as well. IOS also provides excellent context-sensitive command-line help.

In order for IOS to scale between the largest and smallest routers in Cisco's product line, features must be scalable as well. Cisco offers a wide variety of networking protocols and features in IOS, although not all are available on all platforms. Most users will take advantage of less than ten percent of the features available in their version of IOS, and in most cases, that's all they need.

IOS configuration has traditionally been through a command-line interface (CLI). The CLI is a scary place for the accidental administrator and those not familiar with networking in general. Many tools exist to provide a buffer between the network administrator and CLI. These can provide basic configurations and assist in troubleshooting, but all Cisco administrators (accidental or otherwise) should familiarize themselves with the CLI. In a worst-case scenario, it becomes the user interface of last resort.

Non-IOS

The only non-IOS operating system covered in this book is the one used to run the Cisco 700 family of ISDN access routers. This operating system is very different from IOS, providing a much smaller feature set and a much less intuitive CLI. Fortunately, GUI-based tools exist to configure these routers, making basic configurations easier.

This operating system supports only IP and IPX network protocols and comes in three feature sets: Small Office/Home Office (SOHO), Remote Office (RO), and Internet Ready. The SOHO software feature set supports routing of IP and IPX for up to four devices with STAC compression. The RO software feature set supports IP and IPX routing with STAC compression for up to 1,500 devices. The Internet Ready software feature set supports routing of the IP protocol for up to four devices.

Software feature packs are available for the Cisco 700 family of routers. They consist of CD-ROMs that contain software feature set images and a Windows 95 application, which loads the images onto a router. This makes updating the router OS much easier than through the CLI.

Configuration and Management Programs

CiscoView

CiscoView graphically displays a physical view of Cisco devices providing dynamic status, statistics, and comprehensive configuration information for a wide variety of Cisco hardware. It also provides monitoring functions to aid in basic troubleshooting. CiscoView is bundled with CiscoWorks, CiscoWorks for Windows, and CiscoWorks for Switched Internetworks, and is available as a standalone product.

CiscoWorks

CiscoWorks is a highly configurable management tool that works with many different types of Cisco equipment. It consists of four main products: CiscoWorks, CiscoWorks for Windows, CiscoWorks for Switched Internetworks, and CiscoWorks Blue series. This book is only concerned with the first two options, whose platforms' availability is listed in Table 3-1.

CiscoWorks Platform	NMS Platforms Supported
Solaris	Standalone or integrated with Solstice Site Manager, Solstice Domain Manager, Solstice Enterprise Manager, or HP OpenView
HP/UX	Standalone or integrated with HP OpenView
AIX	Standalone or integrated with Tivoli TME/10 NetView

CiscoWorks for Windows Option	Platforms Supported
Microsoft Window 95	Standalone or integrated with CastleRock SNMPc (included) or HP OpenView Professional Suite
Microsoft Windows NT 3.51 or NT 4.0	Standalone or integrated with HP OpenView Network Node Management

CiscoWorks for Switched Internetworks is for managing Cisco network switches in the Catalyst and LightStream series. The CiscoWorks Blue series consists of several individual pieces that manage IBM SNA protocols running over a variety of Cisco equipment.

Cisco Resource Manager

Cisco Resource Manager is a network management suite that delivers an Internet-based solution for managing Cisco networks. It offers rapid, reliable device software upgrades, easy tracking of network changes, and quick isolation of error conditions for Cisco routers and switches. Its applications, together with links to CCO (Cisco Connection Online) service and support, speed network administrative tasks to help you manage your enterprise network.

Cisco ConfigMaker

Cisco ConfigMaker is an easy-to-use Windows 95/NT network and device configuration tool for the Cisco 1000, 1600, 2500, and 3600 series routers. It is a user-friendly alternative to the existing Cisco command-line interface normally used to configure the Cisco router. Using ConfigMaker, you can configure a single device (or create and configure a network of devices), automatically address those devices, and send the configuration files to them. It includes a spiffy computer-based instructional video for learning the basic steps required for using its GUI.

Although ConfigMaker's documentation claims it will only work on certain routers, this is not true: IOS configuration code is portable across all IOS-based routers. It might not be able to configure all available ports on a larger router, but standard ones like Ethernet and serial are the same across all IOS routers.

Fast Step

Fast Step allows ready configurations of Cisco 76x and 77x series routers from a PC that is running Microsoft Windows 95 or NT 4.0. It takes you through a setup wizard that quickly configures the router to connect to the Internet or your corporate network. You can configure the router over the LAN or over a serial cable connected between your PC and the router's console port. The Fast Step wizard also saves the configuration file, so that you can make changes to it later without starting from the beginning.

Cisco IOS

Because Cisco IOS supports so many platforms and features, you need to have a basic understanding of how Cisco manages this awesome task. Without delving too deep, we will discuss the different types of releases available and how they can affect your network. We will also discuss the user interface and learn the different ways to access it.

Cisco's Strategy and Implementation of IOS Code

Cisco breaks up IOS into two main types of releases: *major* releases and *early deployment* releases. *Major* releases support a fixed set of features and platforms through the life of the release. *Early deployment* releases deliver support for new features and platforms in their regular maintenance updates. Both progress through their life cycle by moving through stages of maintenance releases and interim builds. *Maintenance* releases become available during regular maintenance cycles. They include all recent bug fixes and are fully tested. By comparison, Cisco has weekly releases of interim builds (which Cisco does not intend for customer use, except in unusual circumstances). This accelerated release schedule implies that the interim builds are usually not extensively tested.

Only major releases ever reach the *general deployment* stage. Cisco makes *general deployment* releases available only after extensive testing and only when Cisco (and Cisco customers) prove them functional and stable. When a major release reaches general deployment, Cisco considers it ready for unconstrained use in customer networks. A major release becomes general deployment when Cisco is satisfied that the release has been:

- **Proven** through extensive market exposure in diverse networks
- **Quantified** with metrics analyzed for stability and bug trends
- **Qualified** through customer satisfaction surveys

Once a maintenance update for a particular major release achieves general deployment, all subsequent maintenance updates for that release are also said to be general deployment.

Early Deployment Releases

In general, shun early deployment (ED) releases unless you have special needs that only ED releases can fill. Administrators should stick to general deployment releases for enhanced stability. In cases where you must use ED releases, make sure to keep a close watch for the latest scheduled maintenance release of your ED release. These will continue to provide you with the features you need, as well as the latest bug fixes for both the major release and the ED-unique features.

As a group, early deployment releases are based on major releases of Cisco IOS. ED releases are a vehicle to deliver new functionality quickly, and to address the need for new platform support. These releases provide new technologies for customers to deploy in a limited manner on their networks. Note that similar functionality might be available on more than one ED release. For example, a platform might be introduced initially on the 11.1AA release. Support for this platform might also be included in an ED release based on 11.2, like the 11.2P release. Because 11.2P is based on the 11.2 major release, the platform will support additional 11.2 features when deployed on the 11.2P release.

Interim Builds

As part of the normal development process, Cisco creates *interim builds*, which incorporate bug fixes both for major releases and for early deployment releases. Interim build releases occur approximately once a week between maintenance releases. Cisco usually tests each interim build in a limited manner and incorporates fixes in the interim builds into the subsequent maintenance release, which is fully regression tested.

There are situations in which a customer needs a specific bug fix before its commercial availability on a fully regression-tested release. Cisco's Customer Advocacy (CA) Group can provide interim builds to customers on a case-by-case basis if there is an urgent need to correct a bug. Because of the limited testing performed on interim builds, Cisco strongly discourages the use of interim builds in a production environment. A customer given an interim build should deploy it in the network only as necessary to correct the bug. Moreover, any system running an interim build should migrate to the next maintenance release that properly addresses the problem (which should be the next available maintenance release).

Release Numbering

The release number of a major release identifies the major release and its maintenance level. In Table 3-2, *12.0* identifies the major release, and *7* is its maintenance level. The complete release number is *12.0(7)*. Occasionally, a release number has a lowercase letter, as in *12.0(7a)*. The *a* indicates that there have been very few bug fixes applied since the associated maintenance release (in this example, since 12.0(7)). The release is identical to a regular release in every other way. In general, Early Deployment releases are differentiated from major releases by the use of capital letters in their names. For instance, *11.2* is a major release, whereas *11.2P* and *11.2BC* are early deployment releases.

Table 3-2

Deployment definitions and release timing for Cisco IOS versions

Release Type	Description	Timing	Numbering Example
Major Release—FCS	Introduces significant features, functionality, and/or platforms on a stability-oriented release vehicle	As needed to support customer needs	12.0(1)
Major Release—scheduled maintenance updates	Periodic revisions to major releases: • fully regression tested • incorporate the most recent bug fixes • no new platforms or features—focused on stability	Regular maintenance cycles	12.0(7)
Major Release—interim builds	Working builds—usually not regression tested, and not intended for customer use except in unusual circumstances	Weekly	12.0(4.2)
General Deployment	A major release that is appropriate for general, unconstrained use in customers' networks	When stability of release has been proven internally by Cisco and externally by customers	12.0(8), and all subsequent maintenance updates of 12.0 [12.0(9), 12.0(10), etc.]
Early Deployment—FCS	Introduces significant new features, functionality, and/or platforms on a feature-oriented release vehicle: • based on a major release • will not achieve general deployment	As needed to provide support for newly emerging technologies	12.0(1)T
Early Deployment—scheduled maintenance updates	Periodic revisions to ED releases: • fully regression tested • incorporate the most recent bug fixes, including those from major release • usually deliver new platforms and/or features	Regular maintenance cycles	12.0(3)T
Early Deployment—interim builds	Working builds—usually not regression tested, and not intended for customer use except in unusual circumstances	Generally weekly, though some ED releases follow a different policy	12.0(4.2)T

IOS CLI Navigation

The IOS CLI is the most basic level of control over your Cisco router. No matter how many GUI-based tools you use, you should always have a basic competency with the CLI. In emergencies as well as when GUI tools are not available, you'll need to be able to navigate through the CLI in order to manage your routers.

Getting Connected with HyperTerminal

First, think about how to connect to the router. The Windows 95 OS provides two basic methods: HyperTerminal and Telnet. Use HyperTerminal when your router console or auxiliary connects directly to one of your PC serial ports (COM1, COM2, and so on). Use Telnet when your router connects to your network via Ethernet and has a valid IP address. You will need to configure both properly to optimize their access to the CLI. To start HyperTerminal, click on the Windows Start button, then on Programs | Accessories | HyperTerminal, then click on the icon shown in Figure 3-1.

Figure 3-1
The Windows
HyperTerminal icon.

Hypertrm.exe

When HyperTerminal starts, it asks the administrator to name the icon for a new connection. The name entered should be **Direct to COM1**, and any icon may be chosen. Click OK to complete the connection description, as shown in Figure 3-2.

■ ■ ■ ■ ■ ■
Figure 3-2
Creating a new
connection
description in
HyperTerminal.

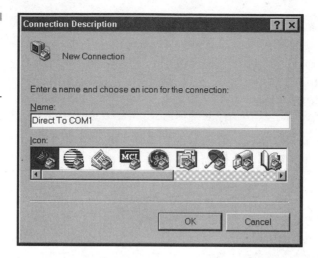

HyperTerminal will present the Phone Number screen next. No data needs to be entered here, but Connect using: needs to be set to Direct to Com 1, as shown in Figure 3-3.

■ ■ ■ ■ ■ ■
Figure 3-3
Choosing a direct
connection to the
serial port in
HyperTerminal.

HyperTerminal will now configure the communications properties for the serial connection to the router. The default settings for the Cisco router console and auxiliary ports are 9600 bits per second (also known as baud), 8 data bits, no parity, one stop bit, and Xon/Xoff flow control. Make sure the Port Settings window on the screen matches the one in Figure 3-4. When complete, click OK.

Figure 3-4
The HyperTerminal serial communications settings must match those used by the Cisco router.

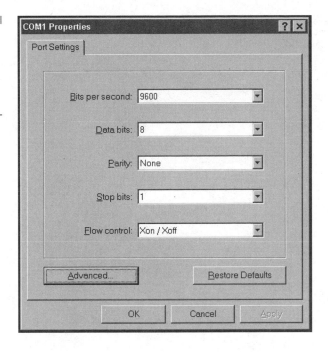

A blank HyperTerminal window connected to your PC's COM1 port will now appear. Before you start to use HyperTerminal to manage your router, make sure the terminal properties are set correctly. Click on the File menu and select Properties, then click on the Settings tab. Make sure your function, arrow, and control keys act as terminal keys, and your terminal emulation is set to VT100. Your scrollback buffer lines should be set to the maximum. This lets you see what changes you've made and gives you a greater history from which to cut and paste. Cut and paste is a lifesaver if you want to save something from the terminal window or enter many lines of data into the router configuration from a text file. Your settings should look like the ones in Figure 3-5.

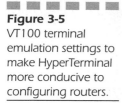

Figure 3-5
VT100 terminal
emulation settings to
make HyperTerminal
more conducive to
configuring routers.

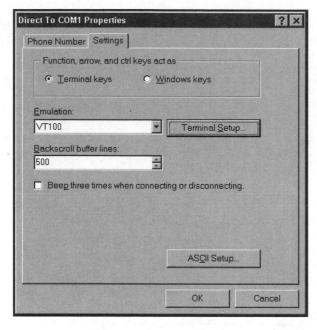

COM1 on your PC now connects to the router. You should be able to press Enter and see the router command prompt in the window. If this doesn't happen, you might have the cable incorrectly connected to the router, or you might have chosen the wrong COM port on your PC. Click on File | Save | Connection | Disconnect, and then on File | Exit. You should now see an icon in the HyperTerminal window for Direct To COM1, as shown in Figure 3-6. The next time you need to manage a router through this serial port, all you need to do is double-click on this icon, and HyperTerminal will restore all your settings for you.

Figure 3-6
The Direct To COM1
icon has been added
to the HyperTerminal
program group.

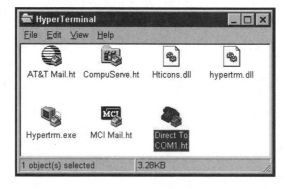

If you have another router connected to COM2 or any other PC COM ports, repeat these steps for each of them.

Serial Cabling

Serial cable connections to PCs can be a problem. In the case of Cisco routers, this is not so. Cisco ships their routers with serial cables. If you use the cables provided by Cisco, you shouldn't have any problems.

Getting Connected with Telnet

Start Telnet by first clicking on the Windows Start button, then on Run, and then enter **Telnet** in the dialog box and press the Enter key. To connect to the router, click on Connect | Remote System and enter the hostname or IP address of a router on your network. Click on Connect to make the connection, as shown in Figure 3-7.

Figure 3-7
Choosing the IP address to connect to in Telnet.

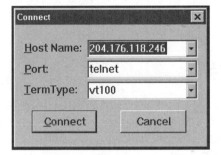

When you connect to an IOS router, it will ask you to enter the password to get access. Telnet connections require a password by default, and they should remain password protected for security purposes. Once you connect to the router for the first time, you'll want to make changes to Telnet's default behavior. Unlike HyperTerminal, where terminal preferences are set per connection, Telnet has only global options for all connections. To set these properly, you should click on Terminal | Preferences and make your screen match the one in Figure 3-8.

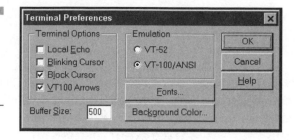

Although extremely limited in its usefulness, the Windows Telnet program deserves coverage by being ubiquitous. If you plan to manage many routers over the network, you should seriously look at acquiring another program to do the job. Many freeware and shareware programs are available on the Internet, and several of these are available from TUCOWS, The Ultimate Collection Of Winsock Software, at http://www.tucows.com.

One fine program is NetTerm. It includes an address book for connections, better handling of backscroll buffers, and the ability to set preferences per connection. It handles both Telnet and serial connections to your router, completely removing the need for Windows Telnet and HyperTerminal. You can get it directly at http://starbase.neosoft.com/~zkrr01.

Levels of Access

Now that you have basic connectivity to the CLI, you need to understand the two default privilege levels in IOS: *access* and *enable*. The *access* privilege level offers only the most basic of IOS commands. Using access privileges, you can log in and get basic information about the health of the router. With access privileges, you can look but not touch (effectively, the router is in *read-only* mode). If you want to see more information and make changes to the router, you must enter the *enable* privilege mode. This mode allows you to read and write configuration changes, as well as monitor more in-depth information about the router. This is equivalent to root access on a UNIX system, administrator access on Windows NT, or supervisor on Novell NetWare. This means you have absolute control of the router, and can do anything you want to it (including dangerous things, like wiping out the configuration file).

By default, the console port of the router puts you into the access level of the CLI without a password. The auxiliary port and all Telnet connections require the access password. The router does not echo the password back to the screen as you type it. If you make a mistake, the Backspace and Delete keys will both erase the last character typed, although you won't be able to see it. This makes it hard to make corrections, but at least gives you a chance. Remember that router passwords are *case sensitive,* so be aware of capital letters and the state of your Caps Lock key. You have three chances to enter the correct access password. If you fail after three attempts, the router will drop your Telnet session, as shown in Figure 3-9.

Figure 3-9   *What you see if you enter three bad passwords in a row.*

```
User Access Verification

Password:
Password:
Password:
% Bad passwords
```

When you succeed and log in to the router, you will see a prompt that shows the router name followed by the greater than sign (>). This is shown in Figure 3-10.

Figure 3-10 *When you successfully log in to the router, you first get to the access level prompt.*

```
User Access Verification

Password:
wan4500>
```

This indicates you are at the access privilege level. In order to reach the enable privilege level, you must enter the command **enable**, press Enter, and then enter the **enable** password or the **enable secret** password. Both control access to enable mode, but the **enable secret** password is automatically encrypted in the configuration file and the **enable** password is in plain text.

If there is an enable secret password, it takes precedence over the non-secret enable password and therefore will be the only one that will place you in enable mode. IOS does not normally encrypt either the enable password or the access password in your configuration file. However, it does automatically encrypt the enable secret password, making it more secure. You should always configure your routers with enable secret passwords.

Once in enable mode you will notice the prompt has changed and the greater than symbol has been replaced by a pound sign (#), or octothorpe. This is shown in Figure 3-11.

Figure 3-11 Notice that the prompt changes when you enter enable mode.

```
User Access Verification

Password:
wan4500>en
Password:
wan4500#
```

Access mode is restricted to 31 commands; enable mode has 51. This is not the only difference, options within commands are limited as well. For example, the **show** command has 78 options in enable mode and only 19 in access mode. Because of the enhanced nature of enable mode, it is always necessary to guard your enable passwords for your routers. These are the keys to your kingdom, and passing them out willy-nilly endangers your network security. On the other hand, you should still protect the access password, although it is much less of a security risk. Because it is usually necessary to have this password before entering enable mode, it is your first line of defense. Take care of it, and it will help take care of you.

CLI Browsing

The CLI is probably unlike any interface you've seen before. Although cryptic to most, it does provide a wide variety of features you should know. Focusing only on basic CLI skills, a list of keystroke commands to help you navigate through the CLI is listed in Table 3-3.

Table 3-3

Listing of some
basic CLI navigation
commands

Keystroke Command	What It Does
Ctrl-P or up arrow	Recall previous command (scroll up through the command history)
Ctrl-N or down arrow	Recall next command (scroll down through the command history)
Ctrl-B or left arrow	Move left over current command at prompt
Ctrl-F or right arrow	Move right over current command at prompt
Ctrl-A	Go to beginning of command line
Ctrl-E	Go to end of command line
Esc B	Go back one word
Esc F	Go forward one word
Delete or Backspace	Erase the character to the left of the cursor
Ctrl-D	Delete the character at the cursor
Ctrl-L or Ctrl-R	Redisplay the current command line

You should practice using the CLI and become proficient in all of the above keystroke commands. By doing so, you will become more aware of your Cisco routers and their configurations. You should also become familiar with using the online help feature.

Cisco IOS provides context-sensitive help using the question mark (?) and Tab keys. Typing a question mark alone shows you all available commands for the current mode. Typing a question mark after typing a partial command shows you all possible commands that will complete the word you started typing. Figure 3-12 shows an example. Typing **c?** in enable mode will show you all the commands that start with *c*. It will also leave the *c* on the command line, so that you can continue typing from the point at which you typed the question mark.

Figure 3-12   Using the question mark will show you available commands to complete what you have started typing.

```
wan4500#c?
calendar clear clock configure connect
copy

wan4500#c
```

You can use the question mark to help you navigate through the CLI. This is especially useful to infrequent CLI users, who might not remember exact commands, such as how to view the status of a certain interface. If you type one or more characters of a command and end with a question mark (**s?**), you will get a list of all commands that start with those characters. If you type enough letters of a command to make it unique, then type a space, and then a question mark (**show inter ?**), you will get a list of all keywords that can be appended to that command. This is shown in Figure 3-13.

Figure 3-13 Typing a question mark after a space will show you all the keywords and options that will help complete the command.

```
wan4500#s?
*s=show    send   setup show slip
start-chat systat

wan4500#show i?
interfaces ip ipx isdn

wan4500#show inter ?
interfaces

wan4500#show inter ?
 BRI        ISDN Basic Rate Interface
 Dialer     Dialer interface
 Ethernet   IEEE 802.3
 Null       Null interface
 Serial     Serial
 Virtual-Access Virtual Access interface
 accounting   Show interface accounting
 crb        Show interface routing/bridging info
 irb        Show interface routing/bridging info
 <cr>

wan4500#show inter e0
Ethernet0 is up, line protocol is up
...
```

The Tab key will complete a word for you when no other words will fit. This allows you to see a whole command without having to type in lengthy words and phrases like **configuration**, **frame-relay**, **payload-compression**, and **packet-by-packet**. Figure 3-14 is an example of the use of the Tab key to show the whole command without typing it all. The bold characters show the characters typed. Each time the Tab key is pressed, the CLI completes the word on the next line, and you can continue typing.

▬▬▬▬▬▬▬▬▬▬▬▬▬▬▬▬▬▬▬▬▬▬▬▬▬▬▬▬▬▬▬▬▬▬

Figure 3-14 The Tab key will fill in words for you as long as no others can complete the command.

```
wan4500#sh<tab>
wan4500#show i<tab>
wan4500#show in<tab>
wan4500#show interfaces e<tab>
wan4500#show interfaces ethernet 0
Ethernet0 is up, line protocol is up
...
```

This is very useful in configuration mode, because you might want to see the whole command spelled out for you, without being forced to type it in. The CLI will let you enter partial commands, as long as the characters you type are unique for one command. For example, there are seven commands in enable mode that start with the letter *s*. If you enter *s?* at the command line, the system will show them to you, as seen in Figure 3-15.

▬▬▬▬▬▬▬▬▬▬▬▬▬▬▬▬▬▬▬▬▬▬▬▬▬▬▬▬▬▬▬▬▬▬

Figure 3-15 Typing *s?* in the CLI will show you all commands that start with the letter *s*.

```
wan4500#s?
*s=show   send   setup show slip
start-chat systat
```

Note two things of interest here: First, there is only one command that starts with *sh*, and it has an asterisk next to it. If you wanted to use the **show** command, all you would normally need to type would be *sh*, the unique first letters of the command name. However, the asterisk indicates that the first letter alone will invoke this command. So, using either *s* or *sh* gives you the same results as typing the whole word **show**. However, simply typing **s<tab>** will not fill in the command line, because there are not enough unique characters. You must type **sh<tab>** if you want the word **show** to appear automatically for you, as shown in Figure 3-16.

Figure 3-16 There must be enough unique letters in a typed command to make the Tab key display the whole word for you.

```
wan4500#s<tab>
wan4500#              Returns a blank line
wan4500#sh<tab>
wan4500#show          Returns the whole word
```

By using short cuts in the CLI, you can become more familiar with it and be more proficient at entering commands. The command-line help character ? (the question mark) should be part of your everyday router programming skills. This will help you remember which commands you want to use, if it has been a long time since you have used the CLI.

CLI Modes

The IOS user interface provides access to several different command modes. Each command mode provides a group of related commands. The five basic CLI modes we will discuss are ROM (Read Only Memory) monitor, Initial Setup, User EXEC, Privileged EXEC or Enable, and Global Configuration mode. These are only a few of the many different modes available in IOS, but you should consider them as all you really need to know in the beginning. Each mode has its own unique command set, giving you access to a particular part of the operating system features. The vast majority of command modes are only available when configuring the router. These all become available to you after entering global configuration mode (which you can only enter from enable mode).

ROM Monitor Mode

Within each Cisco IOS router is a bootable ROM chip that has a very basic operating system on it. During normal operations, you never see this mode; in case of a catastrophe (such as a loss of enable mode password or a corrupt image of IOS), you will need to use it to recover. ROM monitor mode is the most basic fallback position for emergency router maintenance. You should learn the basics of this mode, and hope that you never need to use it.

Entering ROM monitor mode sounds simpler than it is. All you need to do is send a break character down the serial line to the console port within 60 seconds of booting the router. However, the break key on your keyboard might not be the way to do this, depending on how you are accessing the console port. Some methods for sending the break character are listed in Table 3-4. If they don't match your exact software needs, they might be able to take you in the right direction. You should practice entering ROM monitor mode and take notes. This will help you manage any future catastrophe better, because ROM monitor mode will not seem so alien to you.

Table 3-4

Various ways to send a *break* from serial devices and software

Console Access Method	Break Key Sequence
HyperTerminal	Ctrl-Break
NetTerm	Edit -> Send Long Break
UNIX serial utilities: tip and cu	<enter>~%b
Dumb terminal such as VT220	Ctrl-Break

Once you are in ROM monitor mode, you will see something like Figure 3-17 on the screen:

Figure 3-17 What you see when you enter ROM monitor mode.

```
*** System received an abort due to Break Key ***
signal= #3, code= #0, context= #605cdd00
PC = 0x6015b804, Cause = 0x20, Status Reg = 0x34008302
rommon 1 >
```

As in IOS, pressing the question mark key will present you with a list of all available commands. These commands are listed in Figure 3-18.

WARNING

Do not play around in here! You can do really nasty things to your router that you might never be able to undo. The only time you should be working in ROM monitor mode is when you know what you are doing. How do you learn what to do? In most cases that require recovery from a catastrophic failure (such as loss of password or corruption of an IOS image), you can get verbatim instructions from Cisco. Call phone support or access Cisco's troubleshooting engines on the World Wide Web. You will receive a list of step-by-step instructions on how to correct your problem. Once you've completed it, the **reset** command will reboot the router, and move on to the next stage of recovery. ROM monitor mode will not let you fix most problems directly; rather, it allows you to make certain configuration changes that enable you to fix your problem directly in IOS.

Figure 3-18 The ROM monitor command list.

```
alias        set and display aliases command
boot         boot up an external process
break        set/show/clear the breakpoint
confreg      configuration register utility
cont         continue executing a downloaded image
context      display the context of a loaded image
cookie       display contents of cookie PROM in hex
dev          list the device table
dir          list files in file system
dis          disassemble instruction stream
dnld         serial download a program module
frame        print out a selected stack frame
help         monitor builtin command help
history      monitor command history
meminfo      main memory information
repeat       repeat a monitor command
reset        system reset
set          set a monitor variable
stack        produce a stack trace
sync         write monitor environment to NVRAM
sysret       print out info from last system return
unalias      unset an alias
unset        unset a monitor variable
rommon 2 >
```

Initial Setup Mode

When you first receive a router, you should connect it to a serial console device, such as a PC that is running HyperTerminal or a dumb terminal *before* the first boot. If your router came from a third party, someone might have configured it previously and you will not see the initial setup dialog. If the router came from Cisco directly, it should come up in initial configuration mode, which looks like Figure 3-19.

Figure 3-19 *The beginning of the initial configuration dialog.*

```
— System Configuration Dialog —-

At any point you may enter a question mark '?' for help.
Use ctrl-c to abort configuration dialog at any prompt.
Default settings are in square brackets '[]'.

Continue with configuration dialog? [yes]:
```

This mode provides you with an easy-to-understand configuration menu. It takes you quickly and easily through the steps needed to provide basic functionality. Of course, you will need to know how you want the router configured before you begin. Among the information you should have before you start are the protocols you will use (TCP/IP, IPX, AppleTalk, and so on), the addresses for each interface, the routing protocols used, and whether or not to use SNMP.

During the initial setup mode, all you need to do is answer the questions put to you. Most are *yes* or *no* questions, and entering **y** or **n** will suffice. If the answer you wish is already on the command line in square brackets ([ ]), all you need to do is press the Enter key to choose it. A basic configuration dialog for a Cisco 2501 router might look like the one below. In this case, we are using a single direct T1 line to the Internet, a single Ethernet connection to your local network, the RIP routing protocol, and the TCP/IP protocol only. First, start by choosing to enter the configuration dialog and viewing the available interfaces, as shown in Figure 3-20. You should double-check the interface summary against the physical ports on the router, and note any discrepancies.

Figure 3-20 *Viewing the interfaces in initial configuration mode.*

```
Would you like to enter the initial configuration dialog? [yes]:<enter>

First, would you like to see the current interface summary? [yes]:
<enter>

Any interface listed with OK? value "NO" does not have a valid configu-
ration

Interface      IP-Address      OK?      Method      Status      Protocol
Ethernet0      unassigned      NO       not set     up          down
Serial0        unassigned      NO       not set     down        down
Serial1        unassigned      NO       not set     down        down
```

Setup will then ask you to give the router a name and enter all three of its passwords. The first is the enable secret password. This password gets you into enable mode, if it exists. It is encrypted, so that no one seeing the configuration file for the router will know what it is. The next password is the enable password. This is stored in plain text and should be different from the enable secret password. It seems silly for Cisco to force you to enter both, because you will never use the enable password if an enable secret password exists. Finally, the virtual terminal password is entered. This is also stored in plain text. It is the password used to enter user exec mode when logging into the router over the network. This is shown in Figure 3-21.

Figure 3-21 *Entering the router name and passwords in initial configuration mode.*

```
Configuring global parameters:

  Enter host name [Router]: cisco-gwy

The enable secret is a one-way cryptographic secret used
instead of the enable password when it exists.

  Enter enable secret: secret
```

The enable password is used when there is no enable secret
and when using older software and some boot images.

```
Enter enable password: junk
Enter virtual terminal password: login
```

Here we choose to use SNMP network management and set the community to gwy-ro-pass. It is extremely important not to use the default community of *public* for your routers. Most SNMP-capable devices use public as the default community string. Hackers trying to attack your network devices via SNMP will always try a community string of *public* first. This community string acts as the password for reading and writing SNMP data to your router. If you choose the default, you could open your router up to severe problems.

Next, choose not to use the Novell IPX protocol, use TCP/IP, not the IGRP (Interior Gateway Routing Protocol) routing protocol, and use the RIP routing protocol. This is shown in Figure 3-22.

■ ■

Figure 3-22 Choosing the SNMP community string, supported protocols, and routing protocols in initial configuration mode.

```
Configure SNMP Network Management? [yes]: <enter>
  Community string [public]: gwy-ro-pass
 Configure IPX? [no]: <enter>
 Configure IP? [yes]: <enter>
  Configure IGRP routing? [yes]: no
  Configure RIP routing? [no]: y
```

Finally, configure each interface with an IP address and the number of bits in the subnet field. If you are part of a larger network, such as a corporate WAN or the Internet, you will receive the IP address numbers and subnet information from the manager of that network. In the case of the Internet, these will always be your ISP. The interface configurations are listed in Figure 3-23.

Figure 3-23 *Configuring IP addresses and netmasks in initial configuration mode.*

```
Configuring interface parameters:

Configuring interface Ethernet0:
 Is this interface in use? [yes]: <enter>
 Configure IP on this interface? [yes]: <enter>
  IP address for this interface: 208.213.189.1
 .Number of bits in subnet field [0]: <enter>
  Class C network is 208.213.189.0, 0 subnet bits; mask is
255.255.255.0

Configuring interface Serial0:
 Is this interface in use? [yes]: <enter>
 Configure IP on this interface? [yes]: <enter>
 Configure IP unnumbered on this interface? [no]: <enter>
  IP address for this interface: 137.244.12.2
  Number of bits in subnet field [0]: 14
  Class B network is 137.244.0.0, 14 subnet bits; mask is
255.255.255.252

Configuring interface Serial1:
 Is this interface in use? [yes]: n
```

Once complete, Setup will show you the default configuration file. This is shown in Figure 3-24. If it is acceptable, enter **yes**, and Setup will write it to NVRAM (Nonvolatile RAM). The configuration will take effect immediately, and if all else is correct, the router will start doing its job. Note the gibberish in the enable secret line is really the encrypted password.

Figure 3-24 The configuration file created by the initial configuration dialog.

The following configuration command script was created:

```
hostname cisco-gwy
enable secret 5 $1$h7A4$WQexeEMKr.sZ.UiJLTmz5.
enable password junk
line vty 0 4
password login
snmp-server community gwy-ro-pass
!
no ipx routing
ip routing
!
interface Ethernet0
ip address 208.213.189.1 255.255.255.0
!
interface Serial0
ip address 137.244.12.2 255.255.255.252
!
interface Serial1
shutdown
no ip address
!
router rip
network 208.213.189.0
network 137.244.0.0
!
end

Use this configuration? [yes/no]: yes
Building configuration...
Use the enabled mode 'configure' command to modify this configuration.


Press RETURN to get started!
```

User EXEC Mode

User exec mode is the most basic connection to the router. By default, it asks only for a password when you connect to the router over the network. You know you are in user exec mode when your router prompt is the router name followed by a greater than character (>). This is shown in Figure 3-25.

Figure 3-25 The user exec mode prompt is the router name followed by a ">".

```
cisco-gwy>
```

In this mode, a user can investigate the network and get basic information on the router only. In order for them to perform configuration changes, they must be able to get into enable mode.

Regardless of how safe this seems, you do not want common users to have access to your router, even in user exec mode. Protect this password as you would protect the enable mode password. Without it, users cannot get any information about the router, except from the console or aux (auxiliary) ports. You can remedy this by placing the same user exec mode password on the console and aux ports; then no one can get information about your router without a password.

Privileged EXEC or Enable Mode

This mode holds ultimate sway over your router. It is the highest level of security, equal to the root user in UNIX, the system user in Novell, and the administrator user in NT. With it, you can do anything you want to the router (including thoroughly trashing it!). Be careful in this mode, and always have a clear idea about what you are trying to do before entering it. This will help to keep you focused and out of trouble.

Enable mode is indicated by a CLI prompt made up of the router name followed by a pound sign (#) (more formally known as an octothorpe—just visit this site if you don't believe me: http://wombat.doc.ic.ac.uk/foldoc/foldoc.cgi?octothorpe). This is shown in Figure 3-26.

Figure 3-26 The enable mode prompt is the router name followed by an octothorpe.

```
cisco-gwy#
```

To get into enable mode, you must first enter user exec mode. Once there, simply enter **enable** at the CLI, and the router will prompt you for the enable secret password if there is one, or for the enable password if there is not. Once in enable mode, you can do anything to the router: check and reset ports, alter the configuration, and even alter the version of IOS running on the router.

Global Configuration Mode

Global configuration mode allows you to make changes to the router's configuration information. You know you are in global configuration mode when your prompt is the router name followed by the word *config* in parentheses and a pound sign. This is shown in Figure 3-27.

Figure 3-27 The CLI prompt that shows global configuration mode.

```
cisco-gwy(config)#
```

You get into global configuration mode by using the **configure** command (or **conf**, for short.) There are four possible sources of configuration updates, and you can see them by entering **conf ?** at the CLI. This is shown in Figure 3-28.

Figure 3-28 The four ways to enter data into configuration mode.

```
cisco-gwy#conf ?
 memory        Configure from NV memory
 network       Configure from a TFTP network host
 overwrite-network Overwrite NV memory from TFTP network host
 terminal      Configure from the terminal
 <cr>
```

If you enter **conf** only, the router will prompt you to provide a source for the updates. Only three of the four are listed, but you can access the fourth by entering **ov**. This is shown in Figure 3-29.

Figure 3-29 *The router leaves out the overwrite-network choice when you only type conf.*

```
cisco-gwy#conf
Configuring from terminal, memory, or network [terminal]?
```

Configuring the router from the CLI directly is done by using the **configure terminal** or **conf t** command, commonly used for general router maintenance and small configuration changes. This is the only way to get direct access to global configuration mode.

The other three options are memory, network, and overwrite-network, and are all automated. You cannot make changes by hand. **Configure memory** or **conf m** copies the configuration file stored in NVRAM back into the running router configuration. This is useful when you've made mistakes configuring the router with **conf t**. It allows you to reset the state of the router to the last saved configuration, but might not delete added lines. To insure a complete restoration to the previous configuration, you must also reboot the router.

Configure network or **conf n** allows you to read a text configuration file from a TFTP (Trivial File Transfer Protocol) server on the network and copy it into the running router configuration. This copies the file into the running configuration as if you were typing it in line for line through the CLI. This can cause problems, because lines that already exist in the running configuration (but have been removed from the text file) will not be removed from the running configuration. Also, certain types of configurations (i.e., access lists) must be completely cleared from the running configuration before they can be changed. Putting a **no** in front of the configuration line (that is, **no access-list 120**) usually does this. If left uncleared, any new lines will append themselves to the bottom of the existing ones. This is useful when making major changes to a router (and needing a better editor than the CLI), but not when removing lines. When removing lines, you can use **configure overwrite-network** or **conf o**. This erases the current running configuration before loading the new one into memory.

Always take care when updating the router configuration. A good way to manage router configurations is with a TFTP server on the network. You can store your router configurations on the server as text files. This allows you to copy them to other files before making changes, and keep a revision history of router changes. It also allows you to use a more familiar text editor to make your configuration changes.

Most of the other command modes are only visible under global configuration mode. For example, when you want to configure an interface, you enter the interface configuration mode by entering the interface name at the global configuration prompt. This is shown in Figure 3-30.

Figure 3-30 Entering interface configuration mode for Ethernet0.

```
cisco-gwy#conf t
Enter configuration commands, one per line. End with CNTL/Z.
cisco-gwy(config)#interface ethernet0
cisco-gwy(config-if)#
```

To exit a configuration mode under global configuration mode, use the **exit** or **end** command. The **exit** command returns you to global configuration mode. The **end** command (or Ctrl-z) returns you to enable mode. This is shown in Figure 3-31.

Figure 3-31 Using the exit command takes you back to the global configuration; typing end takes you back to exec mode.

```
cisco-gwy(config)#interface ethernet0
cisco-gwy(config-if)#exit
cisco-gwy(config)#interface ethernet0
cisco-gwy(config-if)#end
cisco-gwy#
```

Commands are loaded into the router's running configuration as they are typed or read from a file.

Go back and read that last line again. Now once more. Ponder it for a few seconds. (Are you pondering what I'm pondering, Pinky?) This means that lines typed into the running configuration take effect as soon as you press enter or a complete line is read from the file. Therefore, if you are loading a large configuration change, the order of the configuration lines can be extremely important. Think about what might happen if you logged into a remote router and began changing an interface definition. You could possibly execute a command into the running configuration that would lock you out of the router. Fortunately, this command would not be saved into NVRAM, but you would still need someone physically present to cycle the router power to get it back on the network.

You must always keep this in mind when you are making configuration changes. Some commands take a while to execute on a router, so don't panic if the command prompt doesn't return immediately. If it seems to be taking too long, try to make another Telnet connection to the router, or ping it. If there is a danger of the router's going off the network during a configuration change, make sure you have a backup plan to get the router back online. This might be a person on site, the pager or home phone of someone who lives nearby and has access to the router, or a modem on the auxiliary port for you to dial in to.

Table 3-5 contains a more complete list of IOS CLI modes.

Table 3-5

Some of the many modes available in IOS

Command Mode	Access Method	Prompt	Exit Method
User EXEC	Log in.	Router>	Use the **logout** command.
Privileged EXEC or enable	From user EXEC mode, use the **enable** EXEC command.	Router#	To exit back to user EXEC mode, use the **disable** command. To enter global configuration mode, use the **configure** privileged EXEC command.
Global configuration	From privileged EXEC mode, use the **configure** privileged EXEC command.	Router(config)#	To exit to privileged EXEC mode, use the **exit** or **end** command or press **Ctrl-Z**. To enter interface configuration mode, enter an **interface** configuration command.
Interface configuration	From global configuration mode, enter by specifying an interface with an **interface** command.	Router(config-if)#	To exit to global configuration mode, use the **exit** command. To exit to privileged EXEC mode, use the **exit** command or press **Ctrl-Z**. To enter subinterface configuration mode, specify a subinterface with the **interface** command.
Subinterface configuration	From interface configuration mode, specify a subinterface with an **interface** command.	Router (config-subif)#	To exit to global configuration mode, use the **exit** command. To enter privileged EXEC mode, use the **end** command or press **Ctrl-Z**.
Controller configuration	From global configuration mode, use the **controller** command to configure a channelized T1 interface.	Router (config-controller)#	To exit to global configuration mode, use the **exit** command. To enter privileged EXEC mode, use the **end** command or press **Ctrl-Z**.

(cont.)

Table 3-5 continued

Command Mode	Access Method	Prompt	Exit Method
Hub configuration	From global configuration mode, enter by specifying a hub with the **hub** command.	Router (config-hub)#	To exit to global configuration mode, use the **exit** command. To enter privileged EXEC mode, use the **end** command or press **Ctrl-Z**.
Line configuration	From global configuration mode, enter by specifying a line with a **line** command.	Router (config-line)#	To exit to global configuration mode, use the **exit** command. To enter privileged EXEC mode, use the **end** command or press **Ctrl-Z**.
Router configuration	From global configuration mode, enter by issuing a command that begins with **router** (such as **router igrp**).	Router (config-router)#	To exit to global configuration mode, use the **exit** command. To enter privileged EXEC mode, use the **end** command or press **Ctrl-Z**.
IPX-router configuration	From global configuration mode, enter by issuing the **ipx routing** command, then a command that begins with **ipx router** (such as **ipx router eigrp**).	Router(config-ipx-router)#	To exit to global configuration mode, use the **exit** command.
ROM monitor	From privileged EXEC mode, use the **reload** EXEC command. Press Break during the first 60 seconds while the system is booting.	>	To exit to user EXEC mode, type **continue**.
Interface channel configuration	From global EXEC mode, use the **interface channel** *1/2* command.	Router(config)	To exit to global configuration mode, use the **exit** command.
Initial Setup mode	From global EXEC mode, use the **setup** command or use the **write erase** command followed by the **reload** command.	Would you like to enter the initial configuration dialog? [yes]:	To exit from **setup** command, respond with **no**.
Access-list configuration	From global configuration mode, use the **ip access-list** command.	Router(config-std-nacl)# or Router(config-ext-nacl)#	To exit to global configuration mode, use the **exit** command.

Saving the Configuration

Possibly the most important part of making configuration changes to your router is making sure that they stick around after you make them. Simply editing the configuration does not make it permanent the next time the router starts up. When the router boots, it reads a copy of the configuration file from NVRAM into main memory and then runs it. The configuration changes you make in global configuration mode only affect the running configuration in main memory. You must save the configuration in NVRAM in order for it to be permanent. You should also copy the configuration file to a network server, so you can track changes and revert to an earlier (working) version, if necessary.

There are two commands for saving the configuration file: **write** and **copy**. **Write** or **wr** is the older of the two. It is simpler to use and has fewer options, as seen in Figure 3-32.

Figure 3-32 *The options for the write command.*

```
cisco-gwy#wr ?
 erase    Erase NV memory
 memory   Write to NV memory
 network  Write to network TFTP server
 terminal Write to terminal
 <cr>
```

Write erase or **wr e** erases NVRAM and allows you to start over with a clean configuration. If you reboot a router after erasing the NVRAM, it will boot directly into the initial setup mode. **Write memory** or simply **wr** writes the running configuration to NVRAM. This is the easiest way to save the configuration file, but Cisco prefers the use of the newer **copy** command, probably because it has more options. **Write network** or **wr n** will copy the running configuration file to a TFTP server on the network. TFTP usually requires that a file exist before you can write to it. This means you might have to create an empty file on the server before you can successfully **copy** the file. By default, IOS will name the file **ROUTERNAME-confg**. *If you have saved the file previously, the router will overwrite it without asking you first!* Copy the old file to a new one, and add the date of the change to the file name beforehand. This will make it easier to track the changes you make to configuration files. **Write terminal** or **wr t** displays the running configuration to the screen.

The **copy** command is much more complex, because it works on more than just the running configuration in main memory. It can manipulate the startup configuration in NVRAM and the Flash memory where IOS is stored, and it gives you access to two additional network protocols: MOP (Maintenance Operation Protocol) and RCP (Remote Copy Protocol). **Copy running-config startup-config** or **cop ru s** does the same thing as the **write** command, copying the running configuration file in main memory to the startup configuration file in NVRAM. You can also copy the running configuration to a TFTP server (same as **write network**) or to an RCP server using the commands: **copy running-config tftp** and **copy running-config rcp**.

The **copy** command is very versatile, allowing you to copy the running configuration, the startup configuration, and the IOS images in Flash memory to and from anywhere that makes sense, using the TFTP or RCP protocols. The MOP protocol, in this instance, is only useful for copying an IOS image into Flash memory.

Methodology for Configuration Updates

A good method for managing router configurations is by TFTP server on your network. It will allow you to store configuration files and IOS images on a system you trust. You should make sure it's a secure system, because you might be storing passwords in plain text and you wouldn't want just anyone reading your configuration files. Any system can be a TFTP server, including UNIX, Windows NT, or Windows 95. Remember, the danger of a Windows 95 system is that it has no local file security, so think twice about using it.

You should also know that TFTP security is weak. In order to download a file, you must know its name; in order to upload one, it must already exist and be writeable. Because there is no way to get a directory of files, you might consider it somewhat secure. However, IOS names router configuration files **ROUTERNAME-confg** by default, where **ROUTERNAME** is the hostname of the router. This makes it easy for people to guess configuration file names.

All UNIX systems ship with TFTP servers built in, but usually not enabled. Configuring one is usually as easy as uncommenting it from the file */etc/inetd.conf* and then sending a hang up signal to *inetd* using the **kill -1 PID** command, where **PID** is the process id of *inetd*. You should read the manual entry on **tftpd** or **in.tftpd** to make sure you configure it correctly. To shore up security on TFTP (and any other network daemons), you might want to download and install TCP Wrappers from CERT/CC (The Computer Emergency Response Team/Coordination Center http://www.cert.org/) at ftp://ftp.cert.org/pub/tools/tcp_wrappers/. This will give you control over which machines may communicate with the TFTP daemon, eliminating the threat of unauthorized connections to the server.

For Windows NT and Windows 95, Cisco has a free TFTP daemon that you can download from http://www.cisco.com/pcgi-bin/tablebuild.pl/tftp. It does not have many configuration options and only allows you to pick the directory that TFTP will use to store files. However, it shores up security because you can start and stop it as needed. Best of all, it's free!

Once you have a TFTP server set up and basically secure, you should copy your router configuration files and your IOS images to it. The TFTP directory on your server will become the staging area for your IOS upgrades and router configuration changes. You should also keep backup copies of your router configuration files here. Before making changes to a router, back the file up to ROUTERNAME-confg.MMDDYY, where MM is the two-digit month, DD is the two-digit day, and YY is the two-digit year. If you are making many updates in a single day, you can add a two-digit revision number to the end. With that done, you can edit the file using your favorite text editor (just make sure to save it as plain text [.txt] if you are using a word processor). You can then use the command **copy tftp running-config** to update the router configuration and **write** to save it to NVRAM.

If you make changes to the router configuration at the CLI, connect to your TFTP server first and back up the configuration file stored there before saving your changes to the network. Next, use the **write** command to write to NVRAM and **write network** to copy it to your TFTP server.

Using this method will let you track changes to your network and always give you a fallback position in case of a catastrophe.

Notes about the Configuration File

There are essentially two configuration files in a Cisco router at any given time: the running configuration file and the startup configuration file. When you used the command **show configuration**, you see only the startup configuration file. To avoid confusion, you should be explicit about which configuration file you want to view, and use the commands **show running-configuration** and **show startup-configuration**.

IOS supports the concept of hidden commands, meaning that not all commands in the router configuration are visible. These hidden commands are the IOS default for a particular setting or are considered extraneous.

One example is the **no shutdown** command. **Shutdown** disables an interface in the configuration file and indicates this condition on a port with the word *shutdown* in the configuration file, as seen in Figure 3-33.

Figure 3-33 *The shutdown command indicates the port is administratively disabled.*

```
!
interface Serial0
 ip address 137.244.12.2 255.255.255.252
 shutdown
!
```

When the **no shutdown** command is entered for the same interface, the interface enters an operational state and the **shutdown** flag is removed from the configuration. This is shown in Figure 3-34.

Figure 3-34 *An operational interface does not contain a no shutdown command.*

```
!
interface Serial0
 ip address 137.244.12.2 255.255.255.252
!
```

This does not work universally the same in IOS, and you need to get used to it. For example, the commands **service udp-small-servers** and **service tcp-small-servers** are on by default if you use the initial setup dialog. If you enter the command **no service udp-small-servers** in global configuration mode, your running configuration will show the whole command instead of hiding it like it does with **no shutdown**. This is seen in Figure 3-35.

Figure 3-35 *Not all commands disappear from the configuration when they are turned off with a no command.*

```
no service udp-small-servers
service tcp-small-servers
```

Checking Command Syntax

The user interface provides error isolation in the form of an error indicator, shown as a caret symbol (^). It appears at the point in the command line where you have entered an incorrect command, keyword, or argument. The error location indicator and interactive help system allow you to find and correct syntax errors.

Suppose you want to set the clock on your router. You can use context-sensitive help to check the syntax for setting the clock, as shown in Figure 3-36.

Figure 3-36 Displaying the command syntax.

```
wan4500# clock ?
 set  Set the time and date
wan4500# clock
```

The help output shows that the keyword **set** is required. Next, check the syntax for entering the time, as shown in Figure 3-37.

Figure 3-37 The Help output shows you the information required to complete the command.

```
wan4500# clock set ?
 hh:mm:ss  Current time
wan4500# clock set
```

Enter the current time in HH:MM:SS format, as shown below in Figure 3-38.

Figure 3-38 Although the information is entered properly, it doesn't mean that is all that is needed.

```
wan4500# clock set 13:32:00
% Incomplete command.
wan4500#
```

The error message indicates that you need to provide additional arguments to the CLI to complete the command. Press Ctrl-P or the up arrow key to automatically repeat the previous command. Next, add a space and question mark to see the additional arguments needed to complete the command properly, as shown in Figure 3-39.

Figure 3-39 The command requires more arguments before it is complete.

```
wan4500# clock set 13:32:00 ?
 <1-31>   Day of the month
 MONTH  Month of the year
wan4500# clock set 13:32:00
```

Continue the command by appending the day and month. End with a question mark again to see if any more keywords or arguments are required, as in Figure 3-40.

Figure 3-40 By ending a line with a question mark you can see if any more information is required.

```
wan4500# clock set 13:32:00 23 June ?
 <1993-2035> Year
wan4500# clock set 13:32:00 23 June
```

Finish by entering the year after the date, as in Figure 3-41.

Figure 3-41 The caret symbol shows you where the error in syntax occurred.

```
wan4500# clock set 13:32:00 23 June 98
                                    ^

% Invalid input detected at '^' marker
wan4500# clock set 13:32:00 23 June
```

The caret symbol and error message indicate an error at **98**. To list the correct syntax, enter the command up to the point where the error occurred and then enter a question mark, as shown in Figure 3-42.

Figure 3-42 Viewing the syntax the router wants will help you correct your errors.

```
wan4500# clock set 13:32:00 23 June ?
 <1993-2035> Year
wan4500# clock set 13:32:00 23 June
```

From the help information, you can see that you must enter the year as a four-digit number, not a two-digit number. To complete the command, type the year properly and press the Enter key. This is shown in Figure 3-43.

Figure 3-43 Now the command is complete and the clock is set.

```
wan4500# clock set 13:32:00 23 June 1998
wan4500#
```

IOS Feature Sets

The Cisco IOS software is packaged into *feature sets* (also called *software images*). There are many different feature sets available; each feature set contains a specific subset of Cisco IOS features and protocols. Not all feature sets are available with all platforms. Also, some feature sets support different features when run on different platforms.

There is a very large list of feature sets, and it is not always clear what is included in each one. To select the one that is right for you, you probably need to do some research. The proper place for this is Cisco's Web site, Cisco Connection Online (CCO). You can connect to it at http://www.cisco.com and then follow these steps to reach the IOS documentation section:

- Documentation
- Cisco Product Documentation
- Cisco IOS Software Configuration

From there, you need to select the IOS version you wish to use; after that, you are looking for release notes and the IOS packaging information.

Cisco IOS packaging information contains cross referencing that describes which feature sets are available on which platforms and what features they support. This is required reading for any site administrator who has specific needs. For example, IOS version 11.1 only supports the AppleTalk protocol on Cisco 7500 routers with the following feature sets: Desktop/IBM, Enterprise, Enterprise/APPN, Desktop/IBM/VIP, Enterprise/VIP, and Enterprise/APPN/VIP.

The URLs shown in Table 3-6 will take you directly to the proper Web pages for all recent versions of Cisco IOS versions 10 and 11.

Table 3-6

URLs for IOS major versions

Cisco IOS Version	Web page URL
10.2	http://www.cisco.com/univercd/cc/td/doc/product/software/ios102/rn_rt102/83523.htm
10.3	http://www.cisco.com/univercd/cc/td/doc/product/software/ios103/rn_rt103/83397.htm
11.0	http://www.cisco.com/univercd/cc/td/doc/product/software/ios11/rnrt110/rnrt110.htm
11.1	http://www.cisco.com/univercd/cc/td/doc/product/software/ios111/rnrt111.htm
11.2	http://www.cisco.com/univercd/cc/td/doc/product/software/ios112/rn112.htm
11.3	http://www.cisco.com/univercd/cc/td/doc/product/software/ios113ed/rn113m/rn113mpk.htm

Some feature sets have special designations, such as PLUS, PLUS 40, PLUS 56, and FW (firewall). These add additional features to those specified by the base feature set. For example, you could have three feature sets: IP/IPX/AT/DEC, IP/IPX/AT/DEC PLUS, and IP/IPX/AT/DEC/FW PLUS. The base feature set is IP/IPX/AT/DEC. The additional feature sets add the PLUS feature set to both sets and the firewall features to the last set. The Plus feature set contains a variable set of additional features, depending on the hardware platform selected. PLUS 40 and PLUS 56 include additional 40-bit and 56-bit DES data encryption, respectively.

The variable set of additional features contained in the Plus feature sets can contain such features as network address translation (NAT), data encryption, RADIUS, OSPF, AppleTalk, and Network Time Protocol (NTP). VPDN (L2F tunneling) and RADIUS are available on the Plus feature sets starting with Cisco IOS Release 11.2(10)P and 11.3. Cisco IOS firewall feature sets are available in Releases 11.2(11)P, 11.3(3)T, and up.

The 40-bit DES data encryption may legally be distributed to any party eligible to receive Cisco IOS software; however, it is not a cryptographically strong solution. You should carefully evaluate 40-bit DES before using it. Cisco IOS images that have 56-bit DES might be subject to export or import controls, or both, and might have a limited distribution. For more information, contact your sales representative or distributor, or visit CCO at http://www.cisco.com/wwl/export/encrypt.html, or send e-mail to export@cisco.com.

Choosing an IOS Feature Set

Several concerns must be factored into choosing a feature set: operational necessities, cost, RAM usage, and Flash memory usage. The primary concern is always making sure that you meet your minimal protocol and feature needs. For example, a site that needs only TCP/IP might also need RADIUS authentication, which is usually part of a PLUS feature set. In order to get PLUS, you might need a feature set that supports more than just the TCP/IP protocol (such as IP/IPX/AT/DEC PLUS or Desktop PLUS), because there might not be an IP PLUS feature set available on your platform.

Other concerns are RAM and Flash memory usage. As feature sets add functionality, they usually grow in size and memory requirements. A good example is the Service Provider feature set for the Cisco 2501 router. In version 10.3, the image required 4MB of Flash memory and 4MB of RAM. In version 11.2, the same feature set requires 8MB of Flash memory. Obviously if your router has 4MB of Flash memory, you could not upgrade from 10.3 to 11.2 without upgrading your memory configuration. If you are purchasing a new router, you should make sure to buy as much Flash memory and RAM as you can afford. This will save you time and expense if you should need to upgrade to a substantially larger IOS image later.

Finally, there is the cost of the IOS license itself to consider. While it might be nifty to have an Enterprise feature set license, which includes everything you could possibly use, it also might be cost prohibitive. The Enterprise feature set license cost can be more than twice that of an IP/IPX feature set. If you can get along fine with IP/IPX, why not purchase it instead? It will save you money on RAM, Flash memory, and the license as well. You can always upgrade your license later, and usually with little additional cost than if you had purchased it to begin with.

Non-IOS

The non-IOS-based routers we will be discussing are the Cisco 760 and 770 routers. As previously mentioned, this product line was obtained through the purchase of Combinet, which designed the original router and OS. These series of routers are ISDN-to-Ethernet access routers designed for small, home, and remote office situations. Through enhancements to the OS, Cisco has added an amazing amount of functionality for such an inexpensive product. DHCP, NAT, automatic SPID and ISDN switch sensing, compression, and support for multiple connections are only a few of the highly advanced features available in these routers.

Feature Sets

Three feature sets are available for the 760 and 770 series routers: Internet Ready (IR), Small Office/Home Office (SOHO), and Remote Office (RO). The IR feature set contains support for the TCP/IP protocol and four network devices only. SOHO adds support for the IPX protocol, and RO adds on-the-fly data compression and support for 1,500 network devices.

IR supersedes the SOHO feature set. Customers who have a SOHO license can still find older versions of the OS on Cisco's Web site, but should plan changing to either the IR or RO feature sets, depending on their needs. Those who only need IP and four network devices can continue to upgrade their router OS using the IR feature set. However, if you need IPX and one of the other features in RO (compression or 1,500 network devices), you must upgrade your SOHO license to RO. Only then can you legally download and install this OS on your router.

Each of these feature sets is available in several languages. These languages, listed by country, contain more than just different linguistic command syntax. ISDN standards vary from country to country, and you need to make sure you get the proper version of the OS for your location.

Navigating

Navigating through the CLI in this OS is not nearly as nice as in IOS. There are no special editing keys to fill in commands for you, or allow you to move through the history of previously entered commands. In fact, the CLI for this OS is rather basic. The only really outstanding feature in the CLI is the online help, which is accessible by typing **help** or a question mark. This online help system is only context sensitive in the commands you type. It shows all possible keywords to complete the command if you enter a partial command and a question mark. It will even show you commands that are not valid for your current CLI mode.

The online help shows you all possible commands and the general syntax on how to use them. Unlike IOS, which only shows you the next keyword or option, the 700 series router gives you the whole command. For example, if you wanted to see all possible options for the **show** command, you would enter **show ?**. Unlike in IOS, you must press Enter after typing the question mark. This is shown in Figure 3-44.

Figure 3-44 Example of online help in series 700 routers.

```
access766> show ?
Error on Input string ?
SHow
SHow [<connection>] ADdress
SHow COnfig | NEgotiation | SEcurity [ALl]
SHow CONNections | DEmand | ETher | VOicerouting | STatus | TImeout
SHow DHcp Config
SHow [ <id> ] FIlter
SHow IP COnfig | FIlter | ROute [ALl]
SHow IP PAt
SHow IP RIp SNapshot [ALl]
SHow IPX COnfig | ROute | SErvice [ALl]
SHow IPX CONNections| DEmand | STatistics
SHow IPX FIlter [ALl]
SHow IPX RIp SNapshot [ALl]
SHow MEmstats | SNmp | TYpe
SHow NETBios NAme
SHow [ <connection> | LAn ] PAckets
SHow [ <patternname> ] PATtern
SHow PRofile | USers
access766>
```

You will notice that only the first two or three characters are capitalized. For most commands, you only need to enter the capitalized letters. For example, to view a list of all TCP/IP routes, you could enter **show ip route** or **sh ip ro**. As you become more proficient with the CLI, you will learn more about commands and their associated shorthand.

Profile Use

This OS does not have the concept of command modes, per se. Instead, it has a single global command mode and a user profile command mode. The global command mode allows you to configure parameters for the router as a whole. This includes the ISDN connection to the local telco, DHCP setup, the router system name, and the configuration of the POTS ports, if any exist. User profiles contain the necessary information for each data connection.

There are four user profiles you will see: LAN, internal, standard, and user-defined. The first three are permanent, unerasable profiles. The individual user defines the rest, up to a maximum of 17 profiles. The LAN user profile holds the configuration information for the Ethernet port on the router. Its configuration information includes TCP/IP and IPX/SPX protocol addresses and routing configurations, as well as frame type information. The internal user profile contains the information used to communicate between the LAN and WAN ports. The standard user profile contains the default configuration for the ISDN WAN port.

User-defined profiles create virtual connections to the remote devices with which they are associated. A virtual connection has no physical ISDN channels allocated to it. After its creation, an on-demand call can be made to the remote device to establish a data connection by allocating one or both physical ISDN channels. Virtual and physical connections behave similarly; the difference is that physical connections forward packets to the WAN. Virtual connections monitor packet traffic on the LAN until they identify a packet that is destined for the WAN and initiate a call to the remote device, opening the physical connection. Once the call is established, the virtual connection becomes an active physical connection and the packets move through it.

System mode parameters are modifiable in system mode only. A profile's parameters are modifiable in that profile only. Figure 3-45 shows the prompt indicating you are in system mode by displaying nothing, or the router name followed by the greater than (>) symbol.

Figure 3-45 *The system mode command prompt.*

```
access766>
```

If you are in profile mode, the profile name appears as part of the prompt, separated from the system name by a colon (:). The LAN profile prompt is shown in Figure 3-46.

Figure 3-46 *LAN profile mode prompt.*

```
access766:LAN>
```

System mode parameters affect the router as a whole. Table 3-7 shows the list of system parameters:

Table 3-7

The list of system parameters

Caller ID Parameters	Call waiting	PPP parameters
Date and time	Country group	Screen length
Directory number	Address age time	Screen echo
Delay time	Local and remote access	SNMP parameters
Forwarding mode	Phone 1 and 2	SPIDs
Multidestination dialing	PPP client password	Switch type
Numbering plan	PPP client secret	System password
Patterns	Voice priority	Power Source 1 detect
Passthru		System name

User-profile mode parameters affect connections made through that user profile only. However, an area of the global configuration also stores profile parameters. This area is the profile template. Changes made to profile mode parameters in system mode affect the profile template. When you create a new profile, it inherits the matching system mode parameters from the profile template. Any changes to profile parameters while in profile mode apply to that profile only. When you use the **set profile** command to create a user-defined profile, the default parameters for the new profile are taken from the system mode profile template. Table 3-8 shows the list of profile mode parameters:

Table 3-8

User profile command list

Bridging	Line speed	PPP authentication (outgoing)
Ringback number	Auto calling	All IP parameters, including filters
Compression	Demand	PAP password (client and host)
Passthrough	Timeout	All IPX parameters, including filters
Learning	Called number	CHAP secret (client and host)
Subnet mask	Encapsulation	Bridge filters (address, type, and user-defined)

Windows-based Router Configuration Programs

There are two programs available for configuring Cisco 760 and 770 series routers from the Microsoft Windows GUI: ClickStart and FastStep. Cisco ClickStart is the older GUI tool. If you acquired your router some time ago, it might have come with the router on floppy disks. You should ignore it in favor of the newer FastStep program. Unlike ClickStart, FastStep is current with the latest releases of the OS and, therefore, is better able to help you configure the router. Those who do not have FastStep can download it free from Cisco at http://www.cisco.com/pcgi-bin/tablebuild.pl/faststep. It is available in English, German, French, and Japanese.

Both programs let you set up basic router functionality, including LAN and WAN profile definitions. However, FastStep gives you the ability to configure enhanced functionality in your router. Both programs will configure the router via a serial port, but only FastStep allows you to configure it over the Ethernet network. With the arrival of FastStep version 1.2, you can now use it to set up network address translation. It will even attempt to determine automatically the switch type and SPIDs of your ISDN line.

When you configure your router with FastStep via the network it changes the network settings of the PC that is running it. Two items should concern you any time you let someone else make changes to your networking configuration. First, you will need to return to your original network settings in order to continue using your PC for its daily tasks. In order to make sure that return trip is possible, run **winipcfg** (or **ipconfig /all** under NT) from a DOS prompt. It will bring up your networking information for your default network adapter. Record this information so that you can re-enter it into the system if there is a problem after FastStep completes. Figure 3-47 shows the **winipcfg** configuration window:

Figure 3-47
The winipcfg
window from
Windows 95.

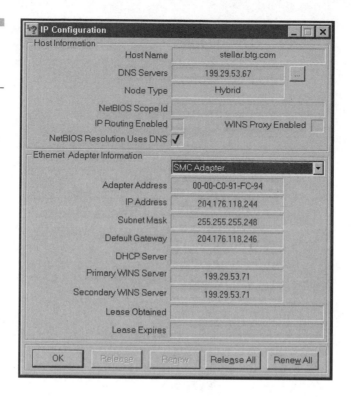

The second problem you might have is the limit on network stations the router can see on the network. If you are using the Internet Ready or SOHO feature set, you are limited to only four devices on the network. If you try to configure a router on a network that has more than four nodes, it's anyone's guess as to whether or not the router will see the PC that is running FastStep. To insure you don't get lost in the crowd, isolate the router and the configuring PC from the rest of your network. Place both on a separate hub that has nothing else connected to it.

If the router is destined for another network, you should configure your PC for that network. FastStep reads your PC's configuration file and will only let you select an IP address for the router that matches it. This happens even if you are configuring the router via the serial cable. Once the configuration of the router is complete, you can send it to its final destination and place your PC back on the local network.

Another method of avoiding these problems is to use the serial port for configuration. This is slower, but presents fewer entanglements in a complex network environment. Unfortunately, FastStep has a tendency to lose the ability to communicate with the router. If this happens, try a few more times. If it still can not talk to the router, exit FastStep and launch HyperTerminal. Press Enter a few times until you see the router prompt, then exit and try FastStep again.

Should the configuration not work on the first try, you might need to run FastStep again and change some options. One hard-to-find problem might be in the channel configuration. Some ISPs only allow certain customers to connect with a single B channel. If your configuration does not work, you should try entering only one phone number to dial and choosing to use only one B channel.

After you run FastStep multiple times, your router configuration might become hopelessly tangled. If this happens, exit FastStep and connect to the router with HyperTerminal. Enter the command **set defaults**. This will return the router to its default configuration and cause it to reboot. Once it has rebooted, you can try configuring it again.

Cisco Configuration and Management Tools

A network can be a colossal mystery to its users and administrators. They become servants to it, rather than its master, and attribute problems to its personality, anthropomorphizing it. A healthy dose of network monitoring and management tools will let you gain the upper hand and start to really understand what is going on inside the network hardware and cables. Cisco makes several software packages to help with these tasks. In this section we'll discuss a few of them.

CiscoWorks

CiscoWorks is the UNIX-based configuration and management tool available for HP/UX, Solaris, and AIX. It can be run by itself or integrated with any of the following network management software: Solstice Site Manager, Solstice Domain Manager, Solstice Enterprise Manager, HP OpenView on Solaris, HP OpenView HP-UX, Tivoli TME/10 NetView AIX. Cisco Works for Windows runs on Microsoft Window 95, NT 3.51, or NT 4.0. CiscoWorks can run standalone or integrated with CastleRock SNMPc, HP OpenView Professional Suite, and HP OpenView Network Node Management on NT. CiscoWorks for Switched Internetworks is for managing

Cisco network switches in the Catalyst and LightStream series. The CiscoWorks Blue series consists of several individual pieces, which manage IBM SNA protocols running over a variety of Cisco equipment.

CiscoWorks is a series of SNMP-based network management software applications. Some of the applications included in CiscoWorks are CiscoView, Configuration File Management, Contacts, Device Management, Global Command Facility, and Software Manager. Configuration File Management provides an audit trail indicating who made changes and when. It can also detect unauthorized configuration changes on your network. Contacts allows you to obtain information about the contact person for a specific device, providing complete name, phone number, e-mail address, title, location, and address. Device Management creates and maintains a database that holds a complete inventory of your network hardware, software, release levels of operational components, responsible individuals, and locations. Global Command Facility allows you to create configuration Snap-Ins that you can apply automatically to groups of routers. Software Manager minimizes upgrade costs by enabling administrators to centrally distribute and manage router software throughout the network. It includes three applications:

- Software Library Manager—Provides a central repository for all Cisco IOS software.

- Software Inventory Manager—Quickly finds the routers you want to upgrade. It automatically tracks software versions running on your network.

- Device Software Manager—Builds on the Flash memory capabilities of Cisco routers, guiding users through a safe and simple upgrade process.

CiscoWorks for Windows

CiscoWorks for Windows is a suite of integrated PC-based network configuration and diagnostic tools for small-to-medium-sized networks. It includes the Configuration Builder, Show Commands, Health Monitor, and CiscoView applications. It comes bundled with CastleRock SNMPc, a complete network management platform for mapping networks, graphing device statistics, and handling alarms. You can also integrate it with HP OpenView Professional Suite and HP OpenView Network Node Manger for Windows NT. Configuration Builder and CiscoView can run as standalone applications.

Configuration Builder allows you to create configuration files for multiple Cisco routers, access servers, and hubs without requiring you to remember complicated command-line language or syntax for the devices. Using Configuration Builder, you can configure a wide variety of Cisco routers, switches, and hubs, including all those listed in the hardware section. Configuration of advanced features must still be done by hand. An Add Commands window allows you to configure features in the router that are not supported by Configuration Builder.

Other features of Configuration Builder include:

- Simultaneous configuration of multiple devices
- Configuration snap-ins
- Duplicate address and configuration checking for IP, IPX, AppleTalk, and DECnet protocols
- Guided router configuration through a sequence of relevant dialog boxes
- Auto detection of hardware information including model type, software version, image type, and number and type of interfaces installed
- Remote configuration capability

Show Commands allows you to quickly display detailed system and protocol information about Cisco routers without requiring you to remember complicated command-line language or syntax. Health Monitor is a dynamic fault and performance management tool that provides real-time statistics on device characteristics, interface status, errors, and protocol utilization. It also provides CPU and environmental card status and indicates changes in conditions through color. This application uses SNMP to monitor and control the Cisco devices.

Cisco Resource Manager

Cisco Resource Manager, based on Web server architecture, takes advantage of today's Internet technology. Its applications are accessible using a standard browser, which simplifies access to information from anywhere in the network. It is composed of Inventory Manager, Software Image Manager, Availability Manager, and Syslog Analyzer applications. It is available as a standalone solution and does not require a management platform or CiscoWorks. It can coexist on the same system with HP OpenView, CiscoWorks, or CiscoWorks for Switched Internetworks and is available for either Solaris or Windows NT.

Inventory Manager quickly collects, displays, and updates router and switch hardware and software inventory information. It can create change reports by automatically detecting hardware and software changes, and it allows users to view past reports. Inventory reports are highly detailed, showing hardware, software, and firmware versions, image type, and physical chassis and interface card information. The inventory information updates automatically each time a device restarts. Custom reports show the Year 2000 certification status of each IOS router image running in your network. These reports are Internet linked to CCO to provide up-to-date information.

Software Manager reduces the time needed to deploy new software images by automating many of the steps associated with scheduling, downloading, and monitoring software upgrades. It can distribute software images to groups of routers, and it supports all the devices in the hardware section of this book. To reduce software upgrade errors, Software Manager validates the proposed image for each target device by checking Cisco IOS release, flash device size, and available RAM requirements. It allows you to schedule a single or multiple upgrade jobs, verifying that each job has completed successfully and providing detailed audit reports on upgrade failures. Software images can be retrieved from the CCO Web site, from another router, or from a local file and stored in the software library for future deployment.

Availability Manager allows quick monitoring of device availability and response time, and reports on offline devices and device reloads. Users can view trend graphs and interface availability information for easier trouble-shooting based on historical information. It also reports device reloads, cause of reload, and offline device status to ensure timely response to network outages.

Syslog Analyzer provides flexible filtering of syslog message reporting that you can use to isolate error conditions on Cisco routers. It provides custom and standard reports that are viewable by device, message type, and severity. These can alert you to configuration changes, high CPU utilization, duplicate IP addresses, Flash memory errors, memory allocation failures, environmental warning, and severity level 0, 1, and 2 syslog errors. Custom filters enable users to select the device and syslog messages displayed along with links to probable cause, recommended action, and user-customized information. A utility to launch a customized script or Web page enables you to extend syslog messages to internal policies and procedures.

When connected to CCO, Cisco Resource Manager provides a dynamic link between your network and CCO service and support. From the Resource Manager desktop, you have access to CCO Web pages, simplifying the task of finding the latest product enhancements, the appropriate software image, Year 2000 certification, diagnostic information, and debugging tools.

Cisco ConfigMaker

ConfigMaker requires no knowledge of IOS and can be used for basic configuration of IP, IPX, and AppleTalk network protocols. It supports network connections over Ethernet, Fast Ethernet, ISDN BRI, ISDN PRI, Frame Relay, PPP, HDLC, and asynchronous lines. It will even configure dial-up connections over modems and ISDN lines.

It works by connecting to a router over a serial line connected to your PC. You can either tell it the type of router or let it discover it on its own. This is handy for modular routers like the 1600 and 3600 series. With those routers, you might spend some time manually adding all the interface cards. Auto configuration saves time and prevents errors by determining this information for you.

Basic testing shows ConfigMaker is extremely capable of creating the configurations necessary for getting your network up and running. You can even provide it a range of network addresses you have available, and it will apportion them in an efficient way. Its major drawback is the need to have the router directly connected to a PC for auto discovery and configuration. Getting this information over a network would make the product much more flexible for network administrators who have routers already in place. Do not let this deter you, because it is quite possible to use ConfigMaker to create new configurations and then use existing methods to update router configurations.

Best of all, it's free. Simply connect to http://www.cisco.com, click on software and support, then on network management products, then on Cisco ConfigMaker Software. You can also go directly to http://www.cisco.com/pcgi-bin/tablebuild.pl/configmaker.

Cisco Dial-Out Utility Software

Those who have Cisco Access Servers should be aware of Cisco Dial-Out Utility Software. This program allows you to connect to an access server and use one of its modems as if it were connected to your computer. It is available free from Cisco's Web site at http://www.cisco.com/cgi-bin/tablebuild.pl/dial-out. You must have a login and password to access the secure area of Cisco's Web site to get this software. If you have a maintenance contract with Cisco and do not have an account, they will be happy to set you up with one. All you need to do is call technical support and ask for a Cisco Connection Online (CCO) account.

This software can turn a typical dial-in server into a dial-in/dial-out access server. This can give your network additional capabilities, such as outbound fax from the desktop and a modem pool from which users can dial out to text-based bulletin board systems (BBS). Before you can use it, you must be running a compatible version of IOS on your access server.

Software Updates from Cisco Connection Online

Users with maintenance contracts for their Cisco routers can get an account on Cisco Connection Online (CCO). Here, Cisco offers all its latest software updates for you to download, including current and previous versions of IOS, Cisco 760 and 770 series OS, and many of the programs described above. You must know your licensing status for each piece of equipment you upgrade with code from this site. If your license only covers the desktop feature set, it is illegal to install an upgraded feature set (such as Enterprise). However, if a new version of Desktop for your router is too large for either Flash or main memory, you can freely use a feature set that has fewer capabilities than Desktop, such as IP/IPX.

As always, you should check with your Cisco sales representative if there are any questions of legality. Your sales rep can also keep your maintenance up-to-date, so your CCO account does not expire at an inopportune time.

Software updates reside under the Software Center heading (look under Software & Support). If you do not have a CCO account, you can still get a great deal of useful software packages, such as FastStep, TACACS (authorization, authentication, and accounting software for dial-in users), RSL (Router Software Loader), and 56K modem firmware updates. Users who have CCO accounts will see all this and more. The area you are most likely to download from is the IOS software area. This area has an extremely helpful program that asks you for your router type, desired IOS version, and desired feature set, and then tells you how much RAM and Flash you will need to install the image. If your router is capable, you can then download that IOS image directly to your hard drive.

Config Registers and IOS Upgrades

Cisco IOS-based routers use a configuration register to determine how the router loads its IOS operating system. The full version of IOS is usually stored in Flash memory, but there is also a crippled version that is stored in a boot ROM or in a separate Flash memory device known as boot Flash. The router can also boot into ROM monitor mode, or download its IOS version off the network. The configuration register setting determines which of these the router boots from.

To check the status of your configuration register, use the **show version** command. At the bottom of the output, you will see the status of all the programmable memory in the router. In Figure 3-48, you can see this router has 128KB of NVRAM, 8MB of system Flash memory, and 4MB of boot Flash. You will also see the current value of the configuration register (in this case 0x2102).

Figure 3-48 The command show version shows many things, including the IOS version in use, the total amount of all types of memory, and the contents of the configuration register.

```
Wan2500# show version
...
128K bytes of non-volatile configuration memory.
8192K bytes of processor board System Flash (Read Only)
4096K bytes of processor board Boot Flash (Read/Write)

Configuration register is 0x2102

Wan2500#
```

Normally, you only use two configuration register settings: 0x2101 and 0x2102. 0x2101 is used to boot from the boot ROM or boot Flash. 0x2102 is used for normal operations where you boot off an IOS image in Flash memory.

If you wish to upgrade your IOS version in Flash memory, you need to make sure that Flash is writeable. Run-from-Flash routers such as the AS5200 or any of the 2500 series require you to change the configuration register to 0x2101 in order to make the Flash writeable. Run-from-RAM routers such as the 4x00 series have Flash memory in read/write mode all the time.

Enter global configuration mode to change the configuration register. All you need to do is enter **config-register NUMBER,** where **NUMBER** is the desired value for the register (normally either 0x2101 or 0x2102). Next, press Ctrl-z to exit global configuration mode. Finally, enter **reload**, choose not to save the configuration, and press Enter to confirm the reload. This is shown in Figure 3-49.

Figure 3-49 *Setting the configuration register.*

```
wan4500#configure t
Enter configuration commands, one per line. End with CNTL/Z.
wan4500(config)#config-register 0x2102
wan4500(config)#^Z
wan4500#reload
%SYS-5-CONFIG_I: Configured from console by console
System configuration has been modified. Save? [yes/no]: no
Proceed with reload? [confirm] <Enter>
```

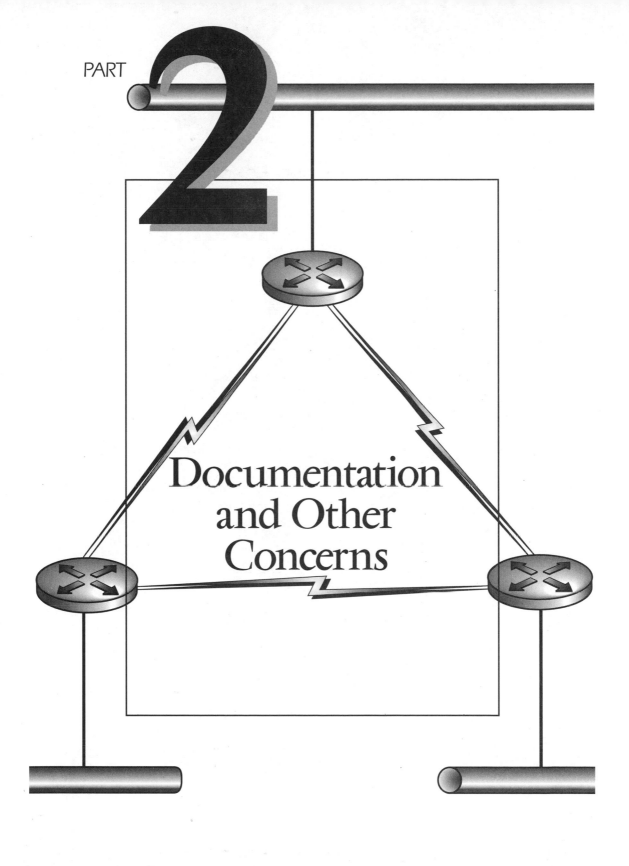

PART

2

Documentation
and Other
Concerns

## CHAPTER 4

Documentation and Support

Cisco provides documentation on CDs and also online. Support is available through a selection of contracts to cover the needs of different types of organizations. In addition, Cisco has a troubleshooting engine, an open forum, and a technical tips section. Beyond these services, users can access a Cisco newsgroup on the Internet. Read on for details on how to get the most out of your Cisco installation documentation.

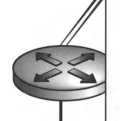

Documentation

This part of the chapter describes the documentation that is supplied by Cisco, the forms it takes, and how to access it.

Documentation CD-ROMs

Cisco includes its documentation CDs (formerly called the Cisco UniverseCD) with every router shipped. These CDs are very important, and many network administrators hold on to them like drowning men holding on to life preservers. For this reason, they seem to accumulate in unorganized piles. The proper action upon receiving a new one is to make it accessible via a Web server on your network and throw out all but the latest two or three versions. It is not uncommon for documentation CDs to be lying around (unopened) years after they arrive. All new CD sets have the creation date silk-screened on the discs themselves, making it easier for you to determine their age.

The Cisco Documentation CDs are a two-disc set. The first disc contains the software you need to install on your computer so that you can view the documentation, which is contained on the second CD. Cisco documentation supports Microsoft Windows 95 or NT, Apple Macintosh, SUN Microsystems SunOS, Solaris 2.4 and higher, IBM AIX 4.1 and higher, and HP/UX 9.0.4, 10.10, and 10.20. All the documentation is in HTML format. Cisco ships Netscape Navigator on the first CD, along with all the tools you will need to enhance it. This includes the Adobe Acrobat Reader plug-in, as well as others.

Because these tools ship on CD, they most likely are not the latest versions available. If you have already installed complementary products or other versions of the same product, they might be corrupted by the installation of software from Cisco's documentation CD. Try loading only the pieces you need, and they will enhance what you already have. For example, if you have Netscape Communicator installed you would not want to load Netscape Navigator, because Communicator is a superset of Navigator. Loading Navigator would have an unpredictable effect on Communicator. Instead, you should load only the plug-ins you don't already have installed; this action would add them to Communicator and enhance its functionality.

Once you have Navigator or Communicator installed with all the plug-ins that Cisco requires, you can access the documentation CD. However, if you don't use Navigator you might experience problems launching the documentation CD from the Start | Programs | Cisco CD-ROM Products menu. Instead of seeing a browser with the documentation CD home page in it, you will have a window that looks like Figure 4-1.

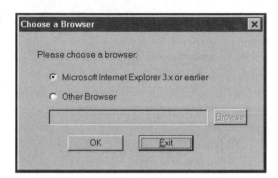

Figure 4-1
Pop-up window asking you to choose a browser.

If this happens, simply click the Other Browser button and browse your file system to choose Communicator. In most cases, you will find it in the directory C:\Program Files\Netscape\Communicator\Program\ netscape.exe. Once you do this, you should bookmark the home page for the documentation CD. You can then return to it simply by launching Communicator and selecting the bookmark.

The documentation on the CD is much like that on Cisco Connection Online (CCO). It has several advantages over CCO, because it is quicker to access and is available without an Internet connection. Of course, the CCO documentation will be up-to-date, while the version on the CD is frozen at one instant in time.

The documentation CD contains information on Cisco's entire product line, including all software, hubs, switches, and routers (from the tiny access router to the forklift-sized Enterprise routers). This is all the current documentation at the time of creation, including information on discontinued products. This CD set is free with each router, but costs a pretty penny if you want to purchase it from Cisco. You can buy it once, or as a monthly subscription. If you don't buy routers every month, you might consider purchasing the CD set a few times a year just to keep current. If you have a support contract you can order it, free of charge, at any time.

Online Documentation

The Cisco online documentation is located on CCO at http://www.cisco.com/public/serv_doc.shtml. If you have a CCO login, it is located at http://www.cisco.com/kobayashi/serv_doc.shtml. The two sites look similar, but there is more information available if you are a CCO subscriber.

The online documentation is the Holy Grail of knowledge for Cisco network administrators. It is always up-to-date, and it's available from anywhere you have Internet access (as long as the Internet is working properly). Anyone who is serious about knowing Cisco products needs a CCO account.

CCO accounts are classified into four categories:

1. Cisco customers who have a SMARTnet or comprehensive support contract with Cisco

2. Cisco customers who receive service from an authorized Cisco Partner

3. Cisco sales partners who have a Reseller, Distributor, or OEM Service Agreement with Cisco

4. Authorized resellers who have a Reseller Service Agreement with Cisco

You can apply for an account online at http://www.cisco.com/public/registration.shtml. Make sure to have the proper documentation available at time of registration. The required information is spelled out for you on the registration page, and you cannot get your account without it.

Support

The basic support offered by Cisco is SMARTnet maintenance. It includes registered access to CCO, technical support required for self-maintenance, software maintenance, and advance hardware replacement. Access to CCO is a must for any Cisco network manager. Technical support is through Cisco's Technical Assistance Center (TAC). Software maintenance allows you to download the latest versions of whatever Cisco software you are licensed to use. Advance hardware replacement means you receive replacement parts from Cisco and then send the broken one back to them.

Types of Contracts

Cisco offers two types of support agreements, SMARTnet and SMARTnet Onsite. Each has three levels of response time: Standard, Enhanced, and Premium.

SMARTnet Standard provides for advance replacement of parts, if calls are received between 9:00 a.m. and 5:00 p.m. local time, five days a week. Parts arrive the next business day. SMARTnet Enhanced speeds up parts replacement by providing four-hour delivery between 9:00 a.m. and 5:00 p.m. local time, five days a week. SMARTnet Premium goes one step further with four-hour parts delivery 24 hours a day, seven days a week, including all holidays.

SMARTnet Onsite includes all the regular SMARTnet services, as well as:

1. All parts, labor, and material required for hardware maintenance
2. Labor for field installation of one software upgrade per year
3. Installation of all mandatory engineering and factory change notices
4. Onsite hardware maintenance

The basic difference among the three levels of SMARTnet Onsite is response time. The Standard level provides for onsite coverage between 9:00 a.m. and 5:00 p.m. local time, Monday through Friday, excluding local Cisco-observed holidays. It also includes guaranteed next-day delivery (Monday through Saturday) of replacement parts. SMARTnet Onsite Enhanced includes onsite coverage between 9:00 a.m. and 5:00 p.m. local time, Monday through Friday, excluding local Cisco-observed holidays. SMARTnet Onsite Premium gives you maximum protection with onsite coverage 24 hours a day, 7 days a week. Both SMARTnet Onsite Enhanced and Premium services include four-hour, onsite delivery of hardware replacements within a 50-mile radius of Cisco Service Centers.

All Cisco support contracts are valid for one year. Larger organizations that require different lengths of time or special features such as co-terminus support agreements on new equipment should contact their Cisco sales representative.

Access to the TAC

The TAC is Cisco's product support organization. They receive your problem reports and respond to you within the time stipulated by your support contract. You can send problem reports to them through the WWW on CCO, or via e-mail, phone, and fax. Likewise, they can respond by e-mail, phone, and fax, as you request. This adds the maximum amount of flexibility to their support organization and allows you access to support in the manner that best fits your situation.

Cisco provides four priority levels for support calls:

1. Production network is down, causing critical impact to business operations if service is not restored quickly. No workaround is available. Cisco and the customer are willing to commit substantial resources around the clock to resolve the situation.

2. Production network is severely degraded, impacting significant aspects of business operations. No workaround is available. Cisco and customer are willing to commit full-time resources during business hours to resolve the situation.

3. Network performance is degraded. Network functionality is noticeably impaired, but most business operations continue.

4. Customer requires information or assistance on Cisco product capabilities, installation, or configuration.

Cisco allows the customer to set the priority level. Obviously you should never ask for Priority Level 1 if you are not willing to go to the extra effort to resolve the problem. The sun will never set on the problem until it is resolved, because Cisco can pass it off to the next spot on the planet where they have a TAC, easily providing constant support. By reporting the current problem status, fresh engineers can pick up where others are preparing to leave work for the day. This provides continuity of the problem status, so the customer doesn't feel as if they are starting over from the beginning.

All trouble reports issued to the TAC via CCO and e-mail are designated low priority by default. If you have a Priority 1 or 2 situation, you should always use the telephone to contact Cisco. The next best option is fax, but you should specify in large letters that this is a high-priority situation. Always make sure the Cisco TAC representatives have several ways to contact you. This will keep you from losing time if you are away from the phone when they call.

The TAC automatically escalates your problem after predetermined amounts of time. The longer your problem goes unresolved, the more people are notified about it. This prevents a call from lingering too long and insures constantly high levels of service. You can see the levels of escalation in Table 4-1 below. If you feel that forward progress or the quality of service is not satisfactory, you should escalate your case by contacting the TAC Duty Manager. Simply ask any TAC representative to connect you to the Duty Manager immediately.

Table 4-1

Automatic Problem
Escalation Timeline

Elapsed Time	Priority 1	Priority 2	Priority 3	Priority 4
1—Hour	CE Manager			
4—Hours	Tech Sup Director	CE Manager		
24—Hours	VP of CA	Tech Sup Director		
48—Hours	Pres. (CEO)	VP of CA		
72—Hours		Pres. (CEO)	CE Manager	
96—Hours			Tech Sup Director	CE Manager

NOTE

Priority 1 problem escalation times are measured in calendar hours, 24 hours per day, 7 days per week. Priority 2, 3, and 4 escalation times correspond with Cisco Technical Assistance Center (TAC) business hours: 6 a.m. to 6 p.m. Pacific Time, Monday through Friday, excluding Cisco holidays.

Troubleshooting Engine

Cisco's troubleshooting engine is a searchable knowledge base of specific troubleshooting questions and answers. You define your search by selecting the LAN protocols, WAN protocols, or platforms that are giving you problems. Then you enter a brief problem description. The troubleshooting engine searches its database for a list of similar problems and attempts to help you troubleshoot it. As you step through it, you can select more in-depth questions with the hope that the search engine will eventually lead you to a solution.

Most of the answers in the troubleshooting engine lead you to specific points in the documentation. If you are asking more general questions, you should use the Open Forum. The troubleshooting engine is only for making changes to configuration.

Open Forum

Cisco's open forum is another searchable knowledge base of specific questions and answers. It provides a broader search base by asking you to enter a brief problem description only. Optionally, you can enter an additional description of the problem, although this is not used in the search. If you can't find a resolution to your problem in the database, you can send the brief and additional description information to a Cisco support engineer and you will be notified when a response is added to the database. The open forum searches its database for a list of similar questions posed to it in the past. By clicking on one of these, you can see the answer that was entered by a Cisco support engineer.

The question list consists of other Cisco customers' questions. When you choose one, you will see the additional description the customer entered and the support engineer's response. If you don't find the answer to the question you entered, you can choose to send it to the forum or try to diagnose it with the troubleshooting engine. If you send it to the forum, a Cisco engineer will look at it and post an answer to it, usually within a few days. You can choose to have the question expire from the open forum and automatically open a case in the TAC. When your question is answered, you are notified by e-mail that the question now has a matching answer and has been entered into the database. The e-mail will contain a URL that will take you directly to the answer to your question.

Technical Tips

Another area of interest to all is the technical tips section. It contains all sorts of useful information on router configuration, cabling, hardware, and white papers. This is the best place to find sample configurations designed more like "how to" articles and not as answers to questions. You can also get technical information about basic and advanced features of Cisco's various products.

Cisco Newsgroups

Outside the realm of Cisco Systems, Inc., there exists the Internet newsgroup comp.dcom.sys.cisco. This is a place where anyone can share ideas and get, or give, help. As always, there are rules that apply. Stick to problems and questions regarding Cisco products and be nice. There are a lot of Cisco professionals and Cisco employees who read the newsgroup threads and help people free of charge. If you cannot afford a maintenance contract, this is one way to get no-cost help. Don't abuse it, though.

## CHAPTER 5

External Concerns

The world of routers does not exist in a vacuum. Somewhere on your network, there will be a device not made by Cisco, or a wide area network connection provided by a third party. These can be classified as external concerns. They are as important to you as each Cisco router on your network, because without them, your routers are useless.

External concerns can be classified into two types: WAN connections and hardware. WAN connections come in many different types, including ISDN, Frame Relay, and point-to-point leased line. They are services provided by telecommunications companies for a fee. Hardware is anything connected to your network (but not made by Cisco) that is necessary for its function. This includes such digital conversion devices as channel service units (CSU), data service units (DSU), and ISDN NT-1s. It also includes modems, external transceivers, hubs, and switches (although we will not be dealing with them in this text).

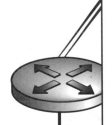
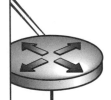

Telephone Companies

Every network administrator, even the accidental ones, can name at least five telecommunications companies fighting for their business. Each week, different arms of the telecom giants cold-call thousands of companies to try to increase their market share in local and long distance voice, Frame Relay, Internet, and leased-line data services. For most network administrators this is an unwanted intrusion, but it does alert you as to which companies are competing for your business.

It is this competition that you must continually consider as you hang up on one aggressive sales person after another. Competition is good, because it drives prices down on your networking costs, whatever they are. Although it is not feasible to change telecom companies on a regular basis, you can always use one phone company to drive down the price of the one you're using. If your prices on a line have been fixed for a while, you might consider having the competition provide you with a quote to replace the service. It's amazing how much money you can save.

Money should not be the only factor in choosing a telecommunications provider. Support, problem escalation, and reliability must also be considered. In the case of an ISP, you must also take into account the costs of changing IP addresses and domain name service (DNS) records. You might find that a few dollars a month doesn't make up for the headaches of converting your network. In addition, some leased lines have startup costs. If you're saving $50 a month but you have to pay a $1000 startup fee, then you would need to keep the line at least 20 months just to break even.

The biggest problem overall is the communications barrier between phone company people and network administrators. Each group has their own set of acronyms and phrases, and they are used to dealing with people who speak their language. When the two groups meet, there is usually a lot of frustration because of insufficient vocabulary on both sides. Never doubt those phone company people want to get your lines working, just don't count on their being able to speak your language. Instead, you should learn some key phrases of their language to make sure you get what you need. Although you might not know exactly what it is you're asking for, Cisco has guidelines for almost all lines that can be ordered from phone companies.

Telco History

Ordering lines from the phone company used to be a straightforward process. Before deregulation, there was only one source for data lines in a Local Access & Transport Area (LATA). A LATA is a geographic area where a specific telecommunications company used to have the exclusive rights to maintain and control the telephone infrastructure. In other words, there used to be only one source for local telephone and data lines. If you wanted to communicate, you had to do business with them.

This was not (and is not) true for connections between LATAs. If you wanted to connect between two or more areas, you had to use a long distance phone company, known as an inter-exchange carrier (IXC). Many such companies exist to provide you this service. Unfortunately, some might not target businesses your size and might remain anonymous to you even though they provide excellent service at a fair price.

Ordering Lines from the Phone Company

When ordering a data line between multiple sites, you don't really need to know whether you are Inter-LATA or Intra-LATA. All you need to do is write up a request for a quote (RFQ), detailing your needs. You should include the name of the local contact, street address, and phone number. You should also ask for rate quotes for one through seven years of service.

The most important pieces of information you provide are the phone numbers for each end of the connection. These will be used to determine which telephone company central office services the various locations and, therefore, what the pricing will be. Telcos actually need only the area code and exchange (first three digits of a seven-digit phone number). However, they will usually not ask you for it in terms non-telco people would understand. Instead, put the acronym NPA/NXX in your personal linguistic computer (your brain) and translate that to something easier to understand: area code and exchange will do, or the first six digits of a ten-digit phone number.

Call all the telco companies you are considering, and contact your salesperson for the appropriate type of service you want installed (ISDN, Frame Relay, T1, and so on), then fax your RFQ to them. This provides a paper trail and makes sure all of them have the same information. Make sure to place a deadline on responses. Two weeks is not outrageous. You might want to give them more time if more responses are important to you.

Undoubtedly, some of those companies you ask to provide a quote won't respond. The good ones will let you know they either can't meet your deadline or don't provide the type of service you want. When you receive all the quotes, you will see they are all in different formats, which makes them hard to compare. This is not done by accident. This is done, in part, to confuse you a bit. Simply convert the quotes into a format that will let you perform an apples-to-apples comparison. Reduce the data by entering it into a spreadsheet, and calculate the cost for one through five years. Companies that have large installation fees and smaller monthly payments might seem attractive, but you need to know where the break-even point will be in comparison with the others.

Once you choose a vendor, make sure you get as much information as possible. This includes phone numbers for their engineering department (which will install the line) and their internal order tracking number. They will commit to an installation date, but don't actually expect them to arrive on time, unless you keep on top of them. Do this by calling both the engineering department and the salesperson three or four days in advance. Make sure you are on their installation schedule and try to lock down a time (usually morning or afternoon) when they will be there. Make sure they have all your contact numbers so that they can get in touch with you when they arrive.

No matter how you try not to answer the question, management always wants an estimate on when new lines will be installed. They don't realize the reason you don't want to answer the question is that you know they will magically transform your estimate into a firm date. So, when things don't happen on that date, they are back at your door asking for an update. By planning for this in advance, you can avoid these problems. Take a page out of the Star Trek Engineers' Manual and add a week or two to what the phone company tells you. This has two benefits: It pads the schedule in your favor if the telco is late (they usually are), and it makes you look like a miracle worker if the installation is done early.

Sample RFQ

Figure 5-1 is a sample RFQ that was sent out to several telcos. Their responses have been summarized below. The data from each has also been reduced to let you see an apples-to-apples comparison. The information shown here is an example of their quote format and how to reduce the data to make comparison easier:

■ ■ ■ ■ ■ ■
Figure 5-1
Sample letter asking
for a leased-line
quote from a
telecommunication
service provider.

Dear Telco Salesperson:

Please provide a quote for a T1 leased line between the following locations:

Location:	Newport News, VA	Fairfax, VA.
NPA/NXX:	757-873	703-383
Address:	2020 Main St.	11225 Fender Dr.
	Newport News, VA 23660	Fairfax, VA 22030
Contact:	Laura Stein	Alex Woo

Please provide pricing discounts for all long-term commitments you offer from one through seven years. This line will be a point-to-point data line with all 24 channels available.

Please fax a quote back to me within 2 weeks of receiving this RFP.

Below are three responses from AT&T, Sprint, and Worldcom. As you can see, the formats are extremely different, and not all the information is easy to pick out. This is partly because of the sales representative's familiarity with the author. Because they knew they were dealing with someone experienced in data line installations, they might not have been as concerned with format as they were with speedy delivery of the quote.

The first quote (Figure 5-2) is from AT&T. You can see they provided pricing for a long-term contract (up to four years.) They are also willing to waive any installation charges if any sort of long-term contract is signed. Before taking a deal like this, make sure you know what the early termination fees are. It would be costly to sign a one-year contract and then have to owe them the installation fee, as well as the difference in price, if the line were terminated early.

Figure 5-2
Actual quote from
AT&T.

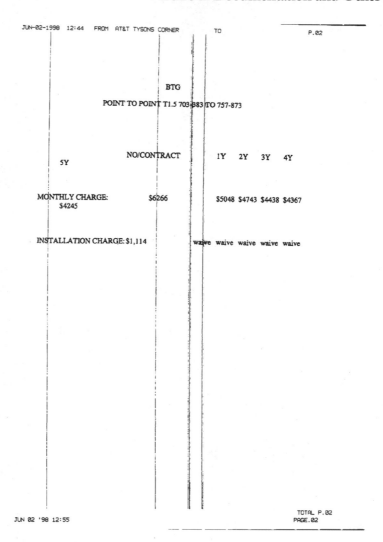

Sprint sent two quotes, one for a one-year term and the other for a two-year term. After follow-up phone calls, they agreed to send several more quotes for longer contract terms. They provided a lot of information, but the formatting made it difficult to determine exactly what costs were being charged. With a little perseverance, the costs became clear and seemed very appealing. An example of a Sprint quote can be seen in Figure 5-3.

Figure 5-3
Actual quote from
Sprint.

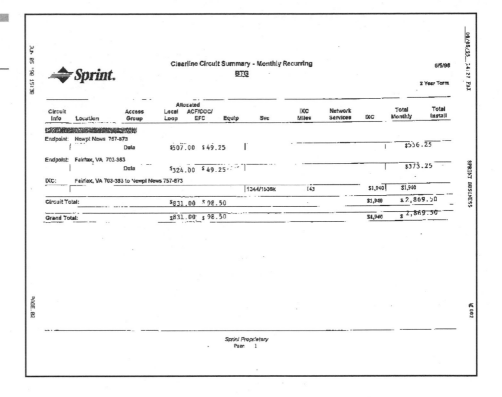

WorldCom provided the most information, faxing out screen dumps from their order quoting system (seen in Figure 5-4). They provided quotes for no contract and for two, three, and five years. They also totaled the monthly recurring costs and the installation costs, which would be your first payment. The novice user might assume this is the total cost every month. This would make WorldCom's pricing look a lot higher than it actually is.

Figure 5-4
Actual quote from
WorldCom.

```
JUN 03 '98 10:11AM                                                    P.2

    TPC215D    USER: IKI    TERMINAL: A136   DATE: 06/03/98   TIME: 08:57:24   PROD
                            WORLDCOM PRIVATE LINE PRICE QUOTE
    MENU OPTION: _____       PRINT? _ (Y/N)
    CUSTOMER:                                    SALES REP: DON S.
    PRIVATE LINE    FROM NORFOLK, VA        757 873 TO RESTON, VA          703 383
    SERVICE: DS1                          LOC A: NRFL VA BSDS0  LOC B: RSTN VA FMCG0
    CHN QTY:      MILES:    154                 TIER: B              TIER: B
         IXC RATE:     3089.27
    IXC FIXED RATE:       0.00
    TYPE 3 LOC A   757 873                         17 MI         642.71
      SIG       .00 COND C        0.00 COND D      0.00
    TYPE 3 LOC B   703 383                          5 MI         487.44
      SIG       .00 COND C        0.00 COND D      0.00
    NON-RECURRING CHARGES:
      IXC                                                       400.00
      LOCAL LOC A     TERM  024                                  51.00
      LOCAL LOC B     TERM  024                                  51.00
                                  TOTAL MONTHLY RATE:         4,219.42
                                  TOTAL NON-RECURRING:          502.00
                                       COMBINED TOTAL:        4,721.42

    PF1 HELP PF2 EXTND HELP PF3 1ST PANEL PF4 MAIN MENU PF8 DETAIL CHGS PF12 RESET




    JUN 03 '98 10:25                                          PAGE.02
```

Figure 5-5 shows the data reduction spreadsheet for all quotes received. The bids received were entered, and the total costs were computed. Whenever a vendor did not provide a quote, that vendor was omitted. This allows you to see only the quotes received for a particular contract length.

Figure 5-5
Spreadsheet of all the information received in the quotes.

No Contract Pricing	Install	Monthly	1-Year Cost
AT&T	$1,114.00	$ 6,266.00	$ 76,306.00
WorldCom	$ 502.00	$ 4,373.09	$ 52,979.08
1-Year Pricing	**Install**	**Monthly**	**1-Year Cost**
AT&T	$ —	$ 5,048.00	$ 60,576.00
Sprint	$ —	$ 3,084.50	$ 37,014.00
2-Year Pricing	**Install**	**Monthly**	**2-Year Cost**
AT&T	$ —	$ 4,743.00	$113,832.00
Sprint	$ —	$ 2,869.50	$ 68,868.00
WorldCom	$ 502.00	$ 4,219.42	$101,768.08
3-Year Pricing	**Install**	**Monthly**	**3-Year Cost**
AT&T	$ —	$ 4,438.00	$159,768.00
WorldCom	$ 502.00	$ 4,118.85	$148,780.60
4-Year Pricing	**Install**	**Monthly**	**4-Year Cost**
AT&T	$ —	$ 4,367.00	$209,616.00
5-Year Pricing	**Install**	**Monthly**	**5-Year Cost**
WorldCom	$ 502.00	$ 3,961.25	$238,177.00

There were only single quotes for four and five years, so no direct comparisons could be made. However, if we move forward the last contract term pricing, we can fill in the blanks in the table. This allows better comparison based on the length of time you expect to be paying for the leased line. This is shown in Figure 5-6.

Figure 5-6
Expanded data reduction extrapolating pricing out to five years.

No Contract Pricing	Install	Monthly	1-Year Cost
AT&T	$1,114.00	$ 6,266.00	$ 76,306.00
Sprint	no bid	no bid	no bid
WorldCom	$ 502.00	$ 4,373.09	$ 52,979.08
1-Year Pricing	**Install**	**Monthly**	**1-Year Cost**
AT&T	$ —	$ 5,048.00	$ 60,576.00
Sprint	$ —	$ 3,084.50	$ 37,014.00
WorldCom	$ 502.00	$ 4,373.09	$ 52,979.08

(cont.)

Figure 5-6
continued

2-Year Pricing	Install	Monthly	2-Year Cost
AT&T	$ —	$ 4,743.00	$113,832.00
Sprint	$ —	$ 2,869.50	$ 68,868.00
WorldCom	$ 502.00	$ 4,219.42	$101,768.08

3-Year Pricing	Install	Monthly	3-Year Cost
AT&T	$ —	$ 4,438.00	$159,768.00
Sprint	$ —	$ 2,869.50	$103,302.00
WorldCom	$ 502.00	$ 4,118.85	$148,780.60

4-Year Pricing	Install	Monthly	4-Year Cost
AT&T	$ —	$ 4,367.00	$209,616.00
Sprint	$ —	$ 2,869.50	$137,736.00
WorldCom	$ 502.00	$ 4,118.85	$198,206.80

5-Year Pricing	Install	Monthly	5-Year Cost
AT&T	$ —	$ 4,367.00	$262,020.00
Sprint	$ —	$ 2,869.50	$172,170.00
WorldCom	$ 502.00	$ 3,961.25	$238,177.00

You can see the price leader in this example is Sprint. The pricing difference is so great that almost all other concerns would be put aside in their favor. However, they might have particularly onerous early termination costs or other problems. Make sure you (or your lawyers) read and understand any contract they send you before you sign.

The important thing is to get the data yourself and make your own analysis. This is a particularly large distance for a leased line, and therefore the cost is extravagant. If you really needed to connect two sites as far away as these, you would be better off pricing out a Frame Relay connection. Frame Relay pricing is much less distance sensitive than a point-to-point leased line.

It is important to note that this pricing was obtained for a leased line in the Commonwealth of Virginia in the United States. Pricing will be different when crossing state boundaries within the United States and in other countries. This pricing should not be used for calculating your leased-line costs, but rather as a case study on how to manage an RFQ.

Factors in Choosing a Vendor

Business is never certain. You no doubt believe that your new site will be around for years, but what if it isn't? If your break-even point is too far in the future, you will have cost your company money. You might think you can save money by choosing a longer time commitment because the monthly charges for longer contracts can be substantially cheaper. However, early termination fees are usually part of a long-term contract. If you choose a seven-year contract and the line is taken down in three years, you will owe the telco money.

The usual formula applied for early termination is the difference between the rate that you should have been paying and the rate you did pay times the number of months the line was active. For example, you order a line that costs $500 a month for a five-year contract and $550 for a three-year contract. You sign a contract for five years, but cancel it in three. Under the standard formula you would owe the telco $50 (the difference between $550 and $500 a month) times 36 months (three years of service), or $1,800. This money will be due at the time of cancellation.

There are some extenuating circumstances concerning line termination fees. First, telecommunications companies don't always remember to go back and charge you. You shouldn't count on being overlooked, but neither should you remind your telco vendor to charge you for early termination. Second, you might be able to get the commitment on the line you are canceling switched over to another line on your network. This will delay your having to pay the early termination fee, although it will extend the commitment on the other line. At the very least, this tactic will delay the eventuality of paying the fee. In the interim, it can reduce the termination fee by extending the cost difference into a lower bracket. Make sure to ask about both early termination fees and moving commitments when you set up a line with a vendor.

Another factor in choosing a vendor is volume. Some vendors give you greater discounts based on the total monthly commitment you make with them. At a certain point you exceed the ability for other telecommunications companies to compete, unless they also get a large chunk of your business. If your company does a lot of local and long distance business with a telco provider who offers volume discounts, you might find they are the least expensive.

Another factor is support and service. The cheapest price in the world won't matter to you if your line is always going down. Unfortunately, you can't measure service by pricing. What you can do is ask each vendor for four or five references in your type of business that have the type of service you want. These will be people who agreed to be references, and you should expect a good response. If a vendor's references can't even give you good feedback, then you should shop elsewhere.

Installation and Placement of Data Jack by Phone Company

The installation of your data line will almost never happen when the sales person says it will and will always take longer than expected. You can speed up the installation by making sure everything is in place before the telco installation engineer arrives. One way to attack the problem is from the destination backward. In this method, you determine exactly where you want the jack to be installed and then determine where the line needs to go to meet the telco lines in the building.

Start by determining where the router will be placed. If you can, install the equipment in advance and evaluate the space it is in. See if it can be accessed easily and if there is proper airflow for cooling. Once everything looks good, pick the location where you want the jack installed. Plan for the eventuality that you might not be there when the installation happens, and mark the spot on the wall, or tape a note there to indicate the location. This will help to eliminate confusion when the engineer arrives to do the installation.

Next, find out where the phone lines come into your office space. This is the area where the phone company's responsibility ends and yours begins. It is called the demarcation point, or in telco slang, simply the 'demarc'. In office buildings the demarc might be a phone closet on each floor. In warehouses and smaller buildings, it might be a box or a sheet of plywood on the wall. When the time comes, you will need access to it. This access might have to come from a building engineer or someone else who manages the facility. Make sure you have multiple ways of finding this person, so that you can reach them when the telco installer finally arrives.

Finally, determine how you want the two points to be connected. The telco installer can usually put the jack anywhere you want. They will charge you time and materials for the work. They are usually skilled and efficient, and you can usually blame wiring problems on the telco if there is a problem at a later time. The price for extending the jack to where you want it from the demarc is usually reasonable, and if you are only installing one line, it is a quick and inexpensive way to get the job done. If you are installing multiple lines from a demarc to a location (for example, your computer room), you might want to contact a professional cable company and have them install a patch panel at each end to make multiple connections easier.

Copyright ⊃ 1997 United Feature Syndicate, Inc.
Redistribution in whole or in part prohibited

Extended Wiring Concerns

One thing to watch when running wiring from the demarc to your router is the path it takes. Electromagnetic interference (EMI) and radio frequency interference (RFI) sources between the demarc and the router can affect the performance of your data lines. You should instruct the cable installer (whether telco or independent) to steer clear of any electrical devices in the ceiling. This includes fans, air conditioning equipment, fluorescent light fixtures, and other sources of EMI or RFI, or both.

If you are running more than a few data lines, you might want to talk to the telephone company about extending your demarc to where your routers will be. By doing this, you extend their responsibility right up to the jack on the wall next to your router. This can make for easier debugging of problems and eliminates finger pointing between the telco and independent cabling companies. Some telcos will try to limit the length of time the extension of the demarc is valid. Ask up front and raise a stink if they try to pull this on you after installation.

Copyright © 1997 United Feature Syndicate, Inc.
Redistribution in whole or in part prohibited

Post-Installation Information

Before the telco installer leaves your site, make sure you have all information regarding the line. Each telco that has anything to do with the line will assign it a circuit identification number. Long distance and Frame Relay lines can have three or more circuit IDs. Dial-up lines will have associated phone numbers. ISDN lines will have System Profile IDs (SPIDs), as well as an ISDN switch type. Frame Relay lines will have DLCI (Data Link Connection Identifier) numbers. You should collect all this information into one place and attach it to the copy of the installation work order and business card left by the installer. If the business card does not have a name or a phone number on it, make sure you write those down as well.

You should attach copies of any contracts relating to this line and the original quote to this cache of information, as well as the name and phone number of the salesperson. Finally, get the phone numbers for reporting trouble on the line from all companies handling the line, and keep this whole cache of information within sight of the circuit ID numbers. With all of this information in one place, you will have an easier time getting problems corrected on your lines.

Options on Carrier Formats

Not every data line is the same. Your challenge is to make sure the lines you order have their options properly set to mesh with your Cisco router. T1 and ISDN line configurations should be clearly conveyed to the telco to make sure they fit your needs. T1 lines have two general configuration options: B8ZS (Bipolar 8 Zero Substitution)/ESF (Extended Superframe Format), and AMI (Alternate Mark Inversion)/SF (Superframe Format). It is not important to know what they mean, but you need to know how they affect the T1 line.

A T1 line is a high-capacity data circuit that contains 24 channels carrying either 56Kbps or 64Kbps in digital data or voice information in each channel. Although you can run voice or data over either configuration, you get more bandwidth for data when configured for 64Kbps per channel. B8ZS/ESF sets the channel speed to 64Kbps, which gives you 1.536Mbps of bandwidth. AMI/SF sets the channel speed to 56Kbps, which gives you 1.344Mbps by comparison. Typically, you want to use B8ZS/ESF for data and AMI/SF for voice. ISDN primary rate interface (PRI) lines, which run on T1 lines, must be set for B8ZS/ESF.

ISDN is a strange beast to configure. Because there are so many different types of telco central office switches for ISDN, there is a broad range of configurations. Some switches have few options, while others have hundreds on the same type of data line. To help you get past this problem, Cisco has provided a detailed list of what options they expect set on the telco ISDN switch in order for their routers to work, as shown in Table 5-1. This list is ordered by switch type.

Table 5-1

Specific ISDN line configuration information for a variety of ISDN switches

ISDN Switch Type	ISDN Connection Type	Data/Voice	Configuration Settings
5ESS Custom	BRI	D	• 2 B-channels for data
			• Point to point
			• Terminal Type=E
			• 1 phone number assigned by telco
			• MTERM=1
			• Request delivery of Calling Line ID on Centrex lines.
			• Might have to set speed of calls to 56Kbps outside the local exchange.

(cont.)

Table 5-1 continued

ISDN Switch Type	ISDN Connection Type	Data/Voice	Configuration Settings
5ESS	BRI	D & V	• Only use this with equipment supporting voice calls (i.e., 760 series, etc.) • 2 B-channels for voice or data • Multipoint • Terminal Type=D • 2 phone numbers, assigned by telco • 2 SPIDs required • MTERM=2 • Number of call appearances=1 • Display=No • Ringing/Idle Call Appearances=Idle • Auto-hold=No • One touch=No • Request delivery of Calling Line ID on Centrex lines. • Might have to set speed of calls to 56Kbps outside the local exchange. • Can have directory number 1 hunt to directory number 2 (it does cost a little extra).
5ESS NI1	BRI	D & V	• Terminal Type=A • 2 B-channels for voice and data • 2 phone numbers, assigned by telco • 2 SPIDs are required • Might have to set speed of calls to 56Kbps outside the local exchange. • Can have directory number 1 hunt to directory number 2 (it does cost a little extra).
DMS-100	BRI	D & V	• 2 B-channels for both voice and data • 2 phone numbers, assigned by telco • 2 SPIDs required • Functional signaling • Dynamic TEI assignment • Maximum number of keys=64

(cont.)

Table 5-1 continued

ISDN Switch Type	ISDN Connection Type	Data/Voice	Configuration Settings
DMS-100 cont.	BRI	D & V	• Release Key=No, or Key Number=No • Ringing Indicator=No • EKTS=No • PVC=1, for all BCS loads up to BCS 34, a PVC=2 means NI1. This causes a problem, because then a 2-digit TID is appended to the SPID. Use PVC=1 • Request delivery of Calling Line ID on Centrex lines. • Might have to set speed of calls to 56Kbps outside the local exchange. • Can have directory number 1 hunt to directory number 2 (it does cost a little extra).
5ESS, 4ESS, and DMS-100	PRI	D & V	• Line format=ESF • Line coding=B8ZS • Call type=23 incoming channels and 23 outgoing channels • Speed=64Kbps rate • Call by Call capability • 23B+D • Trunk Selection Sequence=descending (23 Æ 1) • Set B+D glare=yield • Only 1 phone number, assigned by telco • Might have to set speed of calls to 56Kbps outside the local exchange. • No SPIDs required

Testing and Troubleshooting WAN Connections

When problems arise with WAN connections, your corner of the world will beat a path to your door. Many times the users start calling before the administrator even knows the line is down. Proper testing and troubleshooting methods will help you get your data lines back up quickly, with a limited amount of fuss. These methods stem from being able to break up the many components of your WAN connection into discrete parts and validating their operation one at a time.

Knowing how to test each piece is extremely important. There are many possible points of failure; without a proper debugging methodology, you can quickly become lost. One method of testing lines is from the inside out. To understand this method, you must first understand how a data line is set up. In its simplest configuration, you have something like the diagram in Figure 5-10 below. In this figure, you have two Cisco routers connected to their own CSU/DSU. The CSU/DSU is then connected to the public switched telephone network (PSTN).

Figure 5-10

Generic T1 connection between two sites. Each site has a Cisco router and CSU/DSU. Both are connected to the PSTN (Public Switched Telephone Network), which provides the data communications.

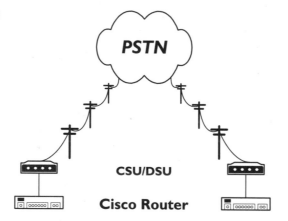

As you can see in Figure 5-10, the PSTN is the center of this connection. Because of this, the best place to start debugging is from the inside, moving toward the router. Your telco provider can test your line from their network all the way to the equipment at your site. This proceeds (in order) from the smart jack, to your demarc, to your computer room jack, to your CSU/DSU, and, finally, to your router.

The first piece of equipment on your site is the smart jack. It is a piece of telco equipment, usually in or near your demarc, and the telco can test it without any assistance from you. If the smart jack is bad, the telco will have to dispatch a repairperson. In this case, you should ask if they will need physical access to your site to make the repair.

The second piece the telco can test is the jack that connects your CSU/DSU to the demarc. You can only test this if you can put the jack into a hard loopback. In a hard loopback, all electrical signals sent by the telco are sent back to them. If you are setting up the line for the first time, you will want to make sure a RJ-45X jack is installed at the demarc and next to the CSU/DSU. A RJ-45X jack automatically goes into a hard loopback when the RJ-45 cable is removed from it. You can also create a loopback cable by cutting the head off one end of a RJ-45 cable and shorting pin 1 to pin 4 and pin 2 to pin 5.

Next, the telco can test all the way up to your CSU/DSU. They do this by trying to put the CSU/DSU into remote loopback. This creates a soft loopback through the CSU/DSU device, but only tests the CSU side. The final test you can perform is on the router serial port, router serial cable, and DSU side of the CSU/DSU. To test these, you need to go into global configuration mode on your router and set "loopback" on the serial port for the T1. This will allow the telco to pass data all the way to your router serial port and have it echoed back to them.

Regardless of the technology in use (ISDN, T1, Frame Relay), starting from the PSTN and working outward toward your router offers the best way to evaluate and solve wide area networking problems. The telco personnel can also run other tests besides loopback tests. One such test is the Bit Error Rate Test, or BERT test. This can be useful in determining whether it is your equipment or theirs that is causing the problem.

Of course, it is always your job to blame their equipment, just as it is their job to blame your equipment. Instead of letting yourself be led into a long round of finger pointing, try this when they say it's on your side: Tell them that you don't think enough testing and troubleshooting has been done, and you would like them to run another set of tests. Then make sure they verify that they are testing your line. It is always possible that, through a simple human error, the telco engineer helping you is testing someone else's line. Hey, it happens! It happened to me!

Remember to always have the circuit ID and any other information about the line (like SPIDs) handy. If you have all the information in front of you, the telco representative can jump right in on the problem, instead of waiting for you to search for vital information.

A Broader Testing Methodology

Advanced troubleshooting starts by answering the question, "What changed?" If a WAN line goes down and you haven't changed anything for weeks, the best bet is to blame the telco. If you've been making changes, you should scrutinize them. In some cases, you might need to ask who has been in the room with the routers (Was it the guy whose new watch always dies after a week?) or if work was done in the telco closet or near the demarc. Your problem could be as simple as someone bumping a piece of equipment, or tripping over a cable and damaging it.

A more likely cause is the telco. In fact, blaming the telco from the start and then investigating your own site could solve the problem more quickly. Changes are always being made at telco facilities that could affect your service for good or ill. Start by placing a call to them and then verifying your equipment. Even if they say it's not their fault, keep blaming them. The chance that it is their fault is usually greater than it's being yours.

After the problem is fixed, telco engineers like saying things like, "I looked at the line and I see no problem on it." Notice they say "no problem" in the present tense. The line goes down, you call, the line comes back up, and they see "no problem." They won't tell you they saw a problem and corrected it, and that brought the line back up. Hearing responses like that should make you wary of your line provider. It's OK to make mistakes once in a while, but it's not OK to lie about it or cover it up.

Whether your telco plays straight with you or not, you should always keep track of line outages. Record them on paper attached to your other information about the individual lines. This will allow you to review the line history after each incident. You should make sure you have all the trouble ticket numbers opened for your case and the explanations of the problem when they are closed. If you are dealing with long distance lines or Frame Relay, there might be several telcos carrying different parts of your line. Because of this, your telco might open trouble tickets with other telco companies to have them investigate the problem. If you have all the trouble ticket and contact numbers, you can inquire about the problem yourself.

The quickest way to a solution is to be a nuisance. Keep calling, stay on the line, and escalate to a supervisor if your line does not come up quickly enough for you. The people at the telco end of the line probably have hundreds of lines to connect, disconnect, and fix. The only way you will become a priority is to be an annoyance that won't go away. If the problem is a low priority, don't bug them about it. If the problem is a high priority, your only way to express this is to keep calling, stay on the line, and escalate the problem. Don't let them call you back, or you are at their mercy.

Of course, there are times when nothing you can do will get the line operational any faster. For example, if a major carrier looses a fiber optic cable bundle somewhere in Middle America because Farmer John caught it while plowing his field, hundreds or thousands of Mbps could be interrupted. If you have a single DS0 (64Kbps) inside that bundle, chances are you will be among the last to be fixed. Simply put, the people who have larger connections (that is, pay the most money) will get attended to first.

Keep Them on the Line

When you are involving telco personnel in solving your problems, remember this nugget. It is corporate policy in many (if not most) of the telcos that they can't hang up on you. This means you can increase your priority and decrease down time, just by sitting on the phone. Usually they will put you on hold to look at something, and then come back to you. If you are not on hold, and they are going to call you back, you might get stuck on a pile with others, and they will get to you when they can. By hanging on the line, you are forcing the engineer at the other end to look at your problem. Remember, never hang up!

At Time of Installation

Be ready for the installation when it comes. If you are, you will certainly suffer fewer headaches than your peers. If all your equipment is in place (at both ends, if it is a point-to-point line), you can test the line while the engineer is still at your site. This will give you quick access to high-level support, because the engineer will really want to leave to go to their next appointment. This is not your problem. If there is a problem when you install the line, you'll want to keep the engineer there as long as possible to keep the lines of communication open.

Extended Test Period before the Line Is Declared Operational for Billing Purposes

WAN lines are not just up or down. A line can be up, but experience high levels of data loss. This will cause poor performance with regard to your data throughput. Many times, these problems can first be detected at installation or shortly after. It is possible to ask the telco to place your line into testing mode for a short period. This is usually a day or two, during which you can perform high throughput data tests and check the lines for errors. In cases where the line is bad, you can actually run the connection in an impaired state for weeks, until the telco fixes the problem. If the line is not officially declared operational, then you are not paying for it. If a problem exists at installation, make sure you don't pay for the line until it works at 100% capacity 100% of the time.

The down side with having a line in testing mode is that it is not going to be stable. As the telco engineers troubleshoot the line, they might take it down repeatedly, sometimes for an extended amount of time. If your users can't stand these types of outages, you should not use the line until it becomes 100% operational.

Understanding Telco Speak (or: A Guide to Translating Telephony Speak Into Computer Speak)

Telco people are just like you. They want to get problems fixed and help their customers. But sometimes it seems like they get frustrated dealing with non-telco people. This is mostly due to the language barrier that exists between telco people and mere mortals, that is, the rest of us. The telco world has its own language, just as programmers, network administrators, and managers do. Someone who is not used to the insiders' language usually has a hard time relating requests and problems. To cut through this, learn some of the telco language and tear down the language barrier. This will lead to quicker solutions to your problems.

Table 5-2 gives you some telco language translations to make your life easier.

Table 5-2

Telco language

Telco slang Telco	Network Manager
What is your line coding? What is your framing?	Are you running B8ZS/EFS or AMI/SF?
Can I loop your CSU remotely?	Do you have remote loopback enabled in your CSU/DSU?
I'll run a Bert test.	I will run a Bit Error Rate Test to see if I can determine the problem.
What is your NPA/NXX?	What are the first six digits of your ten-digit phone number?
Can I do intrusive testing?	Can I take the line completely down to help determine what the problem is?
Can you loop the remote CSU?	If you have remote loopback enabled on the other end of your connection, can you loop that end back to you?

Types of Lines

There are many different types of WAN lines. Each has its own particular setup and troubleshooting quirks, but the overall methodology stays the same. This section contains a quick overview of some of the different types of WAN lines available.

T1

A T1 line is a high-capacity digital leased line. Telco people sometimes call it a DS1. It consists of 24 channels, which can be configured for 56Kbps or 64Kbps. Using all 24 channels for data is called a full T1, or a clear-channel T1. You can also get a fractional T1, which denotes the use of anywhere from one to 23 channels. T1 lines are leased from telco companies and are only point-to-point. Each channel in a T1 is known as a DS0.

E1

An E1 line is a high-capacity digital leased line. It is the rest of the world's equivalent to the T1 used in the United States. It consists of 32 channels, which can be configured for 56Kbps or 64Kbps. Using all 32 channels for data is called a full E1, or a clear-channel E1. You can also get a fractional E1, which denotes the use of anywhere from one to 31 channels. E1 lines are leased from telco companies and are only point-to-point. Each channel in an E1 is known as a DS0.

ISDN

ISDN lines come in two flavors: Basic Rate Interface (BRI) and Primary Rate Interface (PRI). They consist of some number of bearer (or B) channels and one data (or D) channel. In the world of Cisco routers, the B channels carry all WAN data and the D channels carry all the setup/teardown information.

Three types of calls can be placed on ISDN lines: 56Kbps voice, 56Kbps data, and 64Kbps data. Obviously, all voice calls are made at 56Kbps. There are two data options to support local and long distance calls. With long distance calls, the connection might not be ISDN end to end. When this happens, you will likely be using a single channel on a voice T1 line. Because voice T1 lines are set up AMI/SF, their 24 channels have only 56Kbps of bandwidth. This is the situation where you need to make 56Kbps data calls. Local data calls are usually ISDN end to end, and therefore you have a full 64Kbps available for data.

BRI

BRI lines are digital lines, usually procured through the local telco. Most are dial-up, but they can be ordered as leased lines. They consist of two 64Kbps B channels and one 16Kbps D channel. These can be used independent of each other or joined together for a 128Kbps connection to a single site.

Older versions of Cisco IOS only supported the joining together of two B channels for 128Kbps of bandwidth. Starting with IOS version 11.2, Cisco now supports virtually unlimited joining together of channels, allowing you to combine up to 255 channels over multiple PRIs. Cisco only supports MPPP (Multi-link Point-to-Point Protocol) and not the ISDN standard of bonding. Cisco also does not support use of the D channel for anything other than call setup and teardown.

PRI

PRI lines are digital lines, which can be procured through a local or a long distance telco. PRI is an ISDN signaling standard, which is superimposed on a T1 or an E1. A T1 PRI consists of 23 B channels and 1 D channel. An E1 PRI consists of 30 B channels and 2 D channels. Because it runs on a B8ZS/ESF coded T1 or E1 line, all channels, B and D, are 64Kbps. These can be used independent of each other or joined together for a higher bandwidth connection to a single site. Cisco only supports MPPP (Multi-link Point-to-Point Protocol) and not the ISDN standard of bonding.

56/64Kbps

56Kbps and 64Kbps lines are also called DS0s by telco people. 56Kbps lines can be point-to-point leased lines or dial-up, which are called switched 56 lines. 64Kbps lines are only point-to-point leased lines. They offer lower cost connections between WAN sites while providing better reliability at a reasonable bandwidth.

Frame Relay

Frame Relay is technically not a type of WAN line. The data travels not point-to-point, but rather through a Frame Relay provider's network, as shown in Figure 5-12. Connections within the network can change at any point in time, often without the customer's noticing. Your sites lease a WAN line, be it 56/64Kbps, ISDN, or T1, into the Frame Relay provider's local point of presence (POP). Because you only have to pay for a leased line to the Frame Relay POP (and not the whole distance between two sites), the cost for the leased lines is much less.

Figure 5-12

Generic Frame Relay connection. Each site has a router and CSU/DSU. Both connect to the local telco to the nearest Frame Relay POP (Point of Presence).

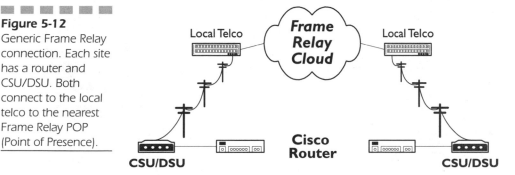

From there, any number of paths route the data through the Frame Relay provider's network. This is why the Frame Relay connection is shown as a cloud.

Once inside the Frame Relay network, your data is routed between your sites based on your contract with the Frame Relay provider. You can have all your sites send their traffic back to a main location, or make a full or partial mesh between all the sites. You do not need to have all the data lines in your Frame Relay network be the same size. If you have several small sites, they might only require 56Kbps or 64Kbps connections to the Frame Relay cloud. Larger sites might get fractional T1 lines utilizing only two or three channels. The main site might have a full T1 to support all the traffic possible from all the remote sites.

Frame Relay has the concept of committed information rates (CIR— pronounced "sear") and burstable information rates (BIR—pronounced "beer" [hic!]). The CIR is the guaranteed minimum bandwidth that will be available for a particular site to communicate through the Frame Relay cloud. No matter how congested the provider's network is, you will always have this minimum available for your networking needs. The BIR is the maximum bandwidth above your CIR that you can burst up to for short periods of time. The CIR and BIR add up to the total port speed for your line. For example, if you have a 128Kbps fractional T1 connection into the Frame Relay cloud, you could have a 64Kbps CIR and a 64Kbps BIR. In this example you would always have a minimum bandwidth of 64Kbps available to you, but when you need it you can burst up to 128Kbps (assuming the network has the extra bandwidth to give you).

You could also set up a line with 0Kbps CIR and 128Kbps BIR, or the reverse. This all depends on your needs and the rules of the Frame Relay provider. Some make you keep your CIR at a minimum of 50% of your port speed. Others might not care, but have other rules regarding service, such as only allocating CIR/BIR rates in 8Kbps or 16Kbps increments.

Some Frame Relay providers have additional services that you can purchase, such as network monitoring and customer-adjustable CIR/BIR settings. The usefulness of network monitoring will depend on the individual customer and product offered by the provider. In some cases, a typical network management system (NMS) like HP Openview will give you the same information. So will some freeware products like MRTG, which graphs router throughput and displays it on a Web page. For more information on MRTG, point your Web browser at:

`http://www.ee.ethz.ch/~oetiker/webtools/mrtg`.

One nice thing about Frame Relay is its flexibility. It requires no customer changes to have the provider change the CIR/BIR ratio. This allows you to respond to user need for extra bandwidth by scheduling ratio changes with your provider. You should find out what the delay is from the time of your request to the time of implementation. This will let your users schedule changes to the network far enough in advance for you to implement them. In fact, some providers offer a service where you can make changes to the CIR/BIR ratios on the fly. This usually costs a premium, but for larger sites it can save more than it costs.

A sample Frame Relay diagram is shown in Figure 5-13. As you can see, there is one central site with a T1 local loop, two remote sites with T1 local loops, and two remote sites with 64Kbps local loops. The main site has a fractional T1 line with a port speed of 256Kbps. This is divided into 128Kbps CIR and 128Kbps BIR. All told, the other sites have 224Kbps CIR and 160Kbps BIR. In this case, all sites communicate only with the central site.

Anyone with simple math skills can see the potential for disaster. If all sites start transmitting at once, they can easily swamp the central site. But how often does this really happen? In truth, it will depend on your network users and applications, but rarely will the central site be flooded with traffic beyond its capacity. This principle is called "overselling bandwidth."

Because not all users on a network transmit or receive data at once, you do not need to provide 100% bandwidth at a central site for all remote sites. You attempt to make an initial guess at the proper oversell ratio (in this case 1:1.75 for CIR). Once the network is up, you monitor it, graphing utilization of your different sites, and adjust your oversell ratio as necessary.

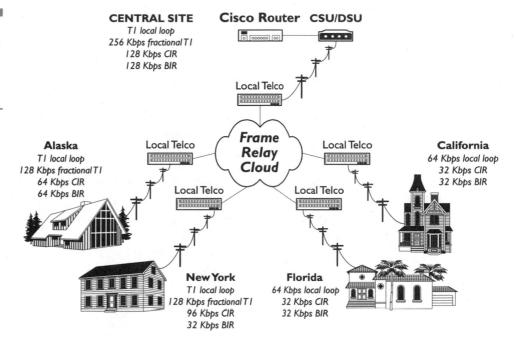

Figure 5-13
A much larger Frame Relay network is shown, with sites all over the United States.

CENTRAL SITE
T1 local loop
256 Kbps fractional T1
128 Kbps CIR
128 Kbps BIR

Cisco Router **CSU/DSU**

Local Telco

Frame Relay Cloud

Alaska
T1 local loop
128 Kbps fractional T1
64 Kbps CIR
64 Kbps BIR

Local Telco

Local Telco

California
64 Kbps local loop
32 Kbps CIR
32 Kbps BIR

Local Telco

Local Telco

New York
T1 local loop
128 Kbps fractional T1
96 Kbps CIR
32 Kbps BIR

Florida
64 Kbps local loop
32 Kbps CIR
32 Kbps BIR

Digital Conversion Devices

Today, most of us are familiar with modems, but how many of us really understand them? The word "modem" is a combination of the words "*mo*dulator" and "*dem*odulator". In simple terms, a modem takes the digital data from your computer and converts it into analog tones that are compatible with the POTS (Plain Old Telephone Service). This is called *modulation*. The modem at the other end converts the tones back into digital data. This is *demodulation*. This is fine for connecting to analog telco lines like POTS, but what about connecting to digital telco lines like T1s and ISDN BRIs?

For digital telco lines, a digital-to-digital converter is used. This is necessary because routers do not speak the same language as telco lines. Each type of digital line requires its own digital conversion device. Each T1, E1,

56Kbps, and 64Kbps require CSU/DSUs; ISDN BRI lines require ISDN NT-1s. T1 and E1 lines use a different type of CSU/DSU than 56Kbps and 64Kbps lines. When you order equipment, you must be extremely precise about what type of data line you will be attaching to it. Many analog modems will handle 56Kbps leased lines, but not 64Kbps. Similarly, some T1 CSU/DSUs only support full T1 and not fractional T1.

ISDN PRI lines require a different digital conversion device altogether. Because the router controls the DSU functions internally, only an external CSU is needed. In this case, a CSU/DSU will not do the job, because CSU/DSUs are integrated into a single unit; their functions cannot be separated from each other. Some Cisco channelized T1/PRI cards require external CSUs, like the one for the Cisco 4x00 series routers. Others, such as those available for the AS5200 and Cisco 3600 series, have the CSU built in, and the telco connection goes right into the router without any external digital conversion devices.

In fact, many of the new Cisco routers, such as the 2524, 1600, 2600, and 3600 series, have internal digital conversion devices. These routers can be configured with an internal NT-1 and CSU/DSU (56/64/T1). In this case, no external devices are needed. This helps reduce the cost of networking hardware, while increasing its functionality. Currently, you have to take special steps to gain remote access to CSU/DSU equipment. When they are fully integrated into IOS, you gain the ability to control and monitor them through the router. This is an extremely powerful tool for the network administrator, because only large companies could previously justify the expense of powerful CSU/DSUs with remote monitoring capabilities.

Table 5-3

List of devices necessary for connecting different types of data lines

Line	Device	Types of External Devices Available
56Kbps	CSU/DSU	• Some normal modems convert EIA-232 to 56Kbps 2-wire or 4-wire leased lines
		• 56Kbps 2-wire CSU/DSU
		• 56/64Kbps 4-wire CSU/DSU
64Kbps	CSU/DSU	• 56/64Kbps 4-wire CSU/DSU
T1	CSU/DSU	• T1 CSU/DSU
E1	CSU/DSU	• E1 CSU/DSU
BRI	NT-1	• ISDN NT-1
PRI	CSU	• T1 or E1 CSU

Cabling

Cabling can be one of those things that sneak up on you and delay your network installation. Cisco has dozens of network connectors available for their routers, and those in turn attach to external devices, which may or may not have the same connector. This gremlin can be avoided with a little bit of research. For example, say you decide to order a channelized T1/PRI card for your Cisco 4500.

Your first step would be to go to Cisco's Web site and look up the installation guide for the Cisco 4500 router at:

```
(http://www.cisco.com/univercd/cc/td/doc/product/ac-
cess/acs_mod/cis4000/4000cn/1000npm.htm).
```

You would then go to the section for installing this particular card. In it, you would see Figure 5-14 below, which shows the female DB-15 connector on the back of the card. Below that you would see Figure 5-15, showing the pin-out for the cable necessary to connect something to that card. Just below that, in Figure 5-16, are the words that indicate that you connect it to an external CSU. Having read the above section, you know that an external CSU is a different device from an external CSU/DSU.

Figure 5-14
External connector on Channelized T1 card.

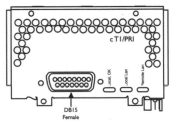

Figure 5-15
Cable diagram for connecting Channelized T1 card to external CSU.

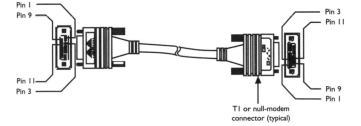

The CT1/PRI interface cables have two male 15-pin DB connectors (one at each end) to connect the CT1 network processor module with the **external CSU**. Table 7 lists the pin-outs for the null-modem CT1 cable, while Table 8 lists the pin-outs for the straight through CT1 cable.

The Cisco documentation only mentions two cables available; both are 15-pin DB to 15-pin DB. One is null modem, and the other is straight through. One would assume from this that all manufacturers of external CSUs provided a 15-pin DB connector on their devices. One manufacturer is Adtran. A quick trip to their Web site at http://www.adtran.com/cpe/t1/t1.csu/t1csuace/t1csuace.html will show you their specifications on the Adtran T1 CSU ACE. If you look at the product specifications, you will notice they say "Physical Interface RJ-48C: 8-Pin Modular."

You now know that a cable is needed to convert the female 15-pin DB connector on the Cisco CT1 card to the female 8-pin RJ48C connector for the Adtran. It does not explicitly say that such a cable ships with the product, which prompts a phone call to Adtran pre-sales technical support. The Adtran technician reports that a female DB-15 to female RJ-48C adapter ships with the T1 CSU ACE. This will do the conversion from DB-15 to RJ-48C. You still need a male-to-male DB-15 cable, and Cisco offers these.

Two standard CT1 serial cables are available for the CT1/PRI module from Cisco Systems: null-modem (part number 72-0800-xx) and straight-through (part number 72-0799-xx). Null-modem cables are used for back-to-back operation and testing. A straight-through cable connects your router to an external CSU (Channel Service Unit).

Going back to the Cisco Web page and looking under cabling, you will see the quote in Figure 5-17. This clearly shows you that you want the straight-through cable. Now all you need is a straight-through RJ48C cable, and the connection will be complete. You can use a short RJ-45 cable (almost any kind will do), silver satin, or CAT 5. You should really use a cable that isolates the send-and-receive pairs, but for very short distances a standard RJ-45 network cable will work fine.

NOTE

Silver satin cabling is called that for the color of the plastic that holds the individual wires together. It is usually flat, and the wires inside it are not twisted. *CAT 5* (IBM Category V type wiring) cable comes in many colors, and the individual wire pairs are twisted. Twisting the cable pairs cancels out the electromagnetic and radio noise they emit and allows you to run them longer and use higher data rates.

As you can see, there is more involved in cabling than meets the eye. By making sure to investigate the equipment and spending a little time on the phone with the various vendors, you can avoid costly delays. Most, if not all, of the information you need is freely available on the World Wide Web; all you need to do is look for it.

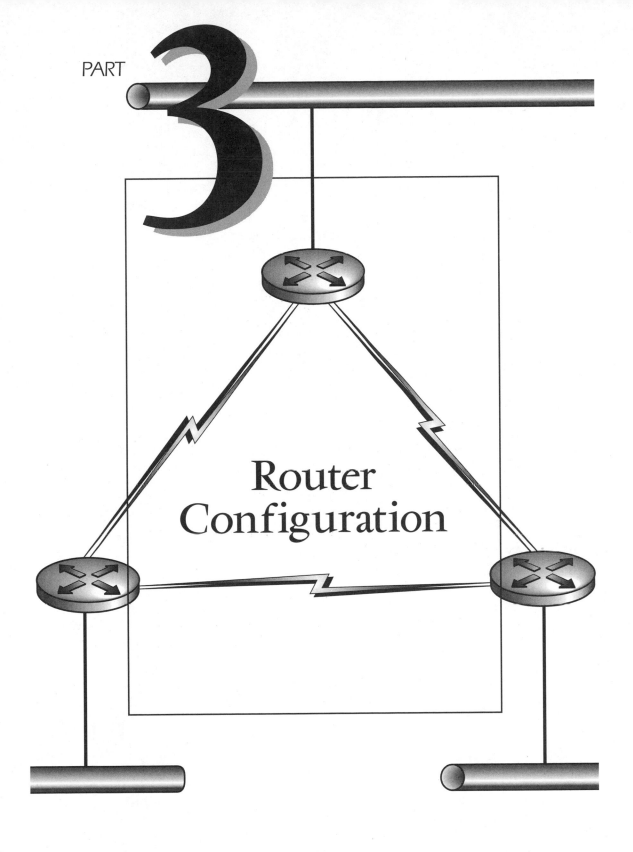

PART

3

Router
Configuration

CHAPTER **6**

Jumping in Feet First

Sometimes the best way to learn something is to jump in feet first. This means immersing yourself in Cisco router command language until you speak it fluently. Your first configurations should be simple ones, based on getting the basic functionality of the router working. This section is devoted to simple configurations. It will get you started with router maintenance and configuration.

Going Backward

Before going forward, make sure that you can go backward. If your routers are already functional, you'll want to back up their configuration files, store the passwords in a safe place, and be able to restore the router to a default configuration.

There are two basic ways to back up the router's configuration file. First, use a terminal emulator like HyperTerminal, Telnet, or NetTerm to connect to the router. Next, use the appropriate command to display the configuration file on the screen. In IOS, the command is **show running-config**, in the 700 series routers, the command is **upload**. Once the whole file has displayed, use cut-and-paste to transfer the file to a text editor like Notepad, WordPad, or vi. Be sure to save the file as a text file (*.txt).

The second method is to write the configuration file to a TFTP server. IOS has long supported TFTP, and the 700 series router OS rev. 4.2 has recently added TFTP support. It does not matter what type of TFTP server you run, just so long as you can write a file to it. You must know the IP address and filename. Some more secure versions of the TFTP server will not create blank files for new file transfers. You must create a blank file and make it writeable before you can copy information into it over the network. This is mostly on UNIX systems; executing the commands in Figure 6-1 will get you around the problem. Note that the directory used, /usr/local/tftpboot, should be replaced with the TFTP home directory used on your UNIX system.

Figure 6-1   *UNIX commands to create a blank file for TFTP uploads.*

```
318 # cd /usr/local/tftpboot

319 # touch config.txt

320 # ls -l config.txt
-rw-r-r—   1 root       sys                 0 Jun 10 11:42 config.txt

323 # chmod a+w config.txt

324 # ls -l config.txt
-rw-rw-rw-   1 root       sys                 0 Jun 10 11:42 config.txt
```

Backing up the Config File in IOS

In IOS, use the command **write network**. IOS will take you through a series of questions, including file name and hostname, or the IP address where you want to TFTP the file. This dialog can be seen in Figure 6-2. WARNING: Remember not to clobber an existing file.

Figure 6-2   The dialog for the write network command.

```
wan4500#write network
Remote host []? rohan
Translating "rohan"...domain server (199.229.53.167) [OK]

Name of configuration file to write [wan4500-confg]? <enter>
Write file wan4500-confg on host 199.29.53.67? [confirm] <enter>
Building configuration...

Writing wan4500-confg !!! [OK]
wan4500#
```

Backing up the Config File in 700 Series Routers

In the 700 series OS, you use the command **UPload TFTP <ip address> <file name>**. "ip address" is the IP address of your TFTP server, and "file name" is the file name into which to write the information on the TFTP server. An example of this is shown in Figure 6-3.

Figure 6-3   Backing up the configuration via TFTP on a Cisco 700 series router.

```
pfischer.isdn> upload tftp 199.229.53.167 paul.txt

TFTP: Starting transfer ...

TFTP: Transfer successful.
pfischer.isdn>
```

Returning the Router to the Factory Default Config

Once you've successfully backed up your existing configuration files, you can start to learn more about your router. If you manage to get the configuration so confused you feel you need to start over, you should do so. The command to erase the configuration on an IOS router is **write erase**. This will wipe out the existing configuration. Next, using the **reload** command, you can reboot the router. It will come up to the initial configuration menu and will only be accessible through the console serial port. The 700 series command to return the router to its factory default state is **set defaults**. It will automatically reboot after you execute this command and, like the IOS router, will only be accessible through the console serial port.

Basic Configurations

Those just jumping into Cisco routers need to become accustomed to Cisco router OS command language. This section will take you through some of the basic parts of the overall router configuration. The goal is to modularize the configuration elements so that they make more sense to you.

These are basic configurations. They are the minimum configurations necessary to verify that the connection works. Once you've completed this section, you should move on to the advanced configurations. These will tell you how to polish your configuration, so that the network performs exactly the way you want it to perform.

Setting up Passwords

All Cisco routers are full of passwords. There are passwords for logging in to the router, passwords for entering enable mode, and passwords for dial-up connections. Each password could be different if you wanted to configure a router that way (not that it makes sense to do it, but it can be done).

Changing passwords periodically is the cornerstone of a good security policy. In this section, we explore how to set up and change passwords for different functions of Cisco routers.

Console and Auxiliary Port Passwords

By default, Cisco does not require passwords to access the console or auxiliary serial ports. This is not usually a problem; however, it can be if there are no controls on physical access. If anyone can walk up to a router and plug in a laptop or terminal, you should definitely configure a password on the console and auxiliary ports. This is especially true if you have connected a modem to the auxiliary port. With a modem connection, you can never be sure who might find the modem number and dial it. If there are no passwords on the router, someone could easily find a way to break into your network.

Setting Console Passwords in IOS

To place a password on IOS router serial ports, you need to enter global configuration mode. Next, select the interface to which you want to apply the password (**con 0** for the console and **aux 0** for the auxiliary port). As you select each interface, use the **password** command to add a password to the port. Be sure to exit and save the configuration to NVRAM.

Figure 6-4   Default configuration information for console and auxiliary ports in IOS.

```
line con 0
line aux 0
```

By default, the console and auxiliary port configuration looks like Figure 6-4 (for IOS version 11.2). Figure 6-5 shows the configuration dialog from enable mode, showing the application of passwords to the console and auxiliary ports. In this example, the passwords have different values so that you can track how the different configuration commands affect the configuration file. Of course, a password is useless if the router never checks for it, so be sure to add the **login** command to the console and auxiliary lines also. This tells the IOS to prompt the user for a password when they try to gain access. Once this section is complete, you can see the passwords in the configuration file. Figure 6-6 shows the passwords in plain text as they appear in the configuration file.

Figure 6-5 *Setting the console and auxiliary port passwords in IOS.*

```
cisco-2501#conf terminal
Enter configuration commands, one per line.  End with CNTL/Z.
cisco-2501(config)#line con 0
cisco-2501(config-line)#login
cisco-2501(config-line)#password 12345
cisco-2501(config-line)#line aux 0
cisco-2501(config-line)#login
cisco-2501(config-line)#password 67890
cisco-2501(config-line)#^Z

%SYS-5-CONFIG_I: Configured from console by console

cisco-2501#copy running-config startup-config
Building configuration...
[OK]
cisco-2501#
```

Figure 6-6 *The passwords for the console and auxiliary ports are listed in plain text.*

```
line con 0
 password 12345
 login
line aux 0
 password 67890
 login
```

Setting Console Passwords in 700 Series Routers

As with IOS, the placement of password access control on a 700 series router is a two-step command. First, the password must be set using the **SEt PAssword SYstem [ENcrypted] [<password>]** command, shown in Figure 6-7. The resulting configuration file change is shown in Figure 6-8. You can only change this password from the global profile environment. It controls access for both console and Telnet sessions. By default, access control is enabled for Telnet connections, but not for the console.

Figure 6-7 Setting the encrypted access password.

```
cisco766> set pa sy 12345
System Protection will be in place after the current session terminates
cisco766>
```

Figure 6-8 The encrypted password as it appears in the configuration file.

```
SET PASSWORD SYSTEM ENCRYPTED 00554155500e
```

Next, enable console password access with the command **SEt LOcalaccess ON | PArtial | PRotected**. This command is shown in Figure 6-9.

Figure 6-9 This command enables password checking on the console port.

```
cisco766> set localaccess protected
System Protection will be in place after the current session terminates
cisco766>
```

You can check to make sure the console is secure using the **logout** command. It will end your authorized session, but the prompt will stay the same. Now, run a command like **upload**, which displays the configuration file. If you receive an error, you know you must use the command **login** and then enter the system password to identify yourself to the router again. Note that the password will not echo back to you as you enter it during login. This command dialog is shown in Figure 6-10.

Figure 6-10 Logout of the router to see if you have properly enabled password checking on the console port.

```
cisco766> logout
cisco766> upload
Login and System password required to process command
cisco766> login
Enter Password:
cisco766> upload
CD
SET SCREENLENGTH 20
SET COUNTRYGROUP 1
...
```

Configuring Telnet Passwords

Protecting the router from unauthorized access via the network is paramount. Unlike physical access, where a cracker risks being seen using the router, Telnet connections allow access to the router from anywhere on the planet, making it much harder to detect break-ins. *Always* password protect Telnet connections to routers.

Configuring Telnet Passwords in IOS

During the initial setup dialog, IOS asks you to **Enter virtual terminal password**. This example uses the phrase **enter-here**, resulting in the configuration changes shown in Figure 6-11. The **line vty 0 4** indicates there are five virtual terminal lines available (0 through 4). Each supports its own Telnet session. All of them allow users to log in to the router if they enter the proper password.

Figure 6-11   The configuration changes showing the Telnet password in plain text.

```
line vty 0 4
 password enter-here
 login
```

The password is the same for all five virtual terminals. You could set the password on each terminal by entering a command sequence such as the one shown in Figure 6-12. (Note the shorthand command **copy run start** used in place of **copy running-config startup-config**.)

Figure 6-12   The command dialog to set each Telnet session to a different password.

```
cisco-2501#configure terminal
Enter configuration commands, one per line.  End with CNTL/Z.
cisco-2501(config)#line vty 0
cisco-2501(config-line)#password number1
cisco-2501(config-line)#line vty 1
cisco-2501(config-line)#password number2
cisco-2501(config-line)#line vty 2
cisco-2501(config-line)#password number3
cisco-2501(config-line)#line vty 3
cisco-2501(config-line)#password number4
cisco-2501(config-line)#line vty 4
cisco-2501(config-line)#password number5
```

```
cisco-2501(config-line)#^Z
cisco-2501#

%SYS-5-CONFIG_I: Configured from console by console

cisco-2501#copy run start
Building configuration...
[OK]
cisco-2501#
```

This resulted in the configuration changes shown in Figure 6-13. Changing the password for each vty individually splits them out in the configuration file from one line (**line vty 0 4**) to five separate lines.

■■ ■■

Figure 6-13 The configuration changes showing each vty line having a different password.

```
line vty 0
 password number1
 login
line vty 1
 password number2
 login
line vty 2
 password number3
 login
line vty 3
 password number4
 login
line vty 4
 password number5
 login
```

This example is not very practical, because a user connecting to the router via Telnet would not know to which port they were connected; therefore, they would have a hard time determining which password to use. To set the passwords for all vty lines to the same string, we would use the dialog in Figure 6-14.

■■

Figure 6-14 *The configuration dialog to make all vty passwords the same.*

```
cisco-2501#conf t
Enter configuration commands, one per line.  End with CNTL/Z.
cisco-2501(config)#line vty 0 4
cisco-2501(config-line)#password open-says-me
cisco-2501(config-line)#^Z
cisco-2501#

%SYS-5-CONFIG_I: Configured from console by console

cisco-2501#cop ru st
Building configuration...
[OK]
cisco-2501#
```

This resulted in the configuration collapsing all five vty lines back to a single entry, as shown in Figure 6-15.

■■

Figure 6-15 *All five vty lines now have the same password, and their entries are collapsed.*

```
line vty 0 4
 password open-says-me
 login
```

Configuring Telnet Passwords in 700 Series Routers

There is only one password protecting the Cisco 7x0 series routers from administrative access. This password gives you access to the router, as well as administrative control. The password is not configured by default and must be added with the command **SEt PAssword SYstem [ENcrypted] [<password>]**. The documentation is slightly incorrect in that the ENcrypted option is always the default, and is therefore never required. The command, shown in Figure 6-16, sets the password and adds the line shown in Figure 6-17 to the configuration file.

■■

Figure 6-16 *Setting the system password.*

```
cisco766> set pa sy 12345
System Protection will be in place after the current session terminates
cisco766>
```

Figure 6-17 The configuration file changes resulting from set password command.

```
SET PASSWORD SYSTEM ENCRYPTED 00554155500e
```

You must be in the global profile to effect this password change. If you change to a subprofile (like LAN), you will get an error message. An example is displayed in Figure 6-18.

Figure 6-18 The system password cannot be set from a profile.

```
cisco766> cd lan
cisco766:LAN> set password system 67890
System parameter can only be modified at system level
cisco766:LAN>
```

By default, Telnet access to this router is protected. This is done through the **SEt REmoteaccess OFF | PArtial | PRotected** command. If, for some reason, you should want to disable Telnet access, you can use the command shown in Figure 6-19.

Figure 6-19 The command used to turn off Telnet access to the router.

```
cisco766> set remoteaccess off
cisco766>
```

This will result in the message *Remote configuration is disabled—ACCESS DENIED* being displayed when you try to Telnet to the router. You can restore it to its default configuration by setting remote access back to *protected*, as shown in Figure 6-20.

Figure 6-20 Telnet access is restored to its normal mode by setting remote access to *protected*.

```
cisco766> set remoteaccess protected
cisco766>
```

Enable and Enable Secret Passwords in IOS

IOS understands the concept of multiple levels of security. In the default setup, you have an access mode and an enable mode. Enable mode gives you complete administrative access to the Cisco router. The normal password for enable mode is the enable password. By default, this password is stored in plain text like the vty, console, and auxiliary passwords. However, if you want more protection, you can create an (encrypted) enable secret password.

If there is an enable password (but not an enable secret password), it will protect access to enable mode. An enable secret password supercedes a mere enable password, and the router will require its use to access enable mode (regardless of the presence of an enable password). The enable secret password is more secure, not only because it is encrypted, but also because it uses stronger encryption than normal (see "Encrypting Passwords" later in this chapter).

To set an enable password, use the **enable password** command (see the dialog in Figure 6-21). This either adds or changes the **enable password** line in the configuration file so that it looks like Figure 6-22.

Figure 6-21 The command dialog to set the enable password.

```
cisco-2501#conf t
Enter configuration commands, one per line.   End with CNTL/Z.
cisco-2501(config)#enable password junk
cisco-2501(config)#^Z
cisco-2501#

%SYS-5-CONFIG_I: Configured from console by console

cisco-2501#cop ru st
Building configuration...
[OK]
cisco-2501#
```

Figure 6-22 The enable password line as it appears in the configuration.

```
enable password junk
```

Figure 6-23 The configuration dialog for creating or changing an enable secret password.

```
cisco-2501#conf t
Enter configuration commands, one per line.   End with CNTL/Z.
cisco-2501(config)#enable secret 12345
cisco-2501(config)#^Z
cisco-2501#

%SYS-5-CONFIG_I: Configured from console by console

cisco-2501#cop ru st
Building configuration...
[OK]
cisco-2501#
```

Figure 6-24 The encrypted enable secret password.

```
enable secret 5 $1$hecz$p.mC8fHOC5Y/8hU6S2xhG.
```

Setting an enable secret password is just as simple. By using the **enable secret** command, you can add or change the encrypted password protecting enable mode. This is shown in Figure 6-23. This either adds or changes the line in the configuration file shown in Figure 6-24. As you can see, the password is not stored in plain text as it is with the enable, vty, console, and auxiliary passwords. This makes your router more secure, because anyone seeing the configuration file (whether over your shoulder or on a print out) will not be able to pick up the password to access enable mode in your router. It also means you cannot rely on text files or printed copies of your configuration file to reference your router passwords. You will have to store them somewhere safe, or you will not be able to get them back if you lose them.

Encrypting Passwords

Encrypting passwords can be scary to someone who is used to reading them in stored configuration files. Getting over this fear is of paramount importance for the security of your network. If anyone looking over your shoulder or reading configuration files on your hard disk can read router passwords in plain text, you are asking for trouble. You need to make it as hard as possible for unauthorized personnel to get into your routers. The first line of defense is encrypting your router password.

Encryption in IOS

There are two types of encryption algorithms in IOS. The first is a hard encryption based on a hashed MD5 algorithm. This hard encryption is used only on the **enable secret** password. The second is much less secure, and has already been broken. Programs to decrypt it are not hard to find on the Internet, and Cisco has known about their existence since 1995. Do not rely on this weak encryption to stop anything more than over-the-shoulder password leaks. For Cisco's official stance on this, see the URL http://www.cisco.com/warp/public/701/64.html/.

Figure 6-25 *The router passwords without weak encryption set.*

```
enable secret 5 $1$hecz$p.mC8fHOC5Y/8hU6S2xhG.
enable password junk
line con 0
 password 12345
 login
line aux 0
 password 67890
 login
line vty 0 4
 password open-says-me
 login
```

Without weak encryption set, the passwords in the configuration file look like Figure 6-25. Turning on the password encryption service in the global configuration mode automatically encrypts all passwords (except the **enable secret**) with weak encryption. Add the password encryption service as per the dialog in Figure 6-26. Once entered, your configuration file will look like Figure 6-27.

Figure 6-26 The command dialog to turn on weak password encryption.

```
cisco-2501#conf t
Enter configuration commands, one per line.  End with CNTL/Z.
cisco-2501(config)#service password-encryption
cisco-2501(config)#^Z
cisco-2501#

%SYS-5-CONFIG_I: Configured from console by console

cisco-2501#cop ru st
Building configuration...
[OK]
cisco-2501#
```

Figure 6-27 The configuration now shows encrypted passwords.

```
service password-encryption
enable secret 5 $1$hecz$p.mC8fHOC5Y/8hU6S2xhG.
enable password 7 09465B0712
line con 0
 password 7 12485744465E
 login
line aux 0
 password 7 1353404A525C
 login
line vty 0 4
 password 7 11060900195F180D1D3966292D
 login
```

Remember that this encryption can be broken and is only meant to
stop people reading over your shoulder. If you have to send a copy of your
configuration file to anyone, make sure to delete or cross out the encrypted
passwords. You can do this by copying the text file aside and changing it
to look something like Figure 6-28.

Figure 6-28 The configuration file after the encrypted passwords have been replaced by a line of Xs.

```
service password-encryption
enable secret 5 XXXXXXXXXXXXX
enable password 7 XXXXXXXXXXXXX
line con 0
 password 7 XXXXXXXXXXXXX
 login
line aux 0
 password 7 XXXXXXXXXXXXX
 login
line vty 0 4
 password 7 XXXXXXXXXXXXX
 login
```

Next, print or e-mail this version with no real passwords. Note that the **enable secret** password was also deleted. Although the encryption used to create it has not been broken, you should not take the chance that someone else might acquire it.

As a side note, you should also make sure to remove any information about SNMP community string names if you send your configuration file to someone else. (See later discussions on security and SNMP for more information.)

Encryption in 700 Series Routers

The 700 series router OS handles encryption in a very straightforward way. The system and PPP passwords can be set using the **encrypted** keyword. The command line help shows the system and PPP passwords being set in the manner shown in Figure 6-29.

Figure 6-29 The command syntax for setting system and PPP passwords. Encryption is optional.

```
SEt PAssword SYstem [ENcrypted] [<password>]
SEt PPp <PAssword | SEcret> <HOst | CLient> {ENcrypted] [<password>]
```

As noted before, if you try to set the system password without using the **encrypted** keyword (as in Figure 6-30), the OS encrypts it anyway, resulting in the configuration entry shown in Figure 6-31.

Figure 6-30 Setting the system password without the encrypted keyword.

```
cisco766> set password system 12345
System Protection will be in place after the current session terminates
cisco766>
```

Figure 6-31 The router encrypts the system password regardless of whether you ask it to or not.

```
SET PASSWORD SYSTEM ENCRYPTED 12485744465e
```

Set the PPP host password with the command shown in Figure 6-32. This also results in an encrypted password in the configuration file, without its being explicitly asked for. This can be seen in Figure 6-33.

Figure 6-32 Setting the PPP host password.

```
cisco766> set ppp password host 67890
cisco766>
```

Figure 6-33 The PPP host password is encrypted regardless of your desire.

```
SET PPP PASSWORD HOST ENCRYPTED 0145515c025b
```

It is puzzling why Cisco includes the **encrypted** keyword as an option, when you always get an encrypted password (whether you use the option or not).

Interface Configuration in IOS

An interface statement in the configuration file controls each physical networking port on a Cisco IOS router. To make changes to an interface, you must enter the interface name first. When you do, you will notice the prompt change from *(config)* in global configuration mode to *(config-if)* in interface configuration mode. You can see this in Figure 6-34.

Figure 6-34 Selecting an interface changes the prompt to let you know you are in interface configuration mode.

```
cisco-2501(config)#interface ethernet 0
cisco-2501(config-if)#
```

Once you are in interface configuration mode, all interface-related commands entered will affect that specific interface only. If you enter a command supported only in global configuration mode, you may revert to that mode. In Figure 6-35 you can see that the administrator is in global configuration mode when the command **interface ethernet 0** is entered. After the command is processed, the prompt changes to *(config-if)* to indicate you are now configuring the interface. Enter the IP address for that interface. Note that you remain in interface configuration mode. However, once you enter the global configuration mode command to create a user, the system reverts to global configuration mode.

Figure 6-35 Entering a global configuration mode command in interface mode automatically exits you from interface configuration mode.

```
cisco-2501(config)#interface ethernet 0
cisco-2501(config-if)#ip address 10.0.0.1 255.255.255.0
cisco-2501(config-if)#user paul password test1
cisco-2501(config)#
```

There will be instances when the commands you are entering are ambiguous to the command-line processor. In this case, the command might be valid, but you cannot enter it from the current mode. To solve this problem, simply **exit** back to the global configuration mode, as shown in Figure 6-36:

Figure 6-36 Using the exit command returns you to global configuration mode.

```
cisco-2501(config)#interface ethernet 0
cisco-2501(config-if)#exit
cisco-2501(config)#
```

Profile Configuration in 700 Series Routers

The 700 series OS does not use the concept of interfaces, but rather one of profiles. Because it is a fixed configuration router with only one Ethernet port and one ISDN BRI port, it doesn't really need to generalize LAN and WAN connections as IOS routers do. Instead, the LAN port has a separate profile from the *user* profiles used to connect via ISDN to WAN sites. To make changes to the Ethernet configuration, you must first be in the LAN profile.

Configuring the Ethernet Port

Explanations follow for configuring the Ethernet interface in IOS and in 700 series routers.

Ethernet Interface Configuration in IOS

The most basic configuration necessary on the Ethernet port is to set the IP address and network mask. Once you do that, the Ethernet port is ready for use, unless it is shut down. In this case, invoke the **no shutdown** command to bring the interface into an active state. On some Cisco routers, you have a choice of connector for certain Ethernet ports. For example, a two-port Ethernet card for a series 4000 router (Figure 6-37) has both AUI and 10-BaseT ports. If an Ethernet interface has multiple connectors, you must choose which one you are going to use in the configuration, using the **media-type** command.

Figure 6-37
The dual Ethernet card for the Cisco 4000 series has two media types for each interface.

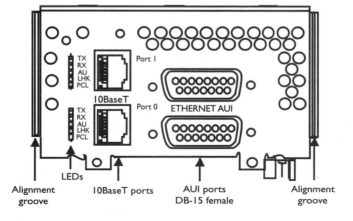

If your network is subnetted, there is a chance that the subnet you are using is illegal, so far as RFC 950 (http://info.internet.isi.edu:80/in-notes/rfc/files/rfc950.txt) is concerned. Although these subnets might be illegal, some people still use them, and they can function without error. Both the first and last subnets of a subnet mask are considered illegal. So, if you wanted four networks of 62 hosts each, you will lose the first and last subnet, unless you override RFC 950.

Cisco is bound to support the RFCs and enforce their proper use. This means that sometimes you will not be able to enter an IP address and netmask. Instead, the router will kick out a *bad mask* error. If you feel that your subnet will work properly, and you want to make the personal decision to override RFC 950 in your network, use the **ip subnet-zero** command.

An example of how to set up an Ethernet interface detailing all the above concerns can be seen in Figure 6-38. The initial configuration for the interface is listed in Figure 6-39. The new configuration, showing the changes entered in Figure 6-38, can be seen in Figure 6-40.

■■

Figure 6-38 *The configuration dialog for setting up a RFC 950 illegal subnet in IOS.*

```
cisco-2501#conf t
Enter configuration commands, one per line.  End with CNTL/Z.
cisco-2501(config)#interface ethernet 0
cisco-2501(config-if)#ip address 10.0.0.1 255.255.255.0
Bad mask /24 for address 10.0.0.1
cisco-2501(config-if)#ip subnet-zero
cisco-2501(config)#interface ethernet 0
cisco-2501(config-if)#ip address 10.0.0.1 255.255.255.0
cisco-2501(config-if)#media-type aui
cisco-2501(config-if)#no shutdown
cisco-2501(config-if)#^Z
cisco-2501#

%SYS-5-CONFIG_I: Configured from console by console

%LINEPROTO-5-UPDOWN: Line protocol on Interface Ethernet0, changed
state to up
%LINK-3-UPDOWN: Interface Ethernet0, changed state to up

cisco-2501#
```

Figure 6-39 The initial state of the interface is shut down with no IP address.

```
interface Ethernet 0
 no ip address
 shutdown
```

Figure 6-40 The new state of the interface has an IP address on an illegal subnet. This can only be done if the
ip subnet-zero command is used.

```
ip subnet-zero
!
interface Ethernet 0
 ip address 10.0.0.1 255.255.255.0
```

Notice that the **ip subnet-zero** command is not part of the interface configuration in Figure 6-40, but rather part of the global configuration. In basic terms, either your router supports RFC 950 illegal subnets or it does not. There is no way to set it on a per-interface basis. Also, notice that the **media-type** command does not show up. Some Cisco routers can automatically sense which port is in use and override the command. On these routers the **media-type** command is not necessary and becomes a hidden command in the configuration file.

Ethernet Interface Configuration in 700 Series Routers

Setting up the Ethernet port for TCP/IP is fairly trivial for Cisco 700 series routers. The only item that might cause you trouble is the Node/Hub switch next to the Ethernet port. This switch configures the Ethernet port to act as a node connected to a hub, or as a hub that has a node connected to it. This is not immediately clear by looking at it, and you might think that it is for selecting what the router is plugged into (it is not). If you are connecting the router to a hub so that multiple devices can route through it, you need to set the switch to node. If you are connecting a single PC directly to the router, it will act as a hub for that PC and you must set the switch to hub.

Statistically speaking, you have a 50—50 chance of selecting the proper setting. If you do not get a link light, you need to change the switch position. You should first shut the router off, then change the switch setting and reboot. If you try changing the switch position while the router is on, you will only get confused. This is because the Ethernet port only seems to check the switch setting at boot and ignores it afterward. By making sure you change the switch position only when the power is off, you decrease your chance of confusion. A rear view of the Cisco 766 router can be seen in Figure 6-41.

Figure 6-41
From left to right, the first three things are the serial console port, the 10BaseT Ethernet port, and the Node/Hub switch.

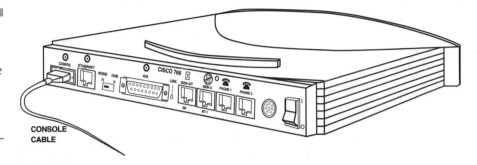

If the link light (shown here as the fifth item) is on, then you have properly connected the router to your other networking equipment.

To set the IP address and netmask on the Ethernet port, you must make configuration changes to the LAN profile. Enter the LAN profile using the **cd lan** command, and then set the IP address with the **set ip address** command. Similarly, the network mask is set with the **set ip netmask** command. This dialog is shown in Figure 6-42.

Figure 6-42 The dialog to set the IP address and network mask on a 700 series router.

```
cisco766> cd lan
cisco766:LAN> set ip address 10.0.0.1
cisco766:LAN> set ip netmask 255.255.255.0
cisco766:LAN>
```

High-capacity Serial Line Basic Configuration

This section contains details for configuring and testing high-capacity lines in IOS. The primary difference between these and ISDN lines is that the connections are permanent and no dialing occurs. This also means there is less configuration, because you don't have to negotiate connections with phone switches.

Getting a High-capacity Serial Line Operational in IOS

The high-capacity lines we will be discussing are the more ubiquitous 56/ 64Kbps (DS0) and 1.544/2.048Mbps T1/E1 (DS1) lines. These lines require more physical setup than they do router configuration. Once the line is installed from Site A to Site B, the first step is to install a CSU/DSU at each end and then make sure the telco can see both of them. Next, try a remote loopback to make sure they can see each other. Only then should you connect a router to the CSU/DSU and attempt to set up the serial interface.

For our example (shown in Figure 6-43), we have two locations, named Site A and Site B. Site A has a Cisco 4000 series router with a four-port serial card and a dual Ethernet card installed. Site B is using a Cisco 2501 router. The two sites use the same external CSU/DSU, and connect via a T1 line provided by the local telco.

Figure 6-43
An example of two sites connected together via a T1 line.

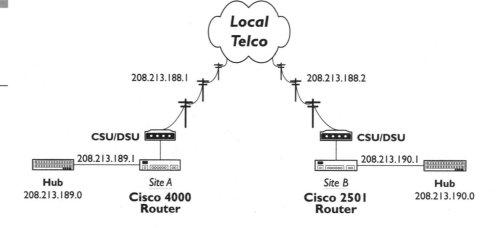

Establishing the Basic Connection

Once the T1 line checks out, the router setup can proceed. This is extremely easy. First, the Ethernet port is set up; we will assume this has been done just as it was in the example above. Next, the serial line receives an IP address, the serial interface is turned on, and we make sure the router is routing.

For our example, we'll use the IP network 208.213.188.0 to connect the two routers. Site A will receive the IP address of 208.213.188.1, and Site B will receive 208.213.188.2. Because an entire class C IP network is used, the netmask is 255.255.255.0.

By default, the configuration of Site A's serial 0 interface is shown in Figure 6-44. It is configured for the Site A configuration with the dialog shown in Figure 6-45.

Figure 6-44 By default a high-speed serial interface is shut down with no IP address.

```
interface Serial0
 no ip address
 shutdown
 no fair-queue
```

Figure 6-45 The dialog to configure Site A's serial interface.

```
wan4500#conf t
Enter configuration commands, one per line.   End with CNTL/Z.
wan4500(config)#interface serial 0
wan4500(config-if)#ip address 208.213.188.1 255.255.255.0
wan4500(config-if)#no shutdown
wan4500(config-if)#exit
wan4500(config)#ip routing
wan4500(config)#^Z
wan4500#
```

First, enter global configuration mode; next, select the interface. Add the IP address to the interface, and activate it with the **no shutdown** command. Finally, issue the **exit** command to return to global configuration mode, and the **ip routing** command to turn on IP routing. (By default, IP routing is on; however, if the router was previously used in bridging mode, the command **no ip routing** would appear in the configuration. The **ip routing** command is a useful double-check that routing is turned on, although it is not necessary in most cases.)

After entering the series of commands in Figure 6-45, the interface configuration looks like Figure 6-46. The setup for Site B is identical. The only difference is the IP address assigned to interface serial 0. In this case, it will be 208.213.188.2.

Figure 6-46 *Site A's serial configuration after the changes are saved.*

```
interface Serial0
 ip address 208.213.188.1 255.255.255.0
 no fair-queue
```

NOTE

Readers should note that the use of an entire class C IP network for a point-to-point link wastes IP address space tremendously. It is shown here only as an example. To avoid this waste, set up a subnet with a netmask of 255.255.255.252. This will provide just two valid IP addresses, one for each side of the point-to-point WAN connection. An even better way of configuring this connection would be with an unnumbered IP address on the serial interfaces. However, since neither subnetting nor unnumbered IP addresses have been discussed, a whole class C is used for this example. If you wish, you can use a whole class C to test a WAN line—as we have done here—but you should never make a configuration like this permanent.

Testing the Basic Connection

Once the line is active, you should see the messages in Figure 6-47 at the console. If you have connected through the network, use the command **terminal monitor** from the enable command prompt to have them pop up on your screen. This must be done each time you log in to the router through the network.

Figure 6-47 *Console information messages show you the line has come up.*

```
%LINK-3-UPDOWN: Interface Serial0, changed state to up
%LINEPROTO-5-UPDOWN: Line protocol on Interface Serial0, changed state
to up
```

The interface state changes to *up* if the router can see the CSU/DSU and the interface is not shutdown. Once both routers have their interfaces up, they attempt to establish the line protocol. That done, the two routers should be talking to each other. You can verify the state of the line at any time using the **show interface** command. This is shown in Figure 6-48.

Figure 6-48 *An example of the copious output received from the show interface Serial0 command.*

```
wan4500#sho int s0
Serial0 is up, line protocol is up
Hardware is HD64570
  Description: To Site B
  Internet address is 208.213.188.1/24
  MTU 1500 bytes, BW 1536 Kbit, DLY 20000 usec, rely 255/255, load 5/
255
  Encapsulation HDLC, loopback not set, keepalive set (10 sec)
  Last input 00:00:05, output 00:00:00, output hang never
  Last clearing of "show interface" counters never
  Input queue: 0/75/0 (size/max/drops); Total output drops: 0
  Queueing strategy: weighted fair
  Output queue: 0/64/0 (size/threshold/drops)
     Conversations  0/8 (active/max active)
     Reserved Conversations 0/0 (allocated/max allocated)
  5 minute input rate 50000 bits/sec, 13 packets/sec
  5 minute output rate 36000 bits/sec, 12 packets/sec
     6677396 packets input, 2555807380 bytes, 0 no buffer
     Received 56735 broadcasts, 0 runts, 0 giants
     19 input errors, 19 CRC, 0 frame, 0 overrun, 0 ignored, 12 abort
     7221491 packets output, 2985787597 bytes, 0 underruns
     0 output errors, 0 collisions, 2 interface resets
     0 output buffer failures, 0 output buffers swapped out
     0 carrier transitions
     DCD=up  DSR=up  DTR=up  RTS=up  CTS=up
wan4500#
```

The first thing to notice from the output of the **show interface serial 0** command is the state of the line. In this case, you see that the interface is up, and so is the line protocol. There is then a whole flurry of information about the state of the line and its configuration, followed by the serial line statistics since they were last reset. At the end, you can see the state of the control line signals.

The control line signals allow the CSU/DSU and the router to gain information about each other. In a working configuration, all the signals should be up. If one of these is down, you might have a problem with the CSU/DSU, the cable, or the T1 connection to the telco.

If all of this looks good, try sending data to the other end. The **ping** command sends a data packet from one router to the other and asks for a reply. You should get a reply all the time on a leased line. If you do not, there might be something wrong with the line or with some of the equipment in between the routers (cable, CSU/DSU, telco equipment). The only exception to this is the first time it is tried. You can issue the **ping** command from user mode or exec mode. This is shown in Figure 6-49.

Figure 6-49 An example of the ping command used to test basic network connectivity.

```
cisco-2501#ping 208.213.188.1

Type escape sequence to abort.
Sending 5, 100-byte ICMP Echos to 208.213.188.1, timeout is 2 seconds:
..!!!
Success rate is 60 percent (3/5), round-trip min/avg/max = 36/37/40 ms
cisco-2501#ping 208.213.188.1

Type escape sequence to abort.
Sending 5, 100-byte ICMP Echos to 208.213.188.1, timeout is 2 seconds:
!!!!!
Success rate is 100 percent (5/5), round-trip min/avg/max = 36/36/36 ms
cisco-2501#
```

Extended Testing with Ping

One way to test a T1 line is to hammer it with **ping** packets and their replies. Using **ping** interactively from the enable mode does this. (**Ping** is interactive only under the enable mode.) You simply enter **ping** on the command line, and the router will prompt you for more information. By choosing a very high number of times to send the **ping** packet, and increasing the datagram size, you can load test the line with data. If no failures occur, you can consider the line clean. In this example, 1,000 packets are sent. Each is 1024 bytes in length. An example of the extended **ping** dialog is shown in Figure 6-50.

Figure 6-50 *An example of the extended ping dialog.*

```
cisco-2501#ping
Protocol [ip]:
Target IP address: 208.213.188.1
Repeat count [5]: 1000
Datagram size [100]: 1024
Timeout in seconds [2]:
Extended commands [n]:
Sweep range of sizes [n]:
Type escape sequence to abort.
Sending 1000, 1024-byte ICMP Echos to 208.213.188.1, timeout is 2 sec-
onds:
!!!!!!!!!!!!!!!!!!!!!!!!!!!!!!!!!!!
...
```

Setting up IP Addresses on all Interfaces

Setting up IP addresses on other interfaces is just as easy. Simply select the interface to which you want to add an IP address, using the **interface** command, and add the IP address. Remember to make sure the interface is not shutdown.

Static and Default Routing

If we take the above example for a T1 connection and look at it from the real world, we will notice something missing. There is nothing communicating over the T1 line except the two Cisco routers! If we add an Ethernet port to each router, the nodes on each of those Ethernet networks can communicate over the T1 line. A diagram of this sample network is shown in Figure 6-51.

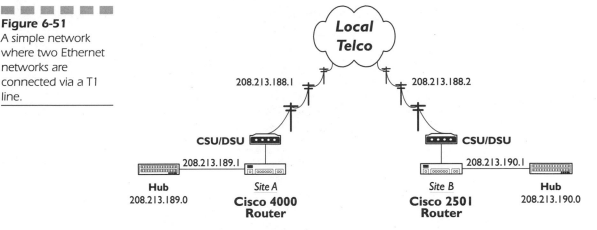

■ ■ ■ ■ ■ ■
Figure 6-51
A simple network
where two Ethernet
networks are
connected via a T1
line.

Before the network on one Ethernet can see the other, you need to route the IP protocol properly. Do this each time from the point of view of the machine you are on. There are two basic point of views per site: the nodes attached to the network and the router. The nodes attached to the network should all have the IP address of the router's Ethernet port as their default gateway. There are several ways to accomplish this, depending on the type of node. The most prevalent are in the Windows 95 desktop system. Begin by clicking on Start | Settings | Control Panel and double-clicking on the Network icon. Choose the TCP/IP setting for the Ethernet card, highlight it, click Properties, and then click on the Gateway tab (shown in Figure 6-52). From here, you should enter the IP address of the router's Ethernet port. If you enter an address not on your local network, the machine will not route properly.

Figure 6-52
The Windows 95 default gateway configuration screen. Note this address should be 208.213.189.1 at site A and 208.213.190.1 at site B.

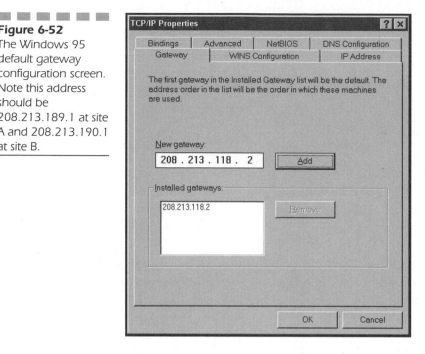

The router automatically knows how to route between networks attached to it, e.g., the LAN and Wan ports.

By having interfaces on the local and the WAN networks, the router already knows how to route between those. What it does not know about is the Ethernet network on the router it talks to over the T1. In order to inform the router about the Ethernet network at the remote site, add a static route to that network. Use the **ip route** command in global configuration mode to do this.

Site A needs a route to the Site B Ethernet network, 208.213.190.0. Site B needs a route to the Site A network, 208.213.189.0. One option is to route the network to the remote WAN IP address, as shown in Figures 6-53 and 6-54.

Figure 6-53 The configuration dialog setting up a static route to Site B's Ethernet on Site A's router.

```
Site-A#conf t
Enter configuration commands, one per line.  End with CNTL/Z.
Site-A(config)#ip route 208.213.190.0 255.255.255.0 208.213.188.2
Site-A(config)#^Z
Site-A#
```

Figure 6-54 The configuration dialog setting up a static route to Site A's Ethernet on Site B's router.

```
Site-B#conf t
Enter configuration commands, one per line.  End with CNTL/Z.
Site-B(config)#ip route 208.213.189.0 255.255.255.0 208.213.188.1
Site-B(config)#^Z
Site-B#
```

Another option is not to use the IP address of the remote router's serial port, but rather to use the local router's interface name. In this case, both routers use Serial0 as the destination for the remote route. This is shown in Figures 6-55 and 6-56.

Figure 6-55 The configuration dialog setting up a static route to Site B's Ethernet on Site A's router using Serial0 as the destination.

```
Site-A#conf t
Enter configuration commands, one per line.  End with CNTL/Z.
Site-A(config)#ip route 208.213.190.0 255.255.255.0 Serial0
Site-A(config)#^Z
Site-A#
```

Figure 6-56 The configuration dialog setting up a static route to Site A's Ethernet on Site B's router using Serial0 as the destination.

```
Site-B#conf t
Enter configuration commands, one per line.  End with CNTL/Z.
Site-B(config)#ip route 208.213.189.0 255.255.255.0 Serial0
Site-B(config)#^Z
Site-B#
```

Another way to simplify the configuration would be to use a default route. In this case, each router effectively says, "route everything I don't otherwise know how to route through this destination." You do this by removing the explicit routes to 208.213.189.0 and 208.213.190.0 and replacing them with routes to 0.0.0.0. (See Figures 6-57 and 6-58.) The network 0.0.0.0 has a network mask of 0.0.0.0. This is what makes it a default route.

Figure 6-57 The configuration dialog setting a default route on Site A's router with Serial0 as its destination.

```
Site-A#conf t
Enter configuration commands, one per line.  End with CNTL/Z.
Site-A(config)# no ip route 208.213.190.0 255.255.255.0 Serial 0
Site-A(config)#ip route 0.0.0.0 0.0.0.0 Serial0
Site-A(config)#^Z
Site-A#
```

Figure 6-58 The configuration dialog setting a default route on Site B's router with Serial0 as its destination.

```
Site-B#conf t
Enter configuration commands, one per line.  End with CNTL/Z.
Site-B(config)# no ip route 208.213.189.0 255.255.255.0 Serial 0
Site-B(config)#ip route 0.0.0.0 0.0.0.0 Serial0
Site-B(config)#^Z
Site-B#
```

While this is a little neater, it could cause you some problems later. For example, what if (as shown by Figure 6-59) Site A gets an Internet connection and connects it to the Serial1 interface? In this case, you must set a default route to the Internet, so that Site A can connect you to all those sites you do not know about. Site B will still function correctly. Its default route will get packets to the Site A network and the Internet. However, Site A must remove the default route to Site B and add one to the Internet. It must also add an explicit route to Site B, or else all packets destined for Site B will be sent out to the Internet.

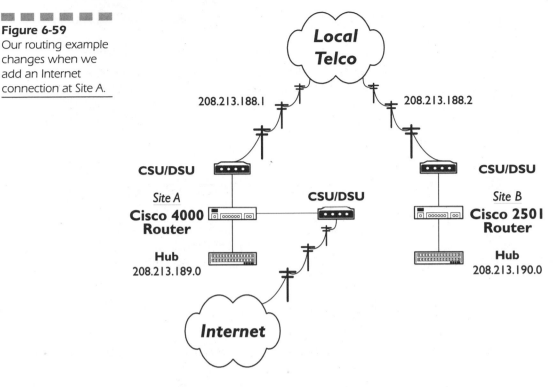

Figure 6-59
Our routing example
changes when we
add an Internet
connection at Site A.

The configuration at Site B stays the same (Figure 6-61); the configuration for Site A changes. Site A gets a default route to the Internet via Serial1 and a static route to Site B, as seen in Figure 6-60.

Figure 6-60 The routing at Site A changes to allow for the Internet connection.

```
Site-A#conf t
Enter configuration commands, one per line.  End with CNTL/Z.
Site-A(config)# no ip route 0.0.0.0.0.0.0.0 Serial 0
Site-A(config)#ip route 0.0.0.0 0.0.0.0 Serial1
Site-A(config)#ip route 208.213.190.0 255.255.255.0 Serial0
Site-A(config)#^Z
Site-A#
```

Figure 6-61 *The routing at Site B stays the same.*

```
Site-B#conf t
Enter configuration commands, one per line.  End with CNTL/Z.
Site-B(config)#ip route 0.0.0.0 0.0.0.0 Serial0
Site-B(config)#^Z
Site-B#
```

ISDN BRI Basic Configuration

This section details the configuration for ISDN dial-up networking. It includes how to set up the line, dial, and authenticate. It also provides you with troubleshooting methodology to help you through each of these stages.

U-loop Versus S/T-loop

ISDN has two electrical signaling standards. The first is U-loop, which is the signaling coming from the telco to your site. U-loop hauls ISDN signal long distances from the telco to your home or office. The second signaling standard is S/T-loop. U-loop converts to S/T-loop at your site. A device called an NT-1 does the conversion.

The S/T-loop signaling permits multiple ISDN devices to share a single ISDN line. If you have an ISDN fax machine (group 4 fax), you might be able to plug it in to the S/T-loop port on your NT-1, even an NT-1 built into a 700 series router. It will all depend on the compatibility of the devices you are using.

Many of the new routers offer built-in NT-1s. However, older routers like the 2503, 2520, and 4000 series do not. If your router does not have a built-in NT-1, you must purchase an external one. If you are setting up a single BRI, a device such as the Adtran NT-1 ACE (http://www.adtran.com/cpe/isdn/netterm/index.html#nt1ace), seen in Figure 6-62, will work for you, as will almost any external NT-1. For higher density BRI connections, you might want to invest in rack-mounted NT-1s, such as the Adtran T400 shelf shown in Figure 6-63 (http://www.adtran.com/cpe/isdn/netterm/t400/t400.html). This works well when you have more BRI connections, such as those provided with the four- and eight-port BRI cards for the 4000 series routers.

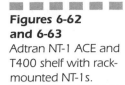

Figures 6-62 and 6-63
Adtran NT-1 ACE and T400 shelf with rack-mounted NT-1s.

The key for determining if your router has a built-in NT-1 is the presence of a U-loop port. If the router does not have a clearly marked U-loop port, it needs an external NT-1. This will take U-loop signaling in from the telco and convert it to S/T-loop signaling. Depending on the external NT-1, you might get more than one S/T-loop connection for external ISDN devices. Other ISDN devices include ISDN fax machines, ISDN credit card verification systems, and ISDN phones.

Configuring the BRI in IOS

Setting up a BRI in IOS is a multistage process. First, you must connect the ISDN line to the telco and configure the line itself (as well as the ISDN switch type your telco is using.) Next, you have to configure the dial-out and dial-in information. Finally, you need to verify routing over the BRI.

Initially, no ISDN switch type is set and there is no really useful configuration information for your BRI interface. This is shown in Figure 6-64.

Figure 6-64 By default the BRI interface is shut down with no IP address.

```
interface BRI0
 no ip address
 no ip route-cache
 no ip mroute-cache
 shutdown
```

The first thing to do is physically connect the ISDN line to the wall jack coming from your telco. This will go into a port on your router labeled *ISDN U-loop.* If your router does not have this port, connect it to the U-loop port on an external NT-1. Next, connect the S/T-loop port on the external NT-1 to your router. Routers like the Cisco 766 have a built-in NT-1 and convert U-loop to S/T-loop internally. With these routers, the U-loop signal from the telco connects directly to the router. The direct U-loop-to-router connection is shown in Figure 6-66. Figure 6-65 shows a router with an external NT-1 connected to the telco's U-loop. It provides S/T-loop for the router's BRI port.

Figure 6-65
ISDN U-loop connected to an external NT-1, which converts the signaling to S/T-loop. The S/T-loop port connects to the router's BRI port.

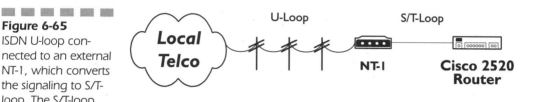

Figure 6-66
Routers like the Cisco 766 and Cisco 3620 can have built-in NT-1 devices.

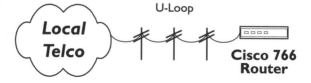

If you have one of these routers, the U-loop connection plugs directly into the router.

Once the router is connected to the telco (whether through an external NT-1 or not), you can start configuring the BRI port in IOS. The first thing to do is to activate the BRI port, so that you can verify that it sees the telco. The command **show isdn status** will display the current state of the BRI line. At this point, all you care about is the layer 1 status. If it shows "DEACTIVATED," you have a problem seeing the telco. This could be a bad connection from the router to the S/T-loop port on an external NT-1, or a bad connection from the U-loop port to the telco. You could also see this if the BRI port is shutdown and the ISDN switch type is set.

To do this, configure the BRI interface using only the **no shutdown** command. Then, in global configuration mode enter the ISDN switch type. This will usually be **basic NI-1** in the United States. The switch type is determined by the local telco, and they should provide this information to you. The **isdn switch-type** command is entered into the global configuration. This must be done before any other ISDN configuration can proceed.

Once you see the port listed as "ACTIVE," you can start looking at the layer 2 status. If you see "TEI_ASSIGNED" you still have a problem. You need to see "MULTIPLE_FRAME_ESTABLISHED" to know the line is working properly. This can happen if the S/T-loop connection is good (which it always is on routers that have internal NT-1 devices) and the U-loop connection does not see the telco. Once you see "ACTIVE" for layer 1 and "MULTIPLE_FRAME_ESTABLISHED" for layer 2, you can move on to configuring the BRI port.

Setting the SPIDs and Directory Numbers

At this point, you can add the SPIDs (System Profile ID numbers) and directory numbers to the BRI interface. The SPIDs are usually the ten-digit phone numbers of the B channels, with some digits prepended or appended, or both, to them. The directory number is always the seven-digit portion of the B channel phone number. For example, if one B channel phone number was (703) 555-4567, the SPID might have the numbers 01 prepended to it and the numbers 0001 appended to it. In this case the SPID would be 0170355545670001 and the directory number would be 5554567. The SPID and directory numbers must be numeric strings without spaces or punctuation in order for the router (and the telco switch) to manipulate them.

The SPID and directory number for each B channel are set on the same line using the **isdn spidX** command, where X is 1 for the first B channel and 2 for the second. Next, add the SPID string, and add the directory number last. This can be seen in Figure 6-67.

Figure 6-67 *The configuration dialog to set the ISDN SPIDs on an IOS router.*

```
cisco-2503#conf t
Enter configuration commands, one per line.  End with CNTL/Z.
cisco-2503(config)#interface bri0
cisco-2503(config-if)#isdn spid1 70331838120101 3183812
cisco-2503(config-if)#isdn spid2 7033188130101 3183813
cisco-2503(config-if)#^Z
cisco-2503#
%SYS-5-CONFIG_I: Configured from console by console
cisco-2503#
```

Once you've entered the SPIDs into the configuration, the output of the **show isdn status** command should change radically for layers 2 and 3. Layer 2 should show lines for **spid1 configured, spid1 sent, spid1 valid** and similar lines for SPID 2. The output should also have "MULTIPLE_FRAME_ESTABLISHED" listed twice (one for each B channel). You should also notice changes in the number of **activated dsl 0 CCBs** in layer 3. It is possible you will not see that, but rather something like Figure 6-68.

Figure 6-68 Errors in the configuration or switch connection can be seen in the output of show isdn status.

```
cisco-2503#sho isdn stat
The current ISDN Switchtype = basic-ni1
ISDN BRI0 interface
    Layer 1 Status:
        ACTIVE
    Layer 2 Status:
        TEI = 64, State = MULTIPLE_FRAME_ESTABLISHED
    Spid Status:
        TEI 64, ces = 1, state = 8(established)
            spid1 configured, spid1 NOT sent, spid1 NOT valid
        TEI Not Assigned, ces = 2, state = 1(terminal down)
            spid2 configured, spid2 NOT sent, spid2 NOT valid
    Layer 3 Status:
        0 Active Layer 3 Call(s)
    Activated dsl 0 CCBs = 0
    Total Allocated ISDN CCBs = 0
cisco-2503#
```

Note that the SPIDs show as both "NOT sent" and "NOT valid." The important point is that they have not been sent to the telco ISDN switch, so there is no way the router can know they are valid. They will eventually be sent to the telco and be verified, but there is no reason to wait. Use the command **clear interface bri0** to reset the port, and the router will immediately try to synchronize with the telco ISDN switch. When it does, you will see output from **show isdn status** like that in Figure 6-69.

██ ██

Figure 6-69 *The output of show isdn status now shows a properly configured BRI port, which has synchro-*
nized with the telco ISDN switch.

```
cisco-2503#sho isdn stat
The current ISDN Switchtype = basic-ni1
ISDN BRI0 interface
    Layer 1 Status:
        ACTIVE
    Layer 2 Status:
        TEI = 64, State = MULTIPLE_FRAME_ESTABLISHED
        TEI = 89, State = MULTIPLE_FRAME_ESTABLISHED
    Spid Status:
        TEI 64, ces = 1, state = 5(init)
            spid1 configured, spid1 sent, spid1 valid
            Endpoint ID Info: epsf = 0, usid = 0, tid = 1
        TEI 89, ces = 2, state = 5(init)
            spid2 configured, spid2 sent, spid2 valid
            Endpoint ID Info: epsf = 0, usid = 1, tid = 1
    Layer 3 Status:
        0 Active Layer 3 Call(s)
    Activated dsl 0 CCBs = 1
        CCB: callid=0x0, sapi=0, ces=1, B-chan=0
    Total Allocated ISDN CCBs = 1
cisco-2503#
```

If one of your SPIDs is wrong, you might see a line saying, **spid 2 NOT
valid**. An example of this is shown in Figure 6-70.

██ ██

Figure 6-70 *Even though it shows multiple frames established, it is clearly shown that one of the SPIDs*
configured was not valid.

```
cisco-2503#sho isdn stat
The current ISDN Switchtype = basic-ni1
ISDN BRI0 interface
    Layer 1 Status:
        ACTIVE
    Layer 2 Status:
        TEI = 64, State = MULTIPLE_FRAME_ESTABLISHED
        TEI = 89, State = MULTIPLE_FRAME_ESTABLISHED
```

```
    Spid Status:
        TEI 64, ces = 1, state = 5(init)
            spid1 configured, spid1 sent, spid1 valid
            Endpoint ID Info: epsf = 0, usid = 0, tid = 1
        TEI 89, ces = 2, state = 5(init)
            spid2 configured, spid2 sent, spid2 NOT valid
            Endpoint ID Info: epsf = 0, usid = 1, tid = 1
    Layer 3 Status:
        0 Active Layer 3 Call(s)
    Activated dsl 0 CCBs = 1
        CCB: callid=0x0, sapi=0, ces=1, B-chan=0
    Total Allocated ISDN CCBs = 1
cisco-2503#
```

In this case, you should reconfigure the SPID to correct the problem. On some routers, the SPIDs might not be reset when you use the command **clear interface bri0**. In this case, you will need to place an ISDN call (which we are not ready to do), or reboot the router. After a reboot, it might still be necessary to clear the interface to synchronize the SPIDs with the telco. Another way to do SPID synchronization is to unplug the BRI line from the router, clear the interface, and then plug it back in. In this case, the output from **show isdn status** will look like Figure 6-71.

Figure 6-71   This time we see that the router has not yet sent the corrected SPID to the telco ISDN switch. It might be necessary to reboot the router or unplug the line to make the router try to synchronize again.

```
cisco-2503#sho isdn stat
The current ISDN Switchtype = basic-ni1
ISDN BRI0 interface
    Layer 1 Status:
        ACTIVE
    Layer 2 Status:
        TEI = 64, State = MULTIPLE_FRAME_ESTABLISHED
    Spid Status:
        TEI 64, ces = 1, state = 5(init)
            spid1 configured, spid1 sent, spid1 valid
            Endpoint ID Info: epsf = 0, usid = 0, tid = 1
```

```
        TEI Not Assigned, ces = 2, state = 3(await establishment)
            spid2 configured, spid2 NOT sent, spid2 NOT valid
    Layer 3 Status:
        0 Active Layer 3 Call(s)
    Activated dsl 0 CCBs = 1
        CCB: callid=0x0, sapi=0, ces=1, B-chan=0
    Total Allocated ISDN CCBs = 1
cisco-2503#
```

Correct the SPID and directory information and synchronize with the telco until you get both B channels working. (This assumes that you have ordered your ISDN line with two B channels. It is possible to order only one B channel, done usually when you want to limit costs and bandwidth.) In the case of only one B channel, the telco will only give you the SPID and directory numbers for one B channel at installation time. Otherwise, they give you two.

Fleshing Out the Configuration

The configuration now needs some expanding. We will be configuring the router for a very basic dial-out connection. First, we need to add an IP address for this router's BRI port. We will also set the line encapsulation to PPP and the authentication to CHAP (Challenge Handshake Authentication Protocol). We will disable CDP (Cisco Discovery Protocol) and enable compression (which might not be supported on all routers) using the STAC algorithm. Additionally, we will use a **dialer map** command to set the phone number and name of the remote router. Finally, we add a default route to the remote router.

We must also declare what packets the router will find interesting. Only interesting packets will make the router place a call and bring up the connection. To define what is interesting, use the **dialer-group** command in the BRI interface. This selects the number of the **dialer-list** which in turn lists the actual protocols.

In this case, our local IP address is 204.176.118.226 with a netmask of 255.255.255.240. This shows that we have subnetted a class C for an ISDN WAN. This is done to prevent wasting IP address space. The **dialer map** command shows we are using the IP protocol and connecting to a router named *wan4500*, which has an IP address of 204.176.118.225. The phone number to reach this router is 3496400. The dialog for entering this information into the router configuration is shown in Figure 6-72.

Figure 6-72 The configuration dialog for setting up the BRI port.

```
cisco-2503#conf t
Enter configuration commands, one per line.  End with CNTL/Z.
cisco-2503(config)#interface bri 0
cisco-2503(config-if)#ip address 204.176.118.226 255.255.255.240
cisco-2503(config-if)#encapsulation ppp
cisco-2503(config-if)#ppp authentication chap
cisco-2503(config-if)#no cdp enable
cisco-2503(config-if)#compress stac
cisco-2503(config-if)#dialer map ip 204.176.118.225 name wan4500
3496400
cisco-2503(config-if)#dialer-group 1
cisco-2503(config-if)#exit
cisco-2503(config)#ip route 0.0.0.0 0.0.0.0 204.176.118.225
cisco-2503(config-if)#dialer-list 1 protocol ip permit
cisco-2503(config)#^Z
cisco-2503#
```

Dial-up Access Authentication

The final piece of the configuration is the creation of a user account and password for the remote router. CHAP does this so the remote router can authenticate the router that is calling it. In this case, we add the user name **wan4500** (as shown in Figure 6-73), because it is the name of the remote router. CHAP uses the name of the remote router as the user name, and the passwords on both routers must match. Hence, each router in a CHAP connection has the other router's name as a user name in its local configuration.

Figure 6-73 The remote router's name is added as a user name on the local router to configure CHAP.

```
cisco-2503#conf t
Enter configuration commands, one per line.  End with CNTL/Z.
cisco-2503(config)#username wan4500 password secret1
cisco-2503(config)#^Z
cisco-2503#
```

You must also add the user name and CHAP password of the local router to the remote router, add a static route to the local router's Ethernet network, and add a **dialer map** statement to route IP back to the remote site. The configuration dialog for this is shown in Figure 6-74. Remember that the passwords must be the same on both routers for CHAP to work properly. Readers will note there is no phone number in the remote router's **dialer map** statement. For the moment, we are only dialing from the remote site (router name cisco-2503) to the central site (router name wan4500). This assumes that the remote router is preconfigured for dial-in ISDN. For this example, we will say that the Ethernet network attached to the local router is 208.213.189.0. Note how this network is routed to the IP address of the local router's BRI port.

Figure 6-74 The CHAP user name and dialer map entry for the remote router must be entered into the remote router.

```
wan4500#conf t
Enter configuration commands, one per line.   End with CNTL/Z.
wan4500 (config)#username cisco-2503 password secret1
wan4500 (config)#ip route 208.213.189.0 255.255.255.0 204.176.118.226
wan4500 (config)#interface BRI0
wan4500 (config-if)#dialer map ip 204.176.118.226 name cisco-2503
wan4500 (config-if)#^Z
wan4500#
```

Testing the Connection

Testing the connection is actually quite easy. All you need to do is use the **ping** command to see if you get a response from the remote router (shown in Figure 6-75). If you arc on the console, you will see standard debugging information. This can be important in troubleshooting the connection for the first time. If you are not on the console, use the command **terminal monitor** from enable mode to see the same information.

Figure 6-75 Using the ping command will bring up the line and make the remote router respond. If you are on the console or have monitoring on, you will see messages about the line being brought up.

```
cisco-2503#ping 204.176.118.225

Type escape sequence to abort.
Sending 5, 100-byte ICMP Echos to 204.176.118.225, timeout is 2 sec-
onds:
.!!!!
Success rate is 80 percent (4/5), round-trip min/avg/max = 24/25/28 ms
cisco-2503#
%LINK-3-UPDOWN: Interface BRI0:1, changed state to up
%LINEPROTO-5-UPDOWN: Line protocol on Interface BRI0:1, changed state
to up
%ISDN-6-CONNECT: Interface BRI0:1 is now connected to 3496400 wan4500
cisco-2503#
```

If this command does not work, you will need to verify your connection and CHAP passwords. You can use debugging built into the router to help you. In order to see the output of the debugging statements, you must be on the console or enter the **terminal monitor** command in enable mode. From there, you can set different debugging options using the **debug** command (this also works from enable mode).

You might be tempted to turn on all sorts of debugging information on your first try. Be aware that you could get more than you need, and debugging has a dramatic impact on router performance. You should try one or two debugging options to get a feel for the verbosity of their output first. When you are finished, use **no debug all** or **undebug all** to turn off all debugging.

You can debug the CHAP authentication session using **debug ppp authentication**. If your CHAP passwords do not match, you will see output like that shown below when trying to ping the remote side. Notice that the CHAP protocol returns a failure with the error message "MD compare failed." This clue—pointing to the passwords not matching—is shown in Figure 6-76.

■ ■
Figure 6-76 If the passwords don't match you will see "MD compare failed" if you have PPP authentication debugging turned on.

```
cisco-2503#ping 204.176.118.225

Type escape sequence to abort.
Sending 5, 100-byte ICMP Echos to 204.176.118.225, timeout is 2 sec-
onds:

%LINK-3-UPDOWN: Interface BRI0:1, changed state to up.
BR0:1 PPP: Treating connection as a callout
BR0:1 PPP: Phase is AUTHENTICATING, by both
BR0:1 CHAP: O CHALLENGE id 27 len 31 from "cisco-2503"
BR0:1 CHAP: I CHALLENGE id 34 len 28 from "wan4500"
BR0:1 CHAP: O RESPONSE id 34 len 31 from "cisco-2503"
BR0:1 CHAP: I RESPONSE id 27 len 28 from "wan4500"
BR0:1 CHAP: O FAILURE id 27 len 21 msg is "MD compare failed"
%LINK-3-UPDOWN: Interface BRI0:1, changed state to down
cisco-2503#
```

Other useful debugging statements are:

- **Debug isdn events**—shows ISDN events in more detail.
- **Debug isdn q921**—shows low-level ISDN protocol communication
- **Debug isdn q931**—shows higher level ISDN protocol communications
- **Debug dialer events**—shows when "interesting" packets cause an outbound dial attempt
- **Debug dialer packets**—copious output showing all packets interesting to the dialer
- **Debug ppp authentication**—shows the CHAP communication between routers
- **Debug ppp negotiation**—shows all PPP associated protocol negotiations, including CHAP, CCP, IPCP, LCP, and PPP.

Configuring the BRI in 700 Series Routers

Configuring the Cisco 700 series router for ISDN is much easier than using IOS in some ways. Because it is a small ISDN-to-Ethernet access router, its operating system and configuration information are already set up for this kind of connection. Assume the Ethernet port and system name have already been set up using the commands shown in Figure 6-77.

Figure 6-77 The dialog used to set up the Ethernet port on a 700 series router.

```
> set user lan
:LAN> set ip routing on
:LAN> set ip address 204.176.117.10
:LAN> set ip netmask 255.255.255.0
:LAN> cd
> set systemname cisco766
cisco766>
```

Setting SPID and Directory Numbers

The first step is to make sure the Cisco 700 series can see the telco ISDN switch. Plug the telco ISDN line into the U-loop port on the back of the router. If your router only has an S/T-loop port, plug your external NT-1 into that, and plug the U-loop cable into the external NT-1. Next, configure the ISDN switch type and the SPID and directory number for both B channels into your router. The configuration dialog for this can be seen in Figure 6-78.

Figure 6-78 Setting up the BRI port configuration on a 700 series router.

```
cisco766> set switch ni-1
cisco766> set 1 spid 70328838120101
You may reboot system to register the new SPID at any time.
cisco766> set 1 directorynumber 2883812
cisco766> set 2 spid 70328838130101
You may reboot system to register the new SPID at any time.
cisco766> set 2 directorynumber 2883813
cisco766>
```

When you enter each SPID, the router will respond "You may reboot system to register the new SPID at any time." This is a polite way of telling you that you will need to reboot the router before the telco will register the SPIDs. You can reboot the router using the **reboot** command. When the router comes back up, you could see a message asking you to wait while the SPIDs register with the telco. Once that time expires, you should see a few more messages telling you that the telco has accepted the SPIDs. An example of this is seen in Figure 6-79.

Figure 6-79 The debugging messages showing the SPIDs being accepted by the telco.

```
Boot version 2.1(1) 11/04/96 17:33
Copyright (c) 1993-1996. All rights reserved.


POST ............ OK (1.5MB).
Validating FLASH ... OK.
Booting up ..........................
01/01/1995 00:00:00  Connection 1 Opened
cisco766> 01/01/1995 00:00:00  L01  0            Started Operation
cisco766> 01/01/1995 00:00:01  L02  0            Line Activated
cisco766>
Please wait for TWAIT timer to expire in 25 seconds
Make a call to bypass this timer
01/01/1995 00:00:26  L18  1                 Terminal Identifier Assigned
cisco766> 01/01/1995 00:00:26  L22  1 70328838120101  Sending SPID
cisco766> 01/01/1995 00:00:26  L18  2                 Terminal Identifier
Assigned
cisco766> 01/01/1995 00:00:26  L23  1 70328838120101  SPID Accepted
cisco766> 01/01/1995 00:00:26  L22  2 70328838130101  Sending SPID
cisco766> 01/01/1995 00:00:28  L19  2                 Terminal Identifier
Unassigned
cisco766> 01/01/1995 00:00:28  L18  2                 Terminal Identifier
Assigned
cisco766> 01/01/1995 00:00:28  L22  2 70328838130101  Sending SPID
cisco766> 01/01/1995 00:00:28  L23  2 70328838130101  SPID Accepted
cisco766>
```

You can check the status of the ISDN line at any time by using the **show status** command. If everything is set up correctly, you should see output like that in Figure 6-80.

Figure 6-80 *The show status command gives you the current state of your ISDN B channels.*

```
cisco766> show status
Status     01/01/1995 00:04:06
Line Status
  Line Activated
  Terminal Identifier Assigned     SPID Accepted
  Terminal Identifier Assigned     SPID Accepted
Port Status                        Interface Connection Link
  Ch:  1        Waiting for Call
  Ch:  2        Waiting for Call
cisco766>
```

Routing Not Bridging

Out of the box, there are some settings you might not want to use. The first is bridging. You can either bridge or route, but not both. Because we want to route, we must turn bridging off in the global configuration, as shown in Figure 6-81.

Figure 6-81 *The command dialog to turn off bridging.*

```
cisco766> set bridging off
cisco766>
```

ISDN WAN User Profile

The next step is to create a user profile for the ISDN port. Because we are still using CHAP and validating passwords in both directions, the name of the user profile must be the name of the router we will be calling (in this case, **wan4500**). This is done using the **set user** command, as shown in Figure 6-82.

Figure 6-82 A new ISDN profile is created using the set user command.

```
cisco766> set user wan4500
New user wan4500 being created
cisco766:wan4500>
```

Now set the IP address, netmask, and phone number to dial, and turn IP routing on. The phone numbers are added with the **set X number** command, where *X* is the number of the B channel. If both B channels dial one number, set them to the same number. This will only work if the number you are calling automatically rolls over to the next line. If this is not the case, you will need to set them to the different numbers. If you only want to use one channel, do not set the second number. By default, multilink PPP is enabled. This is how the two B channels combine into one 128Kbps WAN connection. Multilink PPP must also be enabled on the remote router if it is going to be used. The command dialog for this setup is shown in Figure 6-83.

Figure 6-83 Setting the IP and dial-up information for this WAN profile.

```
cisco766:wan4500> set ip address 204.176.118.234
cisco766:wan4500> set ip netmask 255.255.255.240
cisco766:wan4500> set 1 number 3496400
cisco766:wan4500> set 2 number 3496400
cisco766:wan4500> set ip routing on
cisco766:wan4500>
```

CHAP Authentication

Before you can successfully dial the remote router, you must add the password for the CHAP connection. Remember that the router system name for the local router is the user name on the remote router. The name of the remote router is the profile name on the local router. All that remains is to add the CHAP password to the configuration. In this case, we will use the **set ppp secret client** command, as shown in Figure 6-84. If we had been using the **set ppp password client** command, we would have been setting the PAP password, not the CHAP password. This password must match the one on the remote router.

Figure 6-84 The set ppp secret client command sets the CHAP password for an individual WAN profile.

```
cisco766:wan4500> set ppp secret client secret1
cisco766:wan4500>
```

You should now be able to connect to the remote router. An easy way to test this is to **ping** the IP address of its ISDN port. This should bring up the ISDN line, authenticate the call, and pass the **ping** packet. An example of this is shown in Figure 6-85.

Figure 6-85 Using the ping command to check if the remote router is alive will force the router to make an outbound call.

```
cisco766:wan4500> ping 204.176.118.225
Start sending:  01/01/1995 00:23:28  L05  0       3496400  Outgoing Call
Initiated
cisco766:wan4500> 01/01/1995 00:23:29  L08  1       3496400  Call Con-
nected
cisco766:wan4500> 01/01/1995 00:23:29  Connection 3 Add     Link 1
Channel 1
cisco766:wan4500>  round trip time is 2410 msec.
cisco766:wan4500>
```

The only thing you really care about is the round trip time. This shows that the packets made it to the other side and were answered. If you try this while the line is up, you will see much better response time, and there will not be any confusing status messages about the line coming up and channels being added to a connection. This is shown in Figure 6-86.

Figure 6-86 If this line is up, ping responds quicker and there are no confusing messages.

```
cisco766:wan4500> ping 204.176.118.225
Start sending:   round trip time is 40 msec.
cisco766:wan4500>
```

The Default Route

The final configuration item is to set the default route. The default route tells the router how to route packets for which it does not have an explicit route. The gateway will be the remote router, which could be a corporate ISDN hub or an ISP. This is shown in Figure 6-87.

Figure 6-87 *The configuration dialog for setting a default route to the remote router's ISDN interface.*

```
cisco766:wan4500> SET IP ROUTE DEST 0.0.0.0/0 GATEWAY 204.176.118.225
PROPAGATE OFF COST 1
cisco766:wan4500>
```

Verifying ISDN Communications

If there is a problem with the ISDN line, you will notice that the light labeled NT-1 on the front of the router will blink periodically. (This assumes your router has a built-in NT-1.) Even if it does not blink, the light labeled line will only illuminate if it can see the telco. These should be the first thing you check to make sure the telco connection is operational.

The command **show status** will display the current state of the ISDN connection. If the line to the telco is not working properly, you will see output like that shown in Figure 6-88. Notice that the line status is deactivated.

Figure 6-88 *The show status command can tell you when there is a problem with an ISDN line.*

```
cisco766> show status
Status      01/01/1995 00:01:02
Line Status
  Line DeActivated
 Terminal Identifier Unassigned
Port Status            Interface Connection Link
 Ch:  1       Waiting for Call
 Ch:  2       Waiting for Call
cisco766>
```

If the line is connected, but the wrong switch type or SPIDs are set, you will see output like this. By default, the switch type is set to **5ESS**. If this is not the type of switch you have and you do not change the switch type, you could see something like Figure 6-89.

Figure 6-89 This time show status shows an active line, but unassigned terminal identifier. This could mean incorrect configuration of the SPIDs or the switch type.

```
cisco766> show status
Status      01/01/1995 00:01:57
Line Status
  Line Activated
 Terminal Identifier Unassigned
Port Status           Interface Connection Link
  Ch:  1      Waiting for Call
  Ch:  2      Waiting for Call
cisco766>
```

Proper configuration shows the SPIDs accepted by the telco ISDN switch, as seen in Figure 6-90.

Figure 6-90 A proper configuration will show accepted SPIDs.

```
 cisco766> show status
Status      01/01/1995 00:36:52
Line Status
  Line Activated
  Terminal Identifier Assigned     SPID Accepted
  Terminal Identifier Assigned     SPID Accepted
Port Status             Interface Connection Link
  Ch:  1      Waiting for Call
  Ch:  2      Waiting for Call
cisco766:wan4500>
```

Actual Configurations

Actual configurations are your best guide to seeing how fully integrated routers work in real networks. In this chapter, we prepared our routers for basic configurations, but we also connected to an existing router with a much more advanced setup. The actual setups of those routers are shown here.

As has already been stated, for security reasons you should remove any sensitive information when sending router configurations. Printing them in a book is no different. All passwords, phone numbers, and site names have been changed.

2503 IOS Router Setup for ISDN and T1 Connection

This router was set up for basic IOS T1 and ISDN connection. You can see all the changes to the basic setup in the configurations that were shown above. The complete configuration file is shown in Figure 6-91.

Figure 6-91 The configuration file for our Cisco 2520 router.

```
!
version 11.2
service password-encryption
service udp-small-servers
service tcp-small-servers
!
hostname cisco-2503
!
enable secret 5 NOT_SHOWN
!
username wan4500 password 7 NOT_SHOWN
ip domain-name abc.com
ip name-server 199.29.53.67
ip name-server 199.29.53.118
isdn switch-type basic-ni1
!
```

(cont.)

Figure 6-91 *Continued*

```
interface Ethernet0
 ip address 204.176.117.9 255.255.255.0
 no ip route-cache
 no ip mroute-cache
!
interface Serial0
 ip address 204.176.118.22 255.255.255.252
 no ip route-cache
 no ip mroute-cache
!
interface Serial1
 no ip address
 no ip route-cache
 no ip mroute-cache
 shutdown
!
interface Serial2
 no ip address
 shutdown
!
interface Serial3
 no ip address
 shutdown
!
interface BRI0
 ip address 204.176.118.230 255.255.255.240
 encapsulation ppp
 no ip route-cache
 no ip mroute-cache
 isdn spid1 70331838120101 3183812
 isdn spid2 70331838130101 3183813
 dialer map ip 204.176.118.225 name wan4500 3496400
 dialer-group 1
 compress stac
 no cdp enable
 ppp authentication chap
!
no ip classless
ip route 0.0.0.0 0.0.0.0 204.176.118.225
snmp-server community NOT_SHOWN RO
snmp-server community NOT_SHOWN RW
```

```
dialer-list 1 protocol ip permit
!
line con 0
 exec-timeout 0 0
line aux 0
 transport input all
line vty 0 4
 password 7 NOT_SHOWN
 login
!
end
```

766 ISDN Dial-Up to IOS ISDN Router

This Cisco 766 router configuration was the actual configuration used to connect to the router named **wan4500**. Many of the items shown are system defaults. The complete configuration is listed in Figure 6-92.

Figure 6-92 The complete configuration for our Cisco 766 router.

```
CD
SET SCREENLENGTH 20
SET COUNTRYGROUP 1
SET LAN MODE ANY
SET WAN MODE ONLY
SET AGE OFF
SET MULTIDESTINATION OFF
SET SWITCH NI-1
SET 1 SPID 70331838120101
SET 1 DIRECTORYNUMBER 3183812
SET 2 SPID 70331838130101
SET 2 DIRECTORYNUMBER 3183813
SET AUTODETECTION  OFF
SET CONFERENCE 60
SET TRANSFER 61
SET 1 DELAY 30
SET 2 DELAY 30
SET BRIDGING OFF
SET LEARN ON
SET PASSTHRU OFF
SET SPEED AUTO
SET PLAN NORMAL
```

(cont.)

Figure 6-92 Continued

```
SET 1 AUTO ON
SET 2 AUTO ON
SET 1 NUMBER
SET 2 NUMBER
SET 1 BACKUPNUMBER
SET 2 BACKUPNUMBER
SET 1 RINGBACK
SET 2 RINGBACK
SET 1 CLIVALIDATENUMBER
SET 2 CLIVALIDATENUMBER
SET CLICALLBACK OFF
SET CLIAUTHENTICATION OFF
SET SYSTEMNAME cisco766
LOG CALLS TIME VERBOSE
SET UNICASTFILTER OFF
DEMAND 1 THRESHOLD 0
DEMAND 2 THRESHOLD 48
DEMAND 1 DURATION 1
DEMAND 2 DURATION 1
DEMAND 1 SOURCE LAN
DEMAND 2 SOURCE BOTH
TIMEOUT 1 THRESHOLD 0
TIMEOUT 2 THRESHOLD 48
TIMEOUT 1 DURATION 0
TIMEOUT 2 DURATION 0
TIMEOUT 1 SOURCE LAN
TIMEOUT 2 SOURCE BOTH
SET REMOTEACCESS PROTECTED
SET LOCALACCESS ON
SET CLICKSTART ON
SET LOGOUT 5
SET CALLERID OFF
SET PPP AUTHENTICATION IN CHAP  PAP
SET PPP CHAPREFUSE NONE
SET PPP AUTHENTICATION OUT NONE
SET PPP TAS CLIENT 0.0.0.0
SET PPP TAS CHAPSECRET LOCAL ON
SET PPP CALLBACK REQUEST OFF
SET PPP CALLBACK REPLY OFF
SET PPP NEGOTIATION INTEGRITY 10
SET PPP NEGOTIATION COUNT 10
```

```
SET PPP NEGOTIATION RETRY  3000
SET PPP TERMREQ COUNT 2
SET PPP MULTILINK ON
SET COMPRESSION STAC
SET PPP BACP ON
SET PPP ADDRESS NEGOTIATION LOCAL OFF
SET IP PAT UDPTIMEOUT 5
SET IP PAT TCPTIMEOUT 30
SET CALLDURATION 0
SET SNMP CONTACT ""
SET SNMP LOCATION ""
SET SNMP TRAP COLDSTART OFF
SET SNMP TRAP WARMSTART OFF
SET SNMP TRAP LINKDOWN OFF
SET SNMP TRAP LINKUP OFF
SET SNMP TRAP AUTHENTICATIONFAIL OFF
SET DHCP OFF
SET DHCP DOMAIN
SET DHCP NETBIOS_SCOPE
SET VOICEPRIORITY INCOMING INTERFACE PHONE1 ALWAYS
SET VOICEPRIORITY OUTGOING INTERFACE PHONE1 ALWAYS
SET CALLWAITING INTERFACE PHONE1 ON
SET VOICEPRIORITY INCOMING INTERFACE PHONE2 ALWAYS
SET VOICEPRIORITY OUTGOING INTERFACE PHONE2 ALWAYS
SET CALLWAITING INTERFACE PHONE2 ON
SET CALLTIME VOICE INCOMING OFF
SET CALLTIME VOICE OUTGOING OFF
SET CALLTIME DATA INCOMING OFF
SET CALLTIME DATA OUTGOING OFF
SET USER LAN
SET IP ROUTING ON
SET IP ADDRESS 204.176.117.10
SET IP NETMASK 255.255.255.0
SET IP FRAMING ETHERNET_II
SET IP PROPAGATE ON
SET IP COST 1
SET IP RIP RECEIVE V1
SET IP RIP UPDATE OFF
SET IP RIP VERSION 1
SET USER Internal
SET IP FRAMING ETHERNET_II
SET USER Standard
SET PROFILE ID 000000000000
```

(cont.)

Figure 6-92 Continued

```
SET PROFILE POWERUP ACTIVATE
SET PROFILE DISCONNECT KEEP
SET IP ROUTING ON
SET IP ADDRESS 0.0.0.0
SET IP NETMASK 0.0.0.0
SET IP FRAMING NONE
SET IP RIP RECEIVE V1
SET IP RIP UPDATE OFF
SET IP RIP VERSION 1
SET USER wan4500
SET PROFILE ID 000000000000
SET PROFILE POWERUP ACTIVATE
SET PROFILE DISCONNECT KEEP
SET 1 NUMBER 3496400
SET 2 NUMBER 3496400
SET PPP SECRET CLIENT ENCRYPTED 15010e0f162f3f75
SET IP ROUTING ON
SET IP ADDRESS 204.176.118.234
SET IP NETMASK 255.255.255.240
SET IP FRAMING NONE
SET IP PROPAGATE ON
SET IP COST 1
SET IP RIP RECEIVE V1
SET IP RIP UPDATE OFF
SET IP RIP VERSION 1
SET IP ROUTE DEST 0.0.0.0/0 GATEWAY 204.176.118.225 PROPAGATE OFF COST
1
CD
LOGOUT
```

IOS ISDN BRI Router

A medium-sized core router in a corporation might use this type of setup. In this case, the router is a Cisco 4500 with 8-port BRI, dual Ethernet, and four high-speed serial cards. The complete configuration is shown in Figure 6-93.

Figure 6-93 The configuration file for the central dial-in corporate router.

```
!
version 11.2
service password-encryption
service udp-small-servers
service tcp-small-servers
!
hostname wan4500
!
enable secret 5 NOT_SHOWN
enable password 7 NOT_SHOWN
!
username wan4500 password 7 NOT_SHOWN
username sitea password 7 NOT_SHOWN
username cisco-2503 password 7 NOT_SHOWN
username cisco766 password 7 NOT_SHOWN
no ip source-route
ip domain-name abc.com
ip name-server 199.29.53.67
ip name-server 199.29.53.118
isdn switch-type basic-ni1
!
interface Ethernet0
 ip address 199.29.53.55 255.255.255.0
 media-type 10BaseT
!
interface Serial0
 description To Chantilly Warehouse
 ip address 204.176.118.21 255.255.255.252
 bandwidth 1536
!
interface Serial1
 no ip address
 shutdown
!
interface Serial2
 no ip address
 shutdown
!
interface Serial3
```

(cont.)

Figure 6-93 Continued

```
 no ip address
 shutdown
!
interface BRI0
 description Full time centrex connectiont to Site A
 ip address 204.176.118.45 255.255.255.252
 no ip mroute-cache
 encapsulation ppp
 isdn spid1 7186418419100 6418419
 isdn spid2 7186418422100 6418422
 peer default ip address 204.176.118.46
 dialer idle-timeout 86400
 dialer map ip 204.176.118.46 name sitea broadcast
 dialer-group 2
 no fair-queue
 no cdp enable
 ppp authentication chap
 ppp multilink
!
interface BRI1
 ip unnumbered Dialer1
 no ip mroute-cache
 encapsulation ppp
 isdn spid1 71834964000101 3496400
 isdn spid2 71834964010101 3496401
 no peer default ip address
 dialer rotary-group 1
 dialer-group 1
 no fair-queue
 compress stac
 no cdp enable
!
interface BRI2
 ip unnumbered Dialer1
 no ip mroute-cache
 encapsulation ppp
 isdn spid1 71834964020101 3496402
 isdn spid2 71834964030101 3496403
 no peer default ip address
 dialer rotary-group 1
 dialer-group 1
```

```
 no fair-queue
 compress stac
 no cdp enable
!
interface BRI3
 ip unnumbered Dialer1
 no ip mroute-cache
 encapsulation ppp
 isdn spid1 71834264220101 3426422
 isdn spid2 71834264350101 3426435
 no peer default ip address
 dialer rotary-group 1
 dialer-group 1
 no fair-queue
 compress stac
 no cdp enable
!
interface BRI4
 ip unnumbered Dialer1
 no ip mroute-cache
 encapsulation ppp
 isdn spid1 71834264690101 3426469
 isdn spid2 71834264140101 3426414
 no peer default ip address
 dialer rotary-group 1
 dialer-group 1
 no fair-queue
 compress stac
 no cdp enable
!
interface BRI5
 no ip address
 shutdown
!
interface BRI6
 no ip address
 shutdown
!
interface BRI7
 no ip address
 shutdown
!
```

(cont.)

Figure 6-93 Continued

```
interface Dialer1
 ip address 204.176.118.225 255.255.255.240
 ip tcp header-compression passive
 no ip mroute-cache
 encapsulation ppp
 dialer in-band
 dialer idle-timeout 300
 dialer map ip 204.176.118.230 name cisco-2503
 dialer map ip 204.176.118.231 name sitea
 dialer map ip 204.176.118.234 name cisco766
 dialer-group 1
 no fair-queue
 compress stac
 no cdp enable
 ppp authentication chap
 ppp multilink
!
router rip
 redistribute static
 network 204.176.118.0
 network 199.29.53.0
!
no ip classless
ip route 0.0.0.0 0.0.0.0 199.29.53.4
ip route 204.176.118.20 255.255.255.252 Serial0
ip route 204.176.118.200 255.255.255.248 204.176.118.231
!
snmp-server community NOT_SHOWN RO
snmp-server community NOT_SHOWN RW
dialer-list 1 protocol ip permit
dialer-list 2 protocol ip permit
!
line con 0
 length 22
line aux 0
 transport input all
line vty 0 4
 password 7 NOT_SHOWN
 login
 transport preferred none
!
end
```

CHAPTER **7**

Intermediate Configurations

Basic configurations are fine for getting the line up and running, but there are always more things you'll want to do with your routers. Cisco routers are highly configurable and have many features that will help enhance your network. These features can decrease your site's usage of IP address numbers, enable dynamic routing, and log events to a text file on another machine. You should understand why you want to use these enhancements before you start playing around with them.

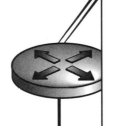

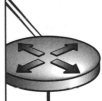

Conserving IP Addresses in IOS

The Internet is growing at a phenomenal rate. Some experts say the number of machines on it doubles every six months. Each machine on the Internet needs an Internet address. Today that includes PCs, Web servers, UNIX boxes, routers, and sometimes hubs and switches. Even users dialing in from home are issued a temporary IP address. They get these from the server or router to which they connect.

Because there is only a limited number of addresses available, many different schemes have evolved to conserve address space. If you think about the T1 connection example in Chapter 6, you'll remember an entire class C network of 256 addresses was used for this connection. This would be a huge waste of address space. Because T1 lines are point-to-point, no more than two IP addresses are necessary (one for each side). One way to conserve address space would be to divide up a Class C network into many small subnetworks, each having only four addresses. Another way would be to unnumber the addresses.

When an interface has an unnumbered address, it takes the IP address of a different interface as its own. Usually the unnumbered interface is a point-to-point WAN connection and the address it takes is that of the primary Ethernet port. In this case, we show a router with a single Ethernet and serial line in use. The serial line's IP address is shown as *unnumbered Ethernet0.*

Figure 7-1 Configuration of Ethernet and serial interfaces. The serial interface IP address is unnumbered and references Ethernet 0.

```
interface Ethernet0
 ip address 208.213.190.1 255.255.255.0
 no ip route-cache
 no ip mroute-cache
!
interface Serial0
 ip unnumbered Ethernet0
 no ip route-cache
 no ip mroute-cache
```

If we had two such routers connecting at separate sites (as we did in the Basic Configurations section), the diagram of the network would look like the one below. In this configuration, you can see that the serial ports have the IP addresses 208.213.188.1 and 208.213.188.2.

■ ■ ■ ■ ■ ■
Figure 7-2
Standard WAN
connection where
each interface on a
router has a unique
IP address.

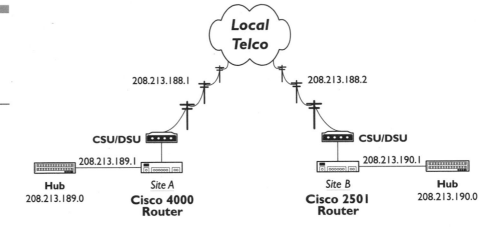

If the routers were converted to an unnumbered IP address scheme, they would be more properly displayed as having one IP address for each router and no specific IP addresses for either LAN or WAN port.

■ ■ ■ ■ ■ ■
Figure 7-3
Unnumbered WAN
connection where
one interface on a
router shares the IP
address of the other
interface.

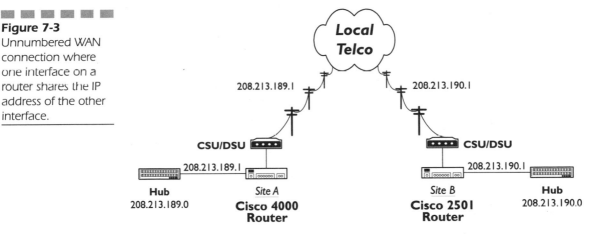

In this configuration, you've saved a whole Class C IP address by using *IP unnumbered* on your WAN interfaces. In most cases, you will save only a small number of IP addresses. However, those IP addresses do add up, and they make a real difference in keeping the Internet running. Think of it as your civic duty to optimize the use of your IP address space.

The final configuration that needs to be done is to route the Class C network on the Ethernet ports to their destination. Because those destinations no longer have IP addresses of their own, the remote network is routed to the local WAN ports themselves. Site B's configuration would look like this:

Figure 7-4　*A static route is added at Site A so packets will reach Site B.*

```
interface Ethernet0
 ip address 208.213.190.1 255.255.255.0
 no ip route-cache
 no ip mroute-cache
!
interface Serial0
 ip unnumbered Ethernet0
 no ip route-cache
 no ip mroute-cache
!
ip route 208.213.189.0 255.255.255.0 Serial0
```

Site A's configuration would look like this:

Figure 7-5　*The same is done at Site B.*

```
interface Ethernet0
 ip address 208.213.189.1 255.255.255.0
 no ip route-cache
 no ip mroute-cache
!
interface Serial0
 ip unnumbered Ethernet0
 no ip route-cache
 no ip mroute-cache
!
ip route 208.213.190.0 255.255.255.0 Serial0
```

Multiple IP Addresses in IOS

Multiple IP addresses on the same interface might not make sense at first. The key is to separate the physical network topology from the logical network. One Ethernet interface on a router can only hook to one port on a hub—this is the physical aspect of the Ethernet port. However, that hub might have traffic for many IP networks traveling over it—this is the logical network aspect. If you are like most people, your physical and logical networks are the same, but there are times when you might want to separate them and add additional logical networks to an existing physical network.

The two most common reasons for having multiple IP addresses on a single interface are to host multiple logical sites on one router and to aid in the transition from one logical network to another. If you want to host multiple sites on one router, you can configure the Ethernet interface to live on multiple logical networks. Machines on one logical network (although on the same physical network) cannot see machines on the other. This helps ensure security, while adding more flexibility to the network configuration. A diagram of this network would look like this:

Figure 7-6
This network shows one router, one hub, and multiple machines on separate logical networks.

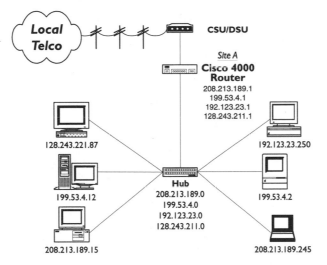

The basic configuration for multiple IP addresses on a single interface looks like this. The keyword **secondary** after the normal IP address information tells the router that this is an additional interface and not replacement information for the existing interface.

Figure 7-7 *Configuration information to add additional IP addresses to a single interface.*

```
interface Ethernet0
  ip address 199.53.4.1 255.255.255.0 secondary
  ip address 192.123.23.1 255.255.255.0 secondary
  ip address 128.243.211.1 255.255.255.0 secondary
  ip address 208.213.189.1 255.255.255.0
  no ip route-cache
  no ip mroute-cache
```

Transition to a New IP Network

The transition from one logical IP network to another is a time-intensive task. This happens most often when companies switch to a different ISP and lose their old Class C network. Most administrators in this situation are forced to switch the router's IP address to the new network first and then start moving stations over one by one. This means all machines on the network are down until an administrator can visit them and get their addresses and gateways changed over to the new network.

By adding a second IP address to the router, a second logical network is added to the existing physical network. The administrator can then keep the site up as he or she visits each machine and move it to the new network at a leisurely pace. This also allows for greater testing of a new ISP connection by letting you keep the existing network in place while the problems with the new one are debugged. This takes care of the LAN side, but on the WAN side you will likely want to go through the added expense of adding the new connection before you take down the old one. In the case of a leased-line WAN connection, you will probably have to buy or borrow an additional router cable and CSU/DSU. In the case of ISDN, you might be out of luck if your router only supports a single BRI. If it supports multiple BRIs, then you can add an additional NT-1 and keep both connections active at the same time.

Assuming you have a leased-line connection, your router configuration might look like the box below. It shows a leased-line connection to each of two ISPs. It also shows a single Ethernet with IP addresses from each Class C given to you from each ISP. Note that a default route to both ISPs is in use. This splits up all outbound traffic evenly between them. If they don't allow packets out to the Internet from each other's networks, you could have problems with this type of configuration. Because this is only a temporary setup, it might not matter much. The network diagram for this configuration looks like Figure 7-9.

Figure 7-8   Router configuration information for connecting to both ISPs while in the process of switching service from one to the other.

```
interface Ethernet0
 ip address 128.243.211.1 255.255.255.0 secondary
 ip address 208.213.189.1 255.255.255.0
 no ip route-cache
 no ip mroute-cache
!
interface Serial0
 ip address 137.39.124.5 255.255.255.252
 no ip route-cache
 no ip mroute-cache
!
interface Serial1
 ip address 168.113.224.62 255.255.255.252
 no ip route-cache
 no ip mroute-cache
!
ip route 0.0.0.0 0.0.0.0 Serial0
ip route 0.0.0.0 0.0.0.0 Serial1
```

Figure 7-9

Diagram of dual ISP connections while transitioning Internet service.

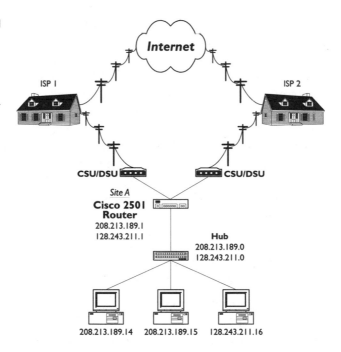

Routing Concerns with Multiple IP Addresses

Routing between the IP networks connected to the Ethernet interface is automatic and needs no special routing statements. However, you must be careful of other machines that sit on both networks. These so-called dual-homed systems might have IP routing turned on by default. Almost all of today's modern operating systems (UNIX, Windows 95, Windows NT) are capable of acting as IP routers. To avoid problems caused by more than one router between two networks, you should make sure that routing is turned off on all these routers. In the case of UNIX systems, make sure "IPFORWARDING" and "IPSENDREDIRECTS" are turned off in the kernel. In Windows operating systems, simply make sure the IP Routing box is not checked.

Dynamic Routing Protocols in IOS

Dynamic routing protocols allow routers to agree among themselves on the best way to route packets through your network. Many different protocols exist, and each has their own characteristics (making some more valuable to your network than others). Some, like RIP (Routing Information Protocol) and OSPF (Open Shortest Path First), are standards and can be used in a heterogeneous router environment. Others, like IGRP (Interior Gateway Routing Protocol) and EIGRP (Enhanced Interior Gateway Routing Protocol), were invented by Cisco and might not work with non-Cisco equipment.

The dynamic routing protocols send out their own packets, attempting to contact other routers on the network. Those routers respond with information about their interfaces and routes. In this way, all routers are able to build a uniform picture of the network. Each protocol has different default times when it sends out inquiry packets and different algorithms for determining the best method of routing to another network.

Some of the routing protocols supported by Cisco include:

- BGP   Border Gateway Protocol
- EGP   Exterior Gateway Protocol
- EIGRP   Enhanced Interior Gateway Routing Protocol
- IGRP   Interior Gateway Routing Protocol
- ISIS   ISO IS-IS
- OSPF   Open Shortest Path First
- RIP   Routing Information Protocol

Before you choose a routing protocol you should learn more about it, because not all routing protocols are created equal. For example, OSPF does exactly what its name says: It routes through the shortest number of hops from the source to the destination. This particular protocol does not always take into account the speeds of the different links between the routers. In the case where four sites were connected together in a box with three T1 lines and a 56Kbps line, OSPF would choose to communicate from Site A to Site D through the 56Kbps line. Clearly you would not want to use it in this type of WAN setup. However, if your WAN links were all about the same speed, it will serve you adequately.

Figure 7-10

Four sites with dual paths to each other prove that all dynamic routing protocols are not equal.

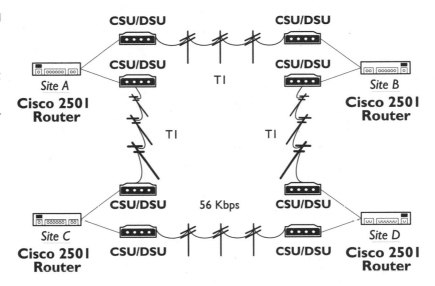

Dynamic routing protocols are most useful when there are multiple routers on a network or multiple paths between remote sites. If you do not have such a setup, then dynamic routing protocols will probably have no value to you.

RIP and EIGRP Protocols

Two more widely used dynamic routing protocols are RIP and EIGRP. RIP is one of the oldest routing protocols, and one of its advantages is that UNIX and NT systems can communicate via RIP. This allows those systems to have a better picture of the network routing tables and communicate more efficiently with other systems. It also lets them be routers themselves and participate in updating the routing protocols. EIGRP, on the other hand, is one of the newest protocols. It is a Cisco proprietary protocol that factors in latency, throughput, and number of hops when determining the best way to route packets.

The first step in configuring a dynamic routing protocol is to add the protocol in global configuration mode. The next step is to add all the networks that your site belongs to. If you have subnetted your network, you should add the main network number and not the subnet number. You can determine what networks your router belongs to by looking at the IP addresses and netmasks of all of your interfaces. A sample configuration is shown in Figure 7-11:

■■

Figure 7-11 Viewing the configuration file shows you the IP addresses for all interfaces. This tells you what networks your router belongs to.

```
interface Ethernet0
 ip address 204.176.117.9 255.255.255.0
!
interface BRI0
 ip address 204.176.118.230 255.255.255.0
```

In this example, the router belongs to two different networks: 204.176.117.0 and 204.176.118.0. Those would be added as networks below the **router rip** or **router eigrp** statement. This is seen in Figure 7-12.

■■

Figure 7-12 Configure the dynamic routing protocol using the router statement, and then add the networks attached to the router.

```
cisco-2503#conf t
Enter configuration commands, one per line.  End with CNTL/Z.
cisco-2503(config)#router rip
cisco-2503(config-router)#network 204.176.117.0
cisco-2503(config-router)#network 204.176.118.0
cisco-2503(config-router)#^Z
cisco-2503#
```

This tells the router to announce that it is connected to these networks using RIP. If you wanted to use EIGRP or some other dynamic routing protocol, you would substitute its name for RIP. Unlike RIP, you must specify an autonomous system number to use EIGRP. This allows you to have routers on the same networks that belong to different groups for the purpose of exchanging routing information. Most sites will usually only use one, and then static route to the Internet. Some might have two: one for the internal network and one that they are assigned by their ISP.

Running Multiple Protocols

Not many sites run multiple routing protocols. This would be redundant, and might even cause problems. As noted above, there are some cases where this might appeal to you, or even be necessary. For example, you might want to run RIP on your internal network, but communicate with your ISP via EIGRP. This is certainly possible, but it is quite an advanced configuration. Those who choose to use multiple routing protocols should make sure they have a good grip on their RIPs and EIGRPs (or other protocols) before they begin.

Announcing Routes Learned from a Different Protocol

If you are using multiple routing protocols and you want to pass information learned from one to the other, you need to specify this explicitly. You could be running EIGRP between your routers and RIP among UNIX systems, which might be acting as routers (or not). If you want the UNIX systems to have the full EIGRP routing information in their local routing tables (and thus route more efficiently), you must tell your routers to redistribute their EIGRP routing tables via RIP. This will send out the updates to your UNIX systems using RIP without stopping your routers from using EIGRP among themselves.

Enabling this is as simple as using the **redistribute** command under the routing section. However, it might seem a little backwards at first. The proper configuration is for RIP to broadcast information that the router has learned through EIGRP, not the other way around. See Figure 7-13.

Figure 7-13 *This configuration shows a router using both RIP and EIGRP. All the information learned by EIGRP is distributed by RIP. No information learned by RIP is distributed by EIGRP.*

```
router eigrp 1
 network 204.176.118.0
 network 204.176.117.0
router rip
 redistribute eigrp 1
 network 204.176.118.0
 network 204.176.117.0
```

If you also wanted the routers to learn about any routes learned by the UNIX systems through RIP, you would tell EIGRP to broadcast that information using **redistribute rip**, as in Figure 7-14.

■■
Figure 7-14   *Now both routing protocols redistribute each other's information.*

```
router eigrp 1
 redistribute rip
 network 204.176.118.0
 network 204.176.117.0
router rip
 redistribute eigrp 1
 network 204.176.118.0
 network 204.176.117.0
```

Propagating Static Routes

Occasionally, you might find one of your routers connected to a device that does not support your routing protocol. Whether the remote router is incapable of it, or it has simply been turned off, you can still map their networks into your dynamic routing tables. To make this happen, simply add the **redistribute static** command into your routing configuration and make sure you have static routes pointing to these networks. In this case, static routes are treated as just another routing information protocol, like RIP or EIGRP. The **redistribute** command is used to propagate information this router knows via a specific routing protocol, so that other routers will also learn about it. See Figure 7-15.

▬▬ ▬▬
Figure 7-15 All routing information learned through static routes is redistributed to all other machines via RIP.

```
router rip
 redistribute static
 network 204.176.118.0
 network 199.29.53.0
!
ip route 208.213.186.0 255.255.255.0 Serial0
ip route 208.213.189.0 255.255.255.0 BRI1
```

When you run the **show ip route** command on another router, you will see the routes that have propagated to it via the dynamic routing protocol. Figure 7-16 shows the routing entries whose lines begin with an "R" for RIP.

▬▬ ▬▬
Figure 7-16 The show ip route command displays how packets are routed and how the information is learned. Here two routes are directly connected and two are learned by RIP.

```
Codes: C - connected, S - static, R - RIP

C    204.176.117.0/24 is directly connected, Ethernet2
     204.176.118.0/24 is variably subnetted, 2 subnets, 2 masks
R       204.176.118.0/24 [120/1] via 204.176.117.9, 00:00:07, Ethernet2
R       204.176.118.224/28 [120/1] via 204.176.117.1, 00:00:06,
Ethernet2
```

One very popular static route is the one that leaves your network and goes to the Internet. If you have multiple routers on a network, only the one directly connected to the Internet should have a static route to your ISP. If you redistribute it via a dynamic routing protocol, all the other routers on the network will use it as their default route (this saves you from having to do it manually). The default route is a network of all zeros with a netmask of all zeros. In this case, it is routed to the remote side of serial port 1. This serial port has an IP address of 208.213.185.5 and is subnetted in such a way that the remote site can only be 208.213.185.6. See Figure 7-17.

Figure 7-17 A static route is added to route packets with unknown destinations to a router that might be able to deliver them, usually through an Internet connection. This is called the default route, and here it is being redistributed to the network via RIP.

```
interface serial 1
 ip address 208.213.185.5 255.255.255.252
router rip
 redistribute static
 network 204.176.118.0
 network 199.29.53.0
!
ip route 208.213.186.0 255.255.255.0 Serial0
ip route 208.213.189.0 255.255.255.0 BRI1
ip route 0.0.0.0 0.0.0.0 208.213.185.6
```

Blocking Dynamic Routing

Another item of concern with dynamic routing protocols is how to block the information passing between two locations. With some routing protocols, you have a routing group number (sometimes called an autonomous system number, or process ID). This group defines which routers listen to other routers about routing information. Hence, two routers on the same physical network that have two different group numbers will not pay attention to each other. Routers that have the same group number will pay attention to each other and exchange routing information.

But what do you do if a site you connect to is already using a group number you use as well? Worse yet, what if you are using RIP, which has no group numbers and listens to all sources and transmits to all destinations? You need to be able to block routing information received from unwanted sources in order to keep your network running properly. You might also want to block the transmission of routing information outside your network for security purposes as well as to keep that information from messing up someone else's network.

You can easily block a router from transmitting routing information on a specific interface by using the **passive-interface** command. This command (under the "router" configuration) tells the router not to send any routing information out from an interface. It can be set on any type of interface, LAN or WAN. See Figure 7-18.

Figure 7-18 Routing information is not sent out from an interface when the passive-interface command is used.

```
router eigrp 2
 redistribute static
 passive-interface Serial0
 network 204.176.117.0
 network 128.5.0.0
```

Ignoring routing information received on a particular interface is more difficult. It is a two-step process, which touches on access lists. Access lists are the building blocks of network security in Cisco routers and can be quite confusing to the uninitiated. In this case, we will use a basic access list to block EIGRP from receiving information through serial interface 0. The first step is to create the access list. This is done with the **access-list** command.

The first option is the basic IP access list number. This is an arbitrary number between 1 and 99. There are other types of access lists, which use different number ranges, but because we are using a basic IP access list, we are limited to this range of numbers. For our example, we will use the number "23." The next option is to select whether to permit or deny packets that match this access list. In our case, we want to deny packets. Finally, we use the keyword **any** to deny packets from any machine. This is shown in Figure 7-19.

Figure 7-19 Blocking routing information from coming in on an interface starts with a basic access list.

```
access-list 23 deny any
```

The access list does nothing by itself; rather, it is used only when referenced by another command. In this case, we want it to block all EIGRP information coming in on serial interface 0. To do this, use the **distribute-list** command to invoke the access list on the interface. The first option to this command is the arbitrary number of the access list (in this case, "23"). Next, select the direction in which you wish the access list to be effective (in or out). Because we are already blocking routing information from going out the interface with the **passive-interface** command, we want to use the inbound direction for the access list. Finally, list the interface on which the access list will take effect (in this case, serial interface 0) seen in Figure 7-20.

Figure 7-20 Applying an access list to a routing protocol allows you to control what information is received.

```
distribute-list 23 in Serial0
```

The final configuration for EIGRP group 2 would look like Figure 7-21.

■ ■
Figure 7-21 The complete configuration to block routing information in both directions on the interface serial 0.

```
router eigrp 2
 redistribute static
 passive-interface Serial0
 network 204.176.117.0
 network 128.5.0.0
 distribute-list 23 in Serial0
!
access-list 23 deny any
```

Checking Routing and Routing Tables

The routing tables are the only way to know how your router is currently routing packets. Routes are added and deleted automatically when interfaces go up and down. You need to check the routing tables from time to time to make sure things are as they should be. The routing table is displayed using the **show ip route** command. A typical small routing table for an EIGRP-based network is shown below.

■ ■
Figure 7-22 The routing tables are viewed with the show ip route command.

```
wan4500#show ip route
Codes: C - connected, S - static, I - IGRP, R - RIP, M - mobile, B -
BGP
       D - EIGRP, EX - EIGRP external, O - OSPF, IA - OSPF inter area
       E1 - OSPF external type 1, E2 - OSPF external type 2, E - EGP
       i - IS-IS, L1 - IS-IS level-1, L2 - IS-IS level-2, * - candidate
default
       U - per-user static route
```

```
Gateway of last resort is 204.176.117.9 to network 0.0.0.0

C    204.176.117.0/24 is directly connected, Ethernet2
S    128.5.0.0/16 [1/0] via 204.176.117.1
D EX 208.213.190.0/24 [170/307200] via 204.176.117.9, 04:53:52,
Ethernet2
D*EX 0.0.0.0/0 [170/307200] via 204.176.117.9, 04:53:52, Ethernet2
wan4500#
```

The letter codes at the beginning of each line tell us whether the route is directly connected to the router (C), statically routed (S), EIGRP (D), or EIGRP external (EX). If the route is directly connected, it will tell you which interface is on that network. If the route is static, it will tell you the destination gateway. If the route is learned through a dynamic routing protocol, it will tell you the destination gateway (which should also be the router that announced the information to it), the time since the route was last updated, and the interface pointing to the destination gateway.

All lines show the route and the netmask as the string xxx.xxx.xxx.xxx/yy, where the x's are the network portion of the IP address and yy is the number of bits in the netmask. In this example, you see a class C network number 208.213.190.0. Class C networks have the netmask 255.255.255.0, so how do they get 24 from this? The answer is simple. Each number in the dotted quad notation of the netmask is eight bits long. If all eight bits are set to one (instead of zero), then they would add up to 255 (128 + 64 + 32 + 16 + 8 + 4 + 2 + 1 = 255). Because you have three sets of eight bits set to one, you have 24 total bits in the netmask field (8 * 3 = 24).

That is all you really need to know; however, some readers might be curious about the numbers inside the square brackets. These numbers (for example, [170/307200] are the administrative distance of the information source and the metric for the route. This probably won't mean a lot to you until you learn more about dynamic routing protocols and how they work.

You can verify routes are operating properly using the **traceroute** command. This command attempts to locate all routers between the local router and the destination. Each intermediate router is called a *hop*. If domain name service has been configured, the router will try to display the name of each router in the path to the destination. Depending on your DNS response times, this could slow down the execution of the command. The **traceroute** command displays the IP address (and sometimes name) of each router as well as the amount of time in milliseconds it took for each system to respond. An asterisk (*) is displayed if no response was available.

Figure 7-23 The traceroute command shows all machines as a packet passes through to reach its destination.

```
wan4500#traceroute 199.29.53.67

Type escape sequence to abort.
Tracing the route to 199.29.53.67

  1 204.176.117.9 0 msec 0 msec 0 msec
  2 204.176.117.1 20 msec 8 msec 8 msec
  3 204.176.118.225 2104 msec 36 msec 56 msec
  4 199.29.53.67 44 msec 36 msec *
wan4500#
```

If you have problems reaching a host, you might get line after line of asterisks. This will continue until the maximum number of 30 hops is reached. This can take some time and cause you much consternation. If you want to stop this, you simply need to enter the abort sequence. This is usually one of the following three key sequences:

1. Ctrl-X
2. Ctrl + Shift + 6 (Hold down Control and Shift and press 6)
3. Ctrl + Shift + 6 (Hold down Control and Shift and press 6), then release them and press x.

Other common errors you run into are *!H* (bang H), which means no route to host, and *!A* (bang A), which means no such address. Examples of this can be seen in Figure 7-24.

Figure 7-24 Examples of output when packets cannot reach a final destination.

```
6 157.130.35.177 40 msec 36 msec 52 msec
7 157.130.35.177 !H   !H   *

5 204.176.119.2 36 msec 32 msec *
6 204.176.119.1 !A   !A   *
```

Routing Protocols on the Cisco 700 Series

Dynamic routing protocols on the Cisco 700 series routers are much simpler than in IOS. Henry Ford said, "You can have it any color you want, as long as it's black." In the same vein, you can use any routing protocol you want, as long as it's RIP. This is a quaint way of saying that RIP is the only dynamic routing protocol available.

Because Cisco 700 series routers are usually used as edge routing devices for SOHO/RO (Small Office Home Office/Remote Office) networks, dynamic routing is not really a requirement. If the remote network is only connected to a single corporate or ISP network via ISDN, the need for dynamic routing protocols is nonexistent. A simple default route to the upstream network will suffice. This is diagramed in Figure 7-25.

Figure 7-25
Basic network diagram for using a 700 series router.

There are, however, many situations where dynamic routing protocols are needed, and not all are immediately visible. The most obscure might be the use of a network management system (NMS) such as HP (Hewlett Packard) Openview Node Manager. Openview and other NMSs might require the use of a routing protocol such as RIP version 2 to automatically map your network.

A less obscure reason for running RIP on a Cisco 700 series router is if your site has more than one internal or external network. In this case, route maintenance is best performed by a dynamic routing protocol like RIP. This allows the network routing tables to adjust to the state of the network.

Figure 7-26
A more complex network diagram using multiple 700 series routers and a Cisco 2514 for Ethernet-to-Ethernet routing.

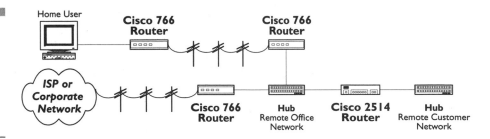

Enabling RIP

There are two main parts to setting up RIP on a 700 series router: sending and receiving. You must determine if you want your router to send out RIP updates and receive them on a per-profile basis. By default, the reception and transmission of RIP packets is turned off. To enable them on a WAN connection, change directory into that profile and enter the following commands in Figure 7-27.

Figure 7-27 Commands for enabling RIP on the ISDN WAN interface of a 700 series router.

```
cisco766> cd wan4500
cisco766:wan4500> set ip rip receive v2
cisco766:wan4500> set ip rip update demand
cisco766:wan4500> set ip rip version 2
cisco766:wan4500>
```

The first command (**set ip rip receive v2**) tells the router to listen for RIP version 2 packets on the WAN. If you are running RIP version 1, you can change the keyword **v2** to **v1**. The keyword **off** disables the reception of RIP packets by the router profile.

The second command (**set ip rip update demand**) tells the router to send RIP updates when the ISDN line first connects and when changes occur in the RIP tables. Use this keyword for WAN connections to avoid bringing up the ISDN line unnecessarily. Other options for this command are **periodic, snapshot, demand**, and **linkup**. The **periodic** keyword tells the router to send updates periodically and when the RIP tables are updated. This is mostly used for LAN connections, but can be used on WAN connections to help insure the ISDN connection stays up full time. Make sure your ISDN billing has been set up for a full-time connection before you do this, or you could be in for a very large phone bill.

The **demand** keyword tells the router to send RIP packets both when the ISDN line first connects and when a change occurs in the RIP table. This can keep the line up if frequent routing changes happen on the Ethernet side of the network. The **linkup** keyword tells the router to send RIP packets only when the ISDN line is connected.

The two periods for **snapshot** routing updates are *quiet* and *active*. During the active period, routing updates occur normally over a particular interface. Once the active period expires, the quiet period begins and the routing table is frozen in that state. There is no RIP activity until the quiet period expires. The **set ip rip snapshot client** and **set ip rip snapshot server** commands are used to configure the quiet and active periods. Those who truly understand dynamic routing protocols and how to configure them should be the only ones using snapshot routing for RIP. Most others, especially accidental administrators, will want to trust the more automatic commands **periodic**, **demand**, and **linkup**.

The **linkup** option is useful on WAN connections. The RIP packets are sent as soon as a connection is established and every 30 seconds thereafter. As long as the connection exists, packets will continue to be sent. If the connection does not exist, RIP updates cease. This prevents the line from being brought up by RIP packets as in the case of the periodic update. Unfortunately, this might keep the line up all the time, because idle counters will be reset every 30 seconds as the RIP updates occur. Later (in Chapter 8) you can learn how to make the router's idle timer ignore RIP packets so that this doesn't happen.

Once you've chosen your RIP update method, you choose the version you want to use with the **set ip rip version** command. Choose either *1* or *2* (unless you are using periodic updates, in which case you also have the option to choose *both*). Whichever version you choose should match the one you chose to receive.

An example of a RIP configuration for a LAN profile can be seen in Figure 7-28.

Figure 7-28 *Commands for enabling RIP on the Ethernet LAN interface of a 700 series router.*

```
cisco766> cd lan
cisco766:LAN> set ip rip receive both
cisco766:LAN> set ip rip update periodic
cisco766:LAN> set ip rip version both
cisco766:LAN>
```

Announcing Ethernet Routes Over the WAN

Most configurations will not require that routes learned over the Ethernet be announced over the WAN. This is because most 700 series network configurations are simple, supporting only SOHO/RO networks. However, in more complex networks you might want to use this feature and, by default, it is turned on. You can double-check this by looking for this command in your LAN and WAN profiles:

Figure 7-29 *Command for enabling ISDN WAN interface to receive RIP information. If RIP updates are sent out the Ethernet port, this information will be passed on as well.*

```
SET IP RIP RECEIVE V2
```

Configuring Static Routes

Static routes are usually all you need to configure 700 series routers, especially in simple SOHO/RO networks. Typically, a single default route is configured to a corporate backbone or ISP in the WAN profile. In some circumstances, you might also want to add other static routes to the configuration. Each one will have its own line in the configuration.

Setting up static routes is fairly simple. The command **set ip route destination** is used. Next, enter the IP network number and, optionally, the number of subnet bits (i.e., 204.176.117.0/24). For the default route use 0.0.0.0/0. Finally, use the keyword **gateway** to define the IP address of the router/server that will know how to route this network (i.e., **gateway 198.17.21.4**). This command also has two options: *propagate* and *cost*. By default, *propagate* will be enabled and the cost will be *1*. Enabling propagation will make the router announce the static route in RIP packets. Examples can be seen in Figure 7-30.

▬▬▬

Figure 7-30 Configuration of static routes on 700 series routers.

```
SET IP ROUTE DEST 208.213.191.0/24 GATEWAY 204.176.117.50 PROPAGATE OFF
COST 1
SET IP ROUTE DEST 0.0.0.0/0 GATEWAY 204.176.118.225 PROPAGATE OFF COST 1
```

The cost associated with a route determines when that route will be used. Lower-cost routes take precedence over ones that have higher costs. This gives you finer control over when a route will be used. For example, you might have two 700 series routers on a small office network. One connects to the corporate network and is operational 24 hours a day. The other is directly connected to the Internet. Both routers only use one B channel for communications, but can bring up a second one if there is sufficient need. They both have WAN profiles for corporate and Internet connections.

Each router would have two static routes. The first router would have a gateway to the local ISP and a cost of 1. The second would have the same gateway and higher cost (probably 10) and would, therefore, become the backup connection. If the first router went down, Internet traffic could begin flowing over its idle B channel. This provides a redundant connection to the Internet. A complementary set of routes to the corporate network would provide a redundant connection to that location. The first router would have a high cost and the second one would have a low cost. If the second router failed, the first would take over for it.

Examining Routing Tables

Viewing the routing tables shows you how the router will route packets to specific networks. The command to view the routing tables is **show ip route**. This command will show you routing information in columns. The first column (**Profile**) tells you which profile a route is learned from (in this case, LAN or wan4500.) The next column (**Type**) tells you the interface for the route (NET for Ethernet or WAN for ISDN.) The **Destination** is the network being routed, and the **Bits** are the subnet bits for that network. The **Gateway** is where the packets for that network will be forwarded. **Prop**(agation) tells you whether this router is announcing this route via RIP. **Cost** displays the cost associated with a particular route. The **Source** column details whether the network is directly connected to a profile, statically routed, or learned from the RIP protocol. **Age** tells you how many minutes the route will remain in the table without being updated.

Figure 7-31   *The show ip route command is used to display routing table information.*

```
cisco766> show ip route
Profile Type  Destination      Bits Gateway        Prop Cost Source   Age
─────────────────────────────────────────────────────────────────────────
wan4500  NET  204.176.118.224   28  DIRECT          ON   1   DIRECT    0
LAN      NET  193.11.115.0      24  204.176.117.8   ON   2   RIP      15
LAN      NET  209.10.10.0       24  193.11.115.1    ON   2   RIP      15
LAN      NET  204.176.118.0     24  193.11.115.1    ON   3   RIP      15
LAN      NET  208.213.191.0     24  204.176.117.50  OFF  1   STATIC    0
LAN      NET  204.176.117.0     24  DIRECT          ON   1   DIRECT    0
LAN      NET  128.5.0.0         16  193.11.115.1    ON   2   RIP      15
wan4500  NET  0.0.0.0            0  204.176.118.225 OFF  1   STATIC    0
cisco766>
```

Logging Events in IOS

If you've watched the console output of your router for a while, you'll notice messages scrolling by on the screen. Mostly they're just general information, but occasionally they have information you might want to see about lines going up and down. Once this information scrolls off the screen, it is normally gone forever. There is no default place where it is logged, but by learning the logging facility, you can change this.

Logging to the Router

Log information can be stored in router RAM. This allows you to keep some of the log history for later viewing. However, this information is not stored permanently. Because there is finite memory in the router for storing messages, a limit on their number is necessary. By default, only the last message is stored. You can increase the number of log messages stored on the router with the **logging history size N** command, where *N* is a number between 1 and 500. Once the log has been filled with messages, new messages will overwrite old ones, automatically rolling the log for you and keeping the last N log messages. Because this information is stored in RAM, it's not permanent. Every time the router is rebooted, the log information will be lost.

Before keeping logs on your router, you should make sure you have enough RAM to store the messages. If your router is already low on RAM, keeping logs could damage your router's performance. Use the **show memory** command to get a general idea of how much memory is available for logging. Then run **show memory failures alloc** to see if any attempts to allocate memory to processes have failed. If they have, you might already be low on memory.

Figure 7-32 IOS commands to show memory status and allocation failures.

```
wan4500#show memory
 Head    Total(b)     Used(b)     Free(b)   Lowest(b)  Largest(b)
Processor   60B7EF50    4722864     1882872    2839992    2630612    2792804
 I/O  40000000   16777216    1837624   14939592   14939592   14939216

wan4500#show memory failures alloc
Caller        Pool          Size    Alignment    When
wan4500#
```

In Figure 7-32, there is 14 MB of I/O memory free with no failures; hence, there is plenty of memory for logging messages. If it is assumed that each log entry takes up 256 bytes, and you want to save the maximum of 500 messages, then you will need 125K (256 bytes x 500 messages) to store your messages. Obviously, 125K can easily fit into 14MB, so there's no problem logging 500 messages on this router.

You might also need to allocate buffer space to log the complete messages, because the message history is only a brief description of what has been logged. This also takes up memory, and it is allocated not by number of messages, but by byte count. The default amount is 8K, and because we have determined we want 125K, the command **logging buffered 128000** can be used to override the default.

Before implementing logging on the local router, consider how the information is displayed. By default, log messages contain information about an event, but no time and date stamp. This makes them nearly worthless for troubleshooting. See the example in Figure 7-33.

Figure 7-33 Typical events logged by the router.

```
%LINK-3-UPDOWN: Interface Ethernet0, changed state to up
%SYS-5-CONFIG_I: Configured from console by vty0 (204.176.117.2)
```

By using the **service timestamps log datetime** command, time and date stamps can be added to each new entry in the log. You might want to add options to this command to display the time down to the millisecond (msec), to use the local time zone information (localtime), or to show the local time zone information (show-timezone). Before using time zone commands, you'll need to set the time zone in the global configuration with the **clock timezone** command. You will also want to set the date and time with the **clock set** command in enable mode.

Figure 7-34 Event log entries with time and date stamp information.

```
*Jul 10 15:27:37.279 UTC: %SYS-5-CONFIG_I: Configured from console by
vty0 (204.176.117.2)
*Jul 10 15:30:35.727 UTC: %LINK-3-UPDOWN: Interface Ethernet0, changed
state to up
*Jul 10 15:30:39.303 UTC: %SYS-5-CONFIG_I: Configured from console by
vty0 (204.176.117.2)
*Jul 10 15:30:39.967 UTC: %LINK-5-CHANGED: Interface Ethernet0, changed
state to administratively down
```

Time stamp information is invaluable to debugging efforts and should be used for all kinds of logging, on router and off. To configure a router with all the options mentioned here, see the example in Figure 7-35.

■■

Figure 7-35 *Commands used to enhance internal logging on the router and provide proper time and date stamp information.*

```
wan4500#clock set 09:16:23 jul 5 1998
wan4500#conf t
Enter configuration commands, one per line.  End with CNTL/Z.
wan4500(config)#service timestamp log datetime msec show-timezone
localtime
wan4500(config)#clock timezone EDT -4
wan4500(config)#logging history size 500
wan4500(config)#logging buffered 128000
wan4500(config)#^Z
wan4500#wr
Building configuration...
[OK]
wan4500#
```

Running the **show logging** command now shows a synopsis of the stored log information, as well as the log messages themselves. The **show logging history** command shows a longer synopsis of the same log information. Note that only **show logging** (and not **show logging history**) displays the time stamp information.

■■

Figure 7-36 *Display of internal log and log history.*

```
wan4500#sho log
Syslog logging: enabled (0 messages dropped, 0 flushes, 0 overruns)
    Console logging: level debugging, 53 messages logged
    Monitor logging: level debugging, 16 messages logged
    Trap logging: level informational, 57 message lines logged
    Buffer logging: level debugging, 48 messages logged

Log Buffer (128000 bytes):

Jul  5 09:18:03.843 EDT: %SYS-5-CONFIG_I: Configured from console by
vty0 (204.176.117.2)
wan4500#sho log history
Syslog History Table:500 maximum table entries,
saving level warnings or higher
 46 messages ignored, 0 dropped, 0 recursion drops
 1 table entries flushed
```

```
SNMP notifications not enabled
   entry number 2 : LINK-3-UPDOWN
    Interface Ethernet2, changed state to up
    timestamp: 715
   entry number 3 : LINK-3-UPDOWN
    Interface Ethernet0, changed state to up
    timestamp: 49963
   entry number 4 : LINK-3-UPDOWN
    Interface Ethernet0, changed state to up
    timestamp: 193848
   entry number 5 : LINK-3-UPDOWN
    Interface Ethernet0, changed state to up
    timestamp: 235575
   entry number 6 : LINK-3-UPDOWN
    Interface Ethernet0, changed state to up
    timestamp: 255877
   entry number 7 : LINK-3-UPDOWN
    Interface Ethernet0, changed state to up
    timestamp: 273556
wan4500#
```

Logging to a Syslog Server

As noted previously, there are some drawbacks to storing log information on routers. First, they take up memory, which could be used for something more important, and the information is lost each time the router is rebooted. If you were using the information to track someone you thought was breaking into your router, all they would need to do would be to reboot the router for your audit trail to be lost.

A more useful method of logging would be to send all the log messages over the network to a log server. This server would then store the messages to its hard disk, where they can be stored almost indefinitely. Cisco uses the standard logging protocol, syslog, to send messages to a server. Most modern UNIX system include a syslog daemon, which is running by default. Typically the configuration file for syslog is **/etc/syslog.conf**.

The router can be configured to send logging information to a syslog server with the command **logging HOST**, where *HOST* is the host name or IP address of the syslog server. You need to set up the router to resolve host names to IP address before you can use the name of the server. If you have not done this, you should use the IP address. Using the IP address is more reliable and uses less overhead, because it does not rely on the DNS server's being alive and does not have to resolve the host name. However, if you have a large number of routers and want the ability to change the location of your logs by changing the DNS pointer to the log server, you will want to use the host name.

▬ ▬

Figure 7-37 *Configuring event log information to be sent to a syslog server.*

```
wan4500#conf t
Enter configuration commands, one per line.  End with CNTL/Z.
wan4500(config)#logging 204.176.117.11
wan4500(config)#^Z
wan4500#wr
Building configuration...
[OK]
wan4500#
```

Once the router is sending logging information to the syslog server, you must make sure the server knows what to do with it. By default, the router uses the syslog definition *local7* to send out all of its alerts. There are eight levels of information used by the *local7* definition; they are listed in Table 7-1.

Table 7-1

The eight levels of syslog information for each log definition

Level Keyword	Severity Level	Description	Syslog Definition
emergencies	0	System unusable	LOG_EMERG
alerts	1	Immediate action needed	LOG_ALERT
critical	2	Critical conditions	LOG_CRIT
errors	3	Error conditions	LOG_ERR
warnings	4	Warning conditions	LOG_WARNING
notifications	5	Normal but significant condition	LOG_NOTICE
informational	6	Informational messages only	LOG_INFO
debugging	7	Debugging messages	LOG_DEBUG

Because the default state of the syslog server is unknown, you should go to the effort to generate your own modifications to the **/etc/syslog.conf** file. It is recommended that a separate file be created for each of the eight levels of logging and that they all be stored separately from the normal syslog information (possibly in another directory). To do this, you should edit the syslog configuration file to look something like this.

■■■

Figure 7-38 *Syslog daemon configuration file sending events for all eight levels to their own files.*

```
local7.emerg      /usr/adm/routers/log.emerg
local7.alert      /usr/adm/routers/log.alert
local7.crit       /usr/adm/routers/log.crit
local7.err        /usr/adm/routers/log.err
local7.warning    /usr/adm/routers/log.warning
local7.notice     /usr/adm/routers/log.notice
local7.info       /usr/adm/routers/log.info
local7.debug      /usr/adm/routers/log.debug
```

Once the file is updated with your information, you will need to create the special directory you want to use (in this case, **/usr/adm/routers**) and then create empty files for the logging information. By default, syslog will not create log files; it will only write to them if they exist. Once this is done, you can restart the syslog daemon, and logging will begin immediately. This procedure is shown in Figure 7-39.

■■■

Figure 7-39 *UNIX system configuration to support logging router events to their own files.*

```
# cd /usr/adm
# mkdir routers
# cd routers
# touch log.emerg log.alert log.crit log.err log.warning log.notice
log.info log.debug
# kill -HUP 'cat /etc/syslog.pid'
```

Tailoring Log Information

One thing you will notice immediately is that something logged to a particular level will also be logged to all other levels below it. Hence, if a log event occurs at level three (error) it will also be logged to levels four, five, six, and seven. This can be extremely obnoxious; in addition, it wastes disk space on your server. There are two ways to stop this: First, stop the router from logging anything above a certain level, and second, stop the server from writing it to the disk.

To stop the router from logging information past a certain level, simply remove those lines from the configuration file. If all you want to see are emergency through warning messages, remove the lines for notifications, information, and debugging. You might also want to change some of the system defaults, such as *.info* or *.debug*. These will log the events for **local7.info** and **local7.debug** wherever the router logs events for the operating system that use different syslog definitions, such as cron and mail. You might want to remove the asterisks in front of these lines and replace them with all other syslog definitions. Many of the syslog definitions are described in Table 7-2.

Table 7-2

Many of the syslog definitions available for use. Cisco uses local7 by default.

Keyword	Description
auth	Authorization system
cron	Cron facility
daemon	System daemon
kern	Kernel
local0-7	Reserved for locally defined messages
lpr	Line printer system
mail	Mail system
news	USENET news
sys9	System use
sys10	System use
sys11	System use
sys12	System use
sys13	System use
sys14	System use
syslog	System log
user	User process
uucp	UNIX-to-UNIX copy system

The **logging trap** command allows you to limit the types of messages sent to the server. It takes one option, a logging level keyword as listed in the table above. If you want to see only levels zero through three (emergency, alert, critical, and error), you would use the keyword **err** as the option to this command.

███

Figure 7-40 Limiting event log information sent from the router to the syslog server with the logging trap command.

```
wan4500#conf t
Enter configuration commands, one per line.  End with CNTL/Z.
wan4500(config)#logging trap err
wan4500(config)#^Z
```

Rotating Log Files

Log files on most UNIX systems will continue to grow forever. Eventually, they will cause the administrator big problems, usually in the form of a full disk and possibly a system crash. You can prevent this by rotating the log files weekly or monthly, depending on how large they get and how much information you want to keep. You can also compress them after they have been moved aside, so that they will take up less space. This will allow you to store more information for longer periods of time.

First, create a script like the one shown in Figure 7-41, which will roll and compress the log files. You will need to specify the special directory name used, the number of iterations of the log file to keep, and the program used to compress the log files. By default the script uses the GNU gzip program. If you don't have gzip, uncomment the lines to use the UNIX compress utility and comment out the lines using gzip. You might want to place the script in a standard directory for system administration scripts, like **/usr/local/etc**. This will help to insure that it will not be lost during operating system upgrades.

███

Figure 7-41 UNIX shell script to rotate log files automatically. This script is available on the World Wide Web at http://paul.tibex.com/Router-Book/newsyslog.

```
#! /bin/sh
#
# Make sure all programs being used are in the PATH
PATH=$PATH:/usr/local/bin

#
# Set the log directory, number of files to keep around, and compres-
sion
# information.
LOG_DIR=/usr/adm/routers
LOG_NAME=log
```

(cont.)

Figure 7-41 continued

```
NUMBER=6
COMPRESS="gzip -9 "
EXT=gz
#
# Uncomment these to use the compress command instead of gzip
#COMPRESS="compress "
#EXT=Z

#
# Change directory into the log directory
cd $LOG_DIR

#
# For each type of log file, move them up the next number.
# The last one in line will be overwritten by the one behind it.
for LOG_EXT in alert debug err notice crit emerg info warning
do
  #
  # Set the log file name.
  LOG=$LOG_NAME.$LOG_EXT
  #
  # Loop while $NUMBER is greater than zero
  while [ "$NUMBER" -gt "0" ]
  do
    NEXT='expr $NUMBER - 1'
    #
    # Move the old logs aside to make room for the new one.
    [ -f $LOG.$NEXT.$EXT ] && mv $LOG.$NEXT.$EXT  $LOG.$NUMBER.$EXT
    NUMBER=$NEXT
  done

#
```

```
# Move the original log aside and give it a .0 extension.
# Then create the new log file and make it work writable
mv $LOG $LOG.0
cp /dev/null $LOG
chmod 666     $LOG


#
# Compress the last log file.
$COMPRESS -9 $LOG.0
done


#
# Restart syslogd so it will start using the new log files.
kill -HUP 'cat /etc/syslog.pid'
```

This script needs to be run periodically. This is configured in the cron tables. The standard command for editing the cron table in most modern UNIX operating systems is **cron -e**. Those not familiar with cron should read their UNIX manual pages before trying to edit the file. If you want to roll the log files weekly, you would use the cron configuration line shown in Figure 7-42. This will cause the script to be executed at 4:01 a.m. every Monday.

Figure 7-42 UNIX cron entry to rotate the log files weekly.

```
1 4 * * 1 /usr/local/etc/newsyslog
```

If you wanted to roll the log files monthly, you would use the configuration line shown in Figure 7-43. It will execute the script at 4:01 a.m. on the first day of each month.

Figure 7-43 UNIX cron entry to rotate the log files monthly.

```
1 4 1 * * /usr/local/etc/newsyslog
```

As with any UNIX shell script, you need to make sure it is executable before it will work. The command shown in Figure 7-44 is all you need to do this.

Figure 7-44 UNIX command to make the log file rotation script executable.

```
# chmod 755 /usr/local/etc/newsyslog
```

Logging Events on 700 Series Routers

Logging on the 700 series routers is extremely simple. All logging is visible on the console port and in Telnet sessions to the router. There is no facility to keep logging information in router memory or send it to a syslog server. Logging is primarily used to debug PPP and LAN problems.

The default setting for logging is *log calls*. Each major call event is logged, and a message displays every time a channel is assigned a connection. This and all other logging is disabled with the command **log none**. Another useful option is **log errors**, which displays error messages that are not otherwise displayed. These include buffer allocation errors, mail delivery errors, and chip level errors. Two options to these commands are **time** and **verbose**. The **time** command displays the time and date of each logged event or message. The **verbose** command modifies the other commands, causing them to give much more information. Be careful using **verbose**, because you might get so much information that you can't figure out what's going on.

Logging on the LAN connection can show traffic or packet information. The command **log lan packets** displays statistics on packet routing once per second. The number of packets filtered, forwarded, and received, and the packet queue lengths are also displayed. The command **log lan traffic** displays a one-character indicator of each packet sent on the connection, or the whole packet when "verbose" is specified. Both methods of logging LAN information can be modified with the **channel** and **verbose** options. The **channel** option allows you to provide the channel number, which is used to log traffic on a channel before the channel is assigned to a connection. This is primarily used to debug PPP negotiation problems. The **verbose** option will give you more information. It also has two options, **inbound** and **outbound**, to restrict the packet content display to either incoming or outgoing packets.

Configuring Domain Name Service

Domain Name Service (DNS) is the protocol that resolves host names (e.g., www.btg.com) to IP addresses (e.g., 204.176.115.69). Although this protocol is not absolutely necessary for router operations, it is easier to remember names rather than long stings of numbers. It also aids in debugging router problems. For example, commands like **traceroute** are able to look up the host names of IP addresses they receive from the network. Debugging using host names is much easier than using IP addresses and having to mentally translate them to hosts or routers on the network. It is for these reasons that most people configure DNS lookup on their routers.

Setting up DNS lookups on your router is very easy. You simply need the domain name to which your network belongs and the IP addresses of your DNS servers. The domain name is added, using the **ip domain-name** command. Each DNS server you want to use is entered individually, using the **ip name-server** command.

Figure 7-45 shows what the output of **traceroute 199.29.53.67** looks like before the DNS is configured:

Figure 7-45 Using the traceroute command shows IP addresses returned instead of system names.

```
wan4500#traceroute 199.29.53.67

Type escape sequence to abort.
Tracing the route to 199.29.53.67

  1 204.176.117.1 4 msec 4 msec 4 msec
  2 204.176.118.225 2056 msec 32 msec 28 msec
  3 199.29.53.67 36 msec 32 msec *
wan4500#
```

Table 7-46 shows the commands used to add DNS lookup services to the router.

Figure 7-46 Commands used to configure DNS resolution in IOS.

```
wan4500#conf t
Enter configuration commands, one per line.  End with CNTL/Z.
wan4500(config)#ip domain-name btg.com
wan4500(config)#ip name-server 199.29.53.67
wan4500(config)#ip name-server 199.29.53.118
wan4500(config)#^Z
wan4500#wr
Building configuration...
[OK]
wan4500#
```

Once DNS is configured, the command can be run using the host name instead of the IP address. Note in Figure 7-47 that the IP addresses of the interim routers are also listed by name.

Figure 7-47 The same traceroute command now resolves IP addresses to host names and host names to IP addresses.

```
wan4500#traceroute rohan
Translating "rohan"...domain server (199.29.53.67) [OK]

Type escape sequence to abort.
Tracing the route to rohan.btg.com (199.29.53.67)

  1 cisco766.gnf.btg.com (204.176.117.1) 4 msec 4 msec 4 msec
  2 corp.isdn.btg.com (204.176.118.225) 32 msec 28 msec 32 msec
  3 rohan.btg.com (199.29.53.67) 32 msec *  32 msec
wan4500#
```

Using the Router as a Network Timeserver

The network time protocol (NTP) is used to set and keep the proper time on your computers. Source clocks on the Internet keep extremely accurate time and usually allow anyone to access them. In fact, many large ISPs have their routers set up as NTP servers, which allows closer access to accurate time. One such server is *rackety.udel.edu*. Normally, you would set up one router to use a source clock server on the Internet, and the rest of your routers to use the first. Your client computers could then get the proper time from their local routers. You should contact your ISP to find out the name and IP address of their NTP servers.

The first step in setting up NTP is to tell the router the timeserver's IP address. This will make the router start getting time information from the Internet immediately. If you are using a dial-up connection, it could cost you extra money, so you might want to investigate it more thoroughly. The command to set the NTP server is **ntp server HOSTNAME**, where *HOSTNAME* is the host name or IP address of the upstream timeserver.

This will update the clock, but not the calendar on the router. You can enter the command **ntp update-calendar** to make sure the calendar gets updated as well. The final configuration necessary is to get the router to broadcast NTP packets to the network. This is done on a per-interface basis. You can also tell slave routers to listen to the broadcast time packets in this way.

A master timeserver on your network would have the NTP configuration shown in Figure 7-48:

Figure 7-48 IOS commands for configuring a network master timeserver.

```
clock timezone EDT -4
interface Ethernet2
 ip address 204.176.117.44
 ntp broadcast
ntp update-calendar
ntp server 128.4.1.1
```

A slave timeserver would have the NTP configuration shown in Figure 7-49:

Figure 7-49 IOS commands for configuring a network slave timeserver.

```
clock timezone EDT -4
interface Ethernet0
 ip address 201.171.117.1
 ntp broadcast
 ntp broadcast client
ntp update-calendar
ntp server 204.176.117.44
```

Configuring your computers to take advantage of time service is beyond the scope of this book. Table 7-3 shows Internet resources you can use to learn more about configuring individual systems.

Table 7-3

List of Internet resources for learning more about NTP.

Resource	Web site
An Introduction to NTP	http://www.eecis.udel.edu/~ntp/
Platform Specific NTP clients	http://www.eecis.udel.edu/~ntp/software.html
Archive of NTP software and related utilities	ftp://ftp.udel.edu/pub/ntp
NTP Version 3 Specification (RFC 1305)	http://ds.internic.net/rfc/rfc1305.txt
Usenet News Group	comp.protocols.time.ntp

Useful Line Settings in IOS

Nothing is more annoying that having your CLI improperly configured. For example, if you make a minor spelling mistake, the router will try to connect you to some nonexistent host. A large number of these problems and annoyances can be corrected with a few minor configuration changes.

To stop the router from trying to resolve every typo, use the command **transport preferred none**. This command needs to be added to every instance of **line** in the configuration (**line** refers to a connection to your router that's used for administration), as shown in Figure 7-50:

▬ ▬

Figure 7-50 IOS command to stop the router from trying to use typos as host names.

```
line con 0
 transport preferred none
line aux 0
 transport preferred none
line vty 0 4
 password 12345
 login
 transport preferred none
```

Do you keep running out of virtual terminals for Telnet sessions? Just add more! Use the **line vty** command to add as many as you need, as shown in Figure 7-51:

▬ ▬

Figure 7-51 Configuring many VTY lines with the same transport and password information.

```
wan4500#conf t
Enter configuration commands, one per line.  End with CNTL/Z.
wan4500(config)#line vty 5 20
wan4500(config-line)#transport preferred none
wan4500(config-line)#password 12345
wan4500(config-line)#^Z
wan4500#wr
Building configuration...
[OK]
wan4500#
```

Pagination not working right? Lines scrolling off the top before the —*more*— prompt allows you to read them? Or maybe you're using a terminal with more than the default 25 lines? Do you like an xterm (X windows terminal program) stretched so that more can be displayed on a single screen? Use the **terminal length N** command, where *N* is the number of lines supported by that terminal. This is done in exec mode and is only valid for that login session.

If you want to do this permanently on some terminal or vty lines, you can add it to the line profile in configuration mode. To do this, use the **length N** command under the specific line you want to change; see Figure 7-52.

Figure 7-52 *Configuring screen lengths for proper pagination in IOS.*

```
wan4500#conf t
Enter configuration commands, one per line.   End with CNTL/Z.
wan4500(config)#line vty 0
wan4500(config-line)#length 36
wan4500(config-line)#line con 0
wan4500(config-line)#length 31
wan4500(config-line)#^Z
wan4500#
```

Finally, are you tired of having the router drop your Telnet connection just because you walked away for a few minutes (or went to lunch)? Change the default time-out! Use the **exec-timeout M S** command, where *M* is minutes and *S* is seconds (as shown in Figure 7-53). If you want to disable automatic logout completely, set M and S to 0. **NOTE:** This is a glaring security hole, because someone can walk up to your machine while you're at lunch and muck with the routers. Make sure not to make this timeout too long, or security will be compromised (even if you use a password-protected screen saver).

Figure 7-53 *Configuring the connections to the router to not automatically log you out.*

```
wan4500#conf t
Enter configuration commands, one per line.   End with CNTL/Z.
wan4500(config)#line vty 0 20
wan4500(config-line)#exec-timeout 0 0
wan4500(config-line)#^Z
wan4500#
```

So, after mucking about with all these things, check out Figure 7-54 to see how your router configuration might look:

Figure 7-54 *The IOS configuration showing the culmination of all the previous edits.*

```
line con 0
 exec-timeout 0 0
 length 31
 transport preferred none
line aux 0
 transport preferred none
line vty 0
 exec-timeout 120 0
 password 12345
 login
 length 36
 transport preferred none
line vty 1 4
 exec-timeout 120 0
 password 12345
 login
 transport preferred none
line vty 5 20
 exec-timeout 120 0
 password 12345
 login
 transport preferred none
```

## CHAPTER 8

Deep Into the Router

There are dark places in the router where many administrators fear to go. In the world of Cisco routers, these places are advanced configurations the likes of which mere mortals rarely see (in fact, few normal network administrators see these configurations either). However, there may come a day when you need to set up these commands in your routers. When you do, this section will be an excellent reference. Until then, you might not want to read this chapter, because if you do, it will only give you ideas. Once these ideas start kicking around in your head, you might want to start trying them.

If you decide to proceed, you need to have a good plan. First, do not implement any new changes that could lock you out of a router or bring the network down during business hours. Second, be sure to back up your original configuration, so you can revert to it if necessary. Finally, make sure you have physical access to the router, so you can break into it through the console port and eliminate a bad configuration. If at all possible, you should try out these configurations on a spare router. If you do not have one, you might try to pick up a used router, which will let you attempt many of these configurations in a non-critical environment.

You have been warned. Some of these configurations, if improperly implemented, can lock you out of a router or, worse, cause serious network problems. It's up to you to make sure you consider the consequences of your actions.

Security with Packet Filters

TCP/IP networking assigns an IP address (or multiple IP addresses) to a single machine (e.g., 204.176.111.4). Port numbers at that IP address reference services that operate on that machine (e.g., 204.176.111.4:23). This allows one machine to have multiple services, such as mail, WWW, and Telnet. Port numbering follows a standard to prevent confusion and allow for ease of communication. Some of these port numbers are 80 for HTTP, 23 for Telnet, and 25 for SMTP (Simple Mail Transport Protocol).

Packet filters block packets based on information found in the packet itself. Packet filtering is the most basic kind of firewall next to the "air-gap firewall" (see Marcus Ranum's installation instructions in Figure 8-1). You can select which packets a router will allow to enter or leave based on the destination port and either the source address, the destination address, or both. You can also choose the interface on which to apply the packet filter. Packet filters can be applied to the IP protocol in general, or to any of its subprotocols: TCP, UDP (User Datagram Protocol), and ICMP (Internet Control Message Protocol). Each selection is entered into a packet filter rule, and all these rules make up an access list.

The ULTIMATELY Secure Firewall (Adaptive Packet Destructive Filter)

Installation Instructions

■ **For best effect** install the firewall between the CPU unit and the wall outlet. Place the jaws of the firewall across the power cord, and bear down firmly. *Be sure to wear rubber gloves while installing the firewall* or assign the task to a junior system manager. If the firewall is installed properly, all the lights on the CPU will turn dark and the fans will grow quiet. This indicates that the system has entered a **secure state**.

■ **For Internet use** install the firewall between the demarc of the T1 to the Internet. Place the jaws of the firewall across the T1 line lead, and bear down firmly. When your Internet service provider's network operations center calls to inform you that they have lost connectivity to your site, the firewall is correctly installed.

If I had a dollar . . .

If I had a dollar for every time I've seen someone post "I need a 100% secure firewall that lets me do everything", I'd be retired by now.

The fact is, if you're connecting your network to anything else, you're running a risk. Period. Usually, that risk can be reduced, often dramatically, by employing basic security precautions such as firewalls. But a firewall is a *risk reduction* system, it is not a *risk mitigation* system — there is, always, some danger that something can go fatally wrong with anything built by humans.

The firewall above is the only 100% *guaranteed* secure solution.
Copyright ©1995 by Marcus J. Ranum. Reprinted with permission.

Figure 8-1
The Marcus Ranum
Ultimate Firewall!

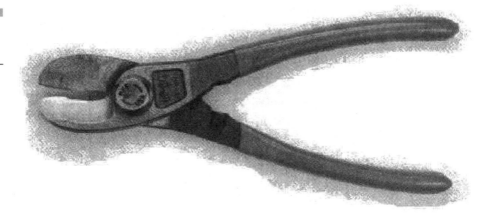

This kind of firewall gives you extremely fine granularity to control access to and between your networks. However, it does come at a cost. Packet filters are difficult to conceptualize for some people, and they are generally hard to set up. Also, they are difficult to edit on the router and cause additional processor overhead (as much as 30 percent on smaller routers like the 700, 1000, and 2500 series); they might also slow down your network connection.

The more rules there are in your packet filter, the slower your connection will become. The filter must compare each packet against each rule until it finds a match. Once a packet matches a rule, comparison ceases and the filter either passes on or discards the packet. This makes packet filter optimization extremely important. Combining as many rules as possible into one rule optimizes packet filters.

The packet filter paradigm is also important. The two choices are *open* or *closed.* An *open paradigm* passes all packets unless specifically denied by a rule. A *closed paradigm* rejects all packets unless specifically permitted by a rule. Balance the specific needs of your network users against the need to secure your network from outside intrusion and tampering. Allowing users to get their work done while securing the network from intrusion is a difficult task, but one that can be accomplished. You might need to read more about network security and firewalls in general before you start to construct packet filters.

Filtering Networks and Wildcard Bits

Filtering networks is done using the network number and wildcard bits. The network number is the network part of the IP address, with the host bits all set to zero. The wildcard bits determine which part of the address the access list will act on. Only bits set to zero are acted upon (bits set to one are ignored). This is the exact opposite of a netmask. Remember that this number is in bits, and you will always have all zeros to the left of the first one, and all ones to the right of the last zero. Table 8-1 shows some examples of netmasks and wildcard bits.

Table 8-1

Examples of netmasks and wildcard bits

Type of Network	Netmask	Wildcard Bits
Class A	255.0.0.0	0.255.255.255
Class B	255.255.0.0	0.0.255.255
Class C	255.255.255.0	0.0.0.255
Class C 2-bit subnet	255.255.255.192	0.0.0.63
Class B 4-bit subnet	255.255.240.0	0.0.31.255

If you do not understand network numbers and netmasks, you should read more about them in a book on TCP/IP networking, such as *TCP/IP Complete* by Edgar Taylor and *Hands-On TCP/IP* by Paul Simoneau.

Configuring Packet Filters in IOS

Creating packet filters in IOS is a two-part task. First, the packet filter is assembled out of a series of rules, created with the **access-list** command. Next, the assembled packet filter is applied to an interface with the **ip access-group** command. Sometimes the entire packet filter is referred to as an *access list.*

There are different types of access lists available in IOS. The access lists are broken up into ranges of numbers, which define what protocols and options are available. Table 8-2 lists protocols that use access lists specified by numbers, and also includes the range of access-list numbers that is valid for each protocol.

Table 8-2

Protocols with access lists specified by numbers

Protocol	Range
IP	1 to 99
Extended IP	100 to 199
Ethernet type code	200 to 299
Ethernet address	700 to 799
Transparent bridging (protocol type)	200 to 299
Transparent bridging (vendor code)	700 to 799
Extended transparent bridging	1100 to 1199
DECnet and extended DECnet	300 to 399
XNS	400 to 499
Extended XNS	500 to 599
AppleTalk	600 to 699
Source-route bridging (protocol type)	200 to 299
Source-route bridging (vendor code)	700 to 799
IPX	800 to 899
Extended IPX	900 to 999
IPX SAP	1000 to 1099

Each protocol has its own set of specific tasks and rules required for you to provide packet filtering. We will focus on IP and extended IP access lists, because those are the most common in the Internet world. You should have a good understanding of the IP protocol to understand packet filters.

Standard IP access lists are simple, and limited in scope. Their access-list range is from 1 to 99. You can use any arbitrary number in this range, because their purpose is simply to match IP addresses when they are applied to an interface or a routing statement (as in Chapter 6). For simplicity's sake, you should start with **1** and increment for each additional list. The next keyword allows you to permit or deny packets with this specific access list. Finally, you can choose the source address of a host or network, or the keyword **any**.

To filter a host, you would first enter the hostname or IP address. To filter a network, you would enter the network number, followed by the wildcard bits. To filter all networks and hosts, you would use the keyword **any**. With standard IP addresses, you are limited to selecting only source addresses. You cannot define port numbers, protocols, or destination information, nor can you log the point when a packet matched the filter. Figure 8-2 shows examples of standard IP access-list commands.

Figure 8-2   *Examples of standard IP access lists.*

```
access-list 1 deny    204.176.111.1
access-list 1 deny    204.176.111.11
access-list 1 deny    204.176.111.0 0.0.0.255
access-list 1 permit any
```

These have more options and will be more useful in many situations. They start the same as standard IP access lists, but their numbers range from 100 through 199. They give you the option **permit** or **deny**, and allow you to set up a dynamic access list. We will not discuss dynamic access lists in this book.

At this point, extended IP access lists begin to diverge from standard IP access lists. Standard IP access lists only have the choices **host**, **network**, or **any**. Extended IP access lists have twelve options and the ability to pick a standard IP protocol number between zero and 255. (You can find the official list of protocol numbers at http://www.isi.edu/in-notes/iana/assignments/protocol-numbers.) All options are listed in Figure 8-3.

Figure 8-3   List of all protocols supported by Extended IP access lists in IOS version 11.2(14).

```
wan4500(config)#access-list 100 permit ?
  <0-255>  An IP protocol number
  eigrp    Cisco's EIGRP routing protocol
  gre      Cisco's GRE tunneling
  icmp     Internet Control Message Protocol
  igmp     Internet Gateway Message Protocol
  igrp     Cisco's IGRP routing protocol
  ip       Any Internet Protocol
  ipinip   IP in IP tunneling
  nos      KA9Q NOS compatible IP over IP tunneling
  ospf     OSPF routing protocol
  tcp      Transmission Control Protocol
  udp      User Datagram Protocol
```

In this book, we'll focus on filtering the IP, ICMP, TCP, and UDP protocols. IP is the underlying protocol for the other three. Anything you filter with IP will also affect the other protocols. Control messages on the network use ICMP packets, as well as programs like **ping** and **traceroute**. Most user protocols employ TCP packets. Programs like **telnet** and **ftp** and Web browsers all use TCP packets. UDP packets are also used by user programs, but less so than TCP. NTP, NFS (Network File System), and TFTP all use UDP packets. Because ICMP, TCP, and UDP packets are all part of the IP protocol, you might sometimes see them referred to as ICMP/IP, TCP/IP, and UDP/IP, although TCP/IP is the most prevalent of these.

The next step in assembling an extended IP access list is to define the source and destination addresses. The source comes first, followed by the destination. You can use the keyword **any** to indicate all hosts. You should use the keyword **host** before listing a host IP address and use the standard network number and wildcard bits notation to define network ranges. Next come protocol-specific options and, finally, the ability to turn logging on for that rule. If you use the command line help, you will see that there are many options available for each subprotocol. We will focus on those that allow you to select ports, log information, and deal with established connections. Figure 8-4 shows some examples of extended IP access lists.

```
access-list 100 permit tcp 204.178.3.0 0.0.0.255 any established
access-list 100 permit tcp any host 204.178.3.55 eq www
access-list 100 permit tcp any host 204.178.3.55 eq smtp
access-list 100 deny   udp any 204.178.3.0 0.0.0.255 eq 2049
access-list 100 deny   icmp any any
```

Designing Packet Filters

There are some major things to keep in mind when designing packet filters. All packet filter rules process from the top down. There is an implicit **deny all** at the end of all access lists. New lines in the configuration always add at the end. In addition, undefined lists referenced by an interface have an implicit **permit any**.

Because all packets undergo top-down evaluation, the order of the access-list commands is vital. If your first rule is an explicit **permit all**, you would never reach any subsequent rules. Conversely, if you bury a rule that matches a majority of packets below many rules that match only a few packets, the earlier, less general rules must be evaluated before the broader rule. This adds a lot of processing overhead to your routers, and would slow down network traffic. Remember, the order of access-list commands counts.

Because there is an implicit **deny all** at the end of all access lists, they might not function the way you think they should. To compensate for this, you should end all your access lists with explicit **permit** or **deny all** statements so they will be easier to read. Easy-to-read access lists are easy to maintain.

When you add lines to an access list, you always do so at the bottom. There is no way to edit them in the middle from the CLI. Because of this, you almost never want to add access lists directly to the router through the CLI. Instead, you should create and edit them in a text editor on a computer that has a TFTP server (remember, Cisco has an MS Windows TFTP server available free at http://www.cisco.com/pcgi-bin/tablebuild.pl/tftp). Whenever you edit your access-list commands, you will need to use the **no access-list NUM** command as the first line in your text file, where *NUM* is the access-list number. This will remove all lines in the existing access-list NUM, and allow your commands to be loaded into the router configuration in the proper order.

The final step in setting up an access list is to assign it to one or more interfaces. This is done using the **ip access-group NUM** command, where *NUM* is the same number used in the access list that you want to apply to the interface. By default, the access list is applied to packets leaving (or going out of) the interface. You should always use the keywords **in** or **out** to make the command easier to read.

Be careful when choosing **in** versus **out**. This option reverses the meanings of the source and destination definitions in your access lists. For example, a packet destined for the local Ethernet would be the destination when coming out that Ethernet port, or going in some other port. It could not be the destination coming in that Ethernet port, because it is on the local network and, therefore, wouldn't be routed anywhere (never entering the router at all).

Another concern when choosing **in** or **out** is router processor overhead. If you use **out**, the packet must enter the router first, be evaluated for routing, and then be evaluated for the access list. If you use **in**, the packet does not enter the router unless it first passes the access list. This requires less processing power for the same job, making it more efficient.

A Basic Packet Filter

As a tutorial, we will create two packet filters for a simple configuration: one mostly closed, the other mostly open. In this example, we have a Cisco 2501 router with a local Ethernet network, and a leased line to an ISP. This is shown in Figure 8-5. We will set up a packet filter inbound on the serial port to protect the router and the company from the Internet. We will allow only inbound WWW and mail traffic to access the Web server and the mail server. We will allow the local users to go anywhere on the Internet they choose, using any protocol. We will also protect against someone on the Internet claiming to be on the local Ethernet. This is called *IP address spoofing*.

In addition, we will block all Telnet connections to the router, in order to prevent someone on the Internet from subverting the router. We will also block all incoming file-sharing protocols, such as those used by Microsoft for peer-to-peer networking and SUN Microsystems' NFS (Network File System). Our router's two IP addresses are 137.39.1.3 on the serial interface and 208.213.189.1 on the Ethernet interface.

Figure 8-5
A basic network
connection with a
leased line to the
Internet, and a local
Ethernet network.

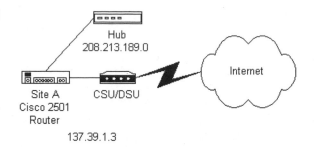

In a mostly closed scenario, we need only specify what we want to permit and then use an explicit **deny all** to block the rest. In a mostly open scenario, we would deny what we do not want and permit the rest with an explicit **permit all** command. In both cases, the first rules deny connections from local networks. Because a packet from our local network will never originate on the Internet (unless someone is trying to spoof our IP network), this should always be blocked. IP spoofing is one way a hacker can trick machines on your network into trusting him.

Mostly Closed Packet Filter

Because no packets coming from the Internet should ever appear to be coming from the local Ethernet, this is the first thing we deny. This stops IP spoofing attacks. Next, we allow established connections back to users. Without this, no outbound connections from the local users to the Internet could happen. Any user on the Internet can connect to the mail server using port 25 (SMTP) and to the Web server using port 80 (www). This fulfills most of our requirements, except for letting the users go anywhere and do anything. Unfortunately, the file transfer protocol (FTP) requires inbound connections on TCP port 20 and on many ports above 1023. In order to allow users to continue to use FTP, we must open these ports as well. We could open all ports above 1023 by ending a command with **gt 1023**, but this might not be necessary. A majority of FTP connections will be destined for the first few thousand ports, so we might use the range of ports between 1024 and 6000. This would be done by ending the command **range 1024 6000**.

The final line is an explicit **deny all**. Although there is already an implicit **deny all** statement in place, this makes the packet filter easier to read. Figure 8-6 shows the command lines used to create the mostly closed filter.

Figure 8-6   A mostly closed basic packet filter.

```
access-list 100 deny    tcp 208.213.189.0 0.0.0.255 any
access-list 100 permit tcp any 208.213.189.0 0.0.0.255 established
access-list 100 permit tcp any host 208.213.189.55 eq www
access-list 100 permit tcp any host 208.213.189.55 eq smtp
access-list 100 permit tcp any any range 1024 6000
access-list 100 permit tcp any any eq ftp-data
access-list 100 deny    ip   any any
```

Mostly Open Packet Filter

Even in a mostly open environment, we start by blocking IP spoofing and allowing established connections. Because we only want to let Web and mail traffic into their respective servers, we add permit statements for this, and then use a deny statement for the whole network. Because the filter undergoes top-down interpretation, Web and mail connection can still take place to the proper servers. Next, we deny access to the router's two IP addresses. Finally, we block TCP/IP ports 137 through 139 and UDP/IP ports 137, 138, and 2049 to block Microsoft and SUN file-sharing protocols.

The final line is an explicit **permit all**. This will override the implicit **deny all** statement that comes after it by default. Figure 8-7 shows the command lines used to create the mostly open filter.

Figure 8-7   The same version of a packet filter in a mostly open scenario.

```
access-list 100 deny    tcp 208.213.189.0 0.0.0.255 any
access-list 100 permit tcp any 208.213.189.0 0.0.0.255 established
access-list 100 permit tcp any host 208.213.189.55 eq www
access-list 100 permit tcp any host 208.213.189.55 eq smtp
access-list 100 deny    tcp any 208.213.189.0 0.0.0.255 eq www
access-list 100 deny    tcp any 208.213.189.0 0.0.0.255 eq smtp
access-list 100 deny    tcp any host 137.39.1.3 eq telnet
access-list 100 deny    tcp any host 208.213.189.1 eq telnet
access-list 100 deny    tcp any 208.213.189.0 0.0.0.255 range 137 139
access-list 100 deny    udp any 208.213.189.0 0.0.0.255 range 137 138
access-list 100 deny    udp any 208.213.189.0 0.0.0.255 eq 2049
access-list 100 permit ip   any any
```

Final Setup for Packet Filters

Once the packet filter has been created and is ready to be put in place, we need to add it to the proper interface. Remember, if we don't explicitly choose the direction our access list will be applied, it defaults to out. The access list is applied to an interface using the **ip access-group** **NUM** command, where *NUM* is the number of the access list you want to apply. Always explicitly append the keywords **in** or **out** to the end of the command.

In Figure 8-8, we add access list 100 to the interface Serial0. The access list filters packets that come in to the serial port.

Figure 8-8   *Access list 101 added inbound on the interface Serial0.*

```
interface Serial0
 ip address 137.39.1.3 255.255.255.248
 ip access-group 100 in
```

Testing Packet Filters

You must also test your packet filters to make sure they are working properly. From inside your network, you should use all possible programs to make sure your users can still get out to the Internet. This is relatively easy, but time consuming. The true challenge comes when you try to test your inbound filters.

Testing inbound filters must happen from the Internet, and for this you will need a way of getting out of your network and coming back in. There are several ways to do this. You can make a dialup connection to the Internet through any ISP (including yours) and content-providing services like America Online and CompuServe, which offer Internet connectivity. You could also make a trip to your local college, mall, library, or Internet café that has an Internet connection. This will let you test, but making corrections will be difficult if you discover a problem. For this, you might be tempted to take a printout of your router configuration file with you. If you do, make sure to obscure any passwords first, just in case someone is leaning over your shoulder. Never leave it anywhere, and do not throw it in the trash. Take it back to the office or home and either burn it or shred it. This is your network security you are carrying around with you. There is no such thing as too much caution.

Another way to test it is to get a UNIX shell account somewhere out on the Internet, usually through an ISP or college. Certain text-based tools will let you test remotely. Chief among these is **telnet**. The **telnet** command allows you to pick which port you connect to on a remote system (by default, port 23). To test the basic packet filter, you could first try to **telnet** back to the router. The router should deny your connection. Next, you could **telnet** to port 80 on your Web server and port 25 on your mail server, and pretend to be a proper client. All you need to do is send the string "GET /" to the Web server and "QUIT" to the mail server to see if they are alive. As you can see in Figure 8-9, the servers respond to the **telnet** command and send back data. This lets you know they are functioning.

■■■

Figure 8-9 *Example of connecting to Web and mail servers using the telnet command.*

```
$ telnet www 80
Trying 204.176.115.69...
Connected to ns3.btg.com.
Escape character is '^]'.
GET /
<!DOCTYPE HTML PUBLIC "-//W3C//DTD HTML 3.2//EN">
<html>
<head>
<TITLE>BTG Opening Page</TITLE>
....

$ telnet mail 25
Trying 199.29.53.67...
Connected to rohan.btg.com.
Escape character is '^]'.
220 rohan.btg.com ESMTP Sendmail 8.8.5/8.7.3; Sat, 11 Jul 1998 18:29:48
-0400 (EDT)
QUIT
221 rohan.btg.com closing connection
Connection closed by foreign host.
```

In order to do a true test of such services as WWW and SMTP, you should also set up dummy hosts with these services and test connecting to them. This will let you know that you have not made a mistake and are allowing all protocols to all servers. You can also test file sharing by contacting someone on the Internet and getting read-only access to NFS- and Microsoft-based servers. You can try to see the NFS server with the UNIX command **showmount -e IP_ADDRESS**. To see a Microsoft Windows machine, you will need to add the hostname and IP address to a file named "lmhosts" (without a file extension) in the C:\WINDOWS directory. After rebooting, right-click on the Network Neighborhood icon and choose Find Computer. Enter the name of the machine you put in the "lmhosts" file. If your packet filters are correct, you should not be able to see either type of system.

Designing Your Own Packet Filters

In order to design and build your own packet filters, you must have a good understanding of what you want to pass through your routers. You also need to be able to know the standard port numbers for the different TCP, UDP, and ICMP services. This information and other hard-core networking standards are located at http://www.iana.org/numbers.html. Of specific interest will be TCP and UDP port numbers listed at http://www.isi.edu/in-notes/iana/assignments/port-numbers and ICMP parameter information at http://www.isi.edu/in-notes/iana/assignments/icmp-parameters.

From there, follow a strict methodology. First, make sure never to experiment on an operational router. Edit your packet filters in a text editor and use the **configure network** command or the cut-and-paste buffer of your GUI to transfer them to the router. Always use the **no access-list NUM** command to clear the old packet filter before entering the new one. Remember that if you lock yourself out of the router before you save the configuration to NVRAM, you should still be able to access the router from the console serial port. If not, you can always reboot it to restore it to the start-up configuration.

Packet Filter for 700 Series Routers

Using dialup routing adds an important new requirement to packet filters—namely, the ability to save money. In many areas, ISDN lines are billed per minute. In the Northeast United States, Bell Atlantic charges as much as two cents per minute per channel for data connections. This makes it possible for your ISDN bill to be several hundred dollars a month if left up for long periods. At those prices, you could probably afford a T1 line. So, how can packet filters keep these costs down?

Unlike IOS routers, the 700 series routers are able to declare packets insignificant to the counters that bring up, and keep up, the ISDN WAN connection. Along with the filter types *block* and *accept,* which allow you to create basic firewalls, you also get two new ones, *demand* and *ignore*. *Block* and *accept* work like *permit* and *deny* in IOS. They allow you to specify which packets are and are not allowed into or out of an interface. *Demand* allows you to declare which packets will affect the WAN threshold and idle time-out counters.

Ignore does the opposite of *demand*. If the WAN connection is up, the router passes packets through without affecting when the WAN connection will come down. If the WAN connection is down, the router drops the packets and will not bring the WAN connection back up.

In IOS, you create packet filters and then assign them to one or more interfaces. The **set ip filter** command creates packet filters directly into individual profiles in the 700 series routers, unlike packet filters in IOS. So if you have several sites you dial into with ISDN, you might want to add packet filters to all of them. In addition, you might want to consider blocking packets from passing between two sites, because it could represent a security risk if you connect one channel to each site simultaneously (see Figure 8-10). A connection like this could allow a clever hacker to enter a corporate network through the home user's ISDN router.

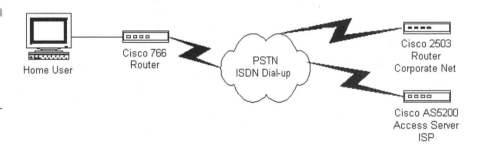

Figure 8-10
A home user connects to the Internet and to a corporate network simultaneously.

This allows for the possible subversion of the corporate network's security through the home user's router.

Packet Filter Syntax

The syntax for the **set ip filter** command is complex. You must specify which type of protocol you want to filter, whether it is an inbound or an outbound filter, and (optionally) the source address, the destination address, or both, and the port you want to filter. Finally, you must choose the action the filter will take. There are seven types of protocols that you can set filters on:

- icmp—Internet Control Message Protocol (ICMP) packets.
- icmpxrd—ICMP packets, except redirect packets.
- icmprd—ICMP redirect packets.
- tcp—Transmission Control Protocol (TCP) packets.
- tcpsyn—TCP SYN (connection establishment) packets.
- tcpxsyn—TCP packets, except SYN.
- udp—User Datagram packets.

These give you a lot of flexibility when setting up filters, but users will most likely stay with the icmp, tcp, and udp types of protocols. Choose inbound or outbound by using the keywords **in** and **out**. Remember that this will affect the meaning of the source and destination addresses. Inbound filters process before the packet enters an interface, and outbound filters process before a packet leaves an interface.

The selection of source and destination can be tricky. You can choose either a source or destination address, or both. Specify a source address with the keyword **source**, and a destination address with the keyword **destination**. Use an equal sign to assign the address to the keyword. In addition to the address itself, you can use the command **/bits** to specify the number of bits in the netmask. This is typically 8 for a class A network, 16 for a class B, 24 for a class C, and 32 for a host. Finally, you can choose the port number on which to filter. The port number follows the IP address and is separated from it by a colon (:).

Port ranges can be set using the plus (+) and minus (–) signs. The plus sign tells the router to filter all ports greater than those listed in your filter. So, **1023+** specifies ports 1024 and up. The minus sign allows you to set a discrete range of ports to filter. For example, **137–139** will make the filter act on packets destined for ports 137, 138, and 139.

The final part of the filter syntax specifies the action: **block**, **accept**, **demand**, or **ignore**. **Block** tells the router not to pass the packet on. **Accept** tells the router to allow the packet to pass unmolested. **Demand** tells the router that the packet is of interest to the threshold queues, which determine when to bring the ISDN line up, and the idle timer, which determines when to bring the ISDN line down. Conversely, the **ignore** command tells the router that the packets are not interesting to the threshold queues or the idle timer, and to drop them if the line is down.

Some examples of packet filters are listed in Figure 8-11.

Figure 8-11 *Sample IP filter commands.*

```
SET IP FILTER   IN   SOURCE=204.176.117.222/32:1023+   BLOCK
SET IP FILTER   IN   SOURCE=204.176.117.222/32:2000-3000   BLOCK
SET IP FILTER TCP IN  SOURCE=198.95.216.125/32:25  ACCEPT
SET IP FILTER TCP OUT DESTINATION=204.176.115.69/32:80 BLOCK
SET IP FILTER TCP OUT  SOURCE=204.176.117.0/24:138   IGNORE
```

The router processes any packets that fail to match a filter in order of precedence, as follows:

- If any one of the filters is set to **accept**, a packet that does not match at least one filter is blocked.
- If all the filters are set to **block**, a packet that does not match any filter is accepted.
- If any one of the filters is set to **demand**, a packet that does not match a **demand** filter is ignored.
- If **ignore** filters are used, a packet that does not match an **ignore** filter is treated as **demand**.

To block packets between specific machines on a specific port, you must specify an IP subprotocol. If you do not, the router will filter on the IP. Just as in IOS, you cannot filter port numbers in the IP protocol, but only on a subprotocol, such as UDP, TCP, or ICMP. Unlike IOS, the 700 series routers will allow you to specify a port number without choosing a subprotocol. This allows you to create a configuration where the port number is ignored, but you can still see it in the configuration. This is confusing to no end if you do it by mistake, so make sure to add your subprotocol type information.

A good example of this problem is listed in Figure 8-12. In the first line, you can see an invalid command that does not use a subprotocol, but has a port number. This command attempted to block WWW traffic between the two IP addresses only, while letting those machines continue to communicate with each other on all other protocols. The second line shows what the command really does—block all traffic between those machines. The third line shows the correct command, with the TCP subprotocol chosen.

■ ■

Figure 8-12 Sample packet filters showing the problems with trying to filter port numbers without choosing an IP subprotocol. (Each command is two lines long in this listing.)

```
SET IP FILTER  OUT  SOURCE=204.176.117.2/32 DESTINATION=204.176.115.69/
32:80  BLOCK
SET IP FILTER  OUT  SOURCE=204.176.117.2/32 DESTINATION=204.176.115.69/
32 BLOCK
SET IP FILTER  TCP OUT  SOURCE=204.176.117.2/32 DESTINA-
TION=204.176.115.69/32:80  BLOCK
```

700 Series User Problems and Concerns

Series 700 users sometimes face different problems than normal WAN users face. Obviously, if they connect to the Internet directly, they need to use packet filters to provide some measure of security for their data. However, if they are part of a corporate network, they might have security provided for them by the corporate firewall. This might remove the need for security packet filters, but there is still the need for money-saving packet filters.

One problem that many 700 series users see is the line's staying up too long. This can be caused by any number of network protocols chattering on the LAN, but two big ones are Microsoft Windows NT browsers and Microsoft Windows 95 shared directories. Microsoft NT announcing it has shares available will chatter incessantly to the local broadcast address. If it is running the License Manager, it will also chat on the network. Windows 95 sends packets to the undirected broadcast address (255.255.255.255) and ports 137, 138, and 139 if it is sharing its resources. If you block these types of packets from passing through your router, you will have problems sharing files or licenses.

Rather than blocking these protocols, a better way to handle this would be **ignore** all packets to these addresses and ports. When using **ignore** or **demand** to filter any packets, you must set the filters on the outbound side of the WAN profile. Figure 8-13 shows the packet filter commands used to help reduce ISDN usage. This will not block these packets, but it will keep them from bringing up or keeping up the ISDN line. You can see that all packets destined for the undirected (255.255.255.255) and local (204.176.117.255) broadcast addresses are being ignored. The router ignores all packets from the local network using the Microsoft file-sharing ports as well.

Figure 8-13 IP filter commands to keep Microsoft from costing you more money.

```
SET IP FILTER TCP OUT   DESTINATION=255.255.255.255/32   IGNORE
SET IP FILTER TCP OUT   DESTINATION=204.176.117.255/32   IGNORE
SET IP FILTER TCP OUT   SOURCE=204.176.117.0/24:137-139  IGNORE
SET IP FILTER UDP OUT   SOURCE=204.176.117.0/24:137-138  IGNORE
```

The packet filter designs for mostly open and mostly closed scenarios detailed earlier in this section are also valid for the 700 series routers. Only the implementation will change, because of the different configuration syntax. First, we will set up a packet filter inbound on the WAN profile for protection from the Internet. Only inbound Internet traffic will have permission to access the Web server. The SOHO/RO users will have access to anywhere on the Internet. We will also protect against IP address spoofing.

In addition, we will make sure to block all Telnet connections into the network, because we offer no public Telnet services. We will also block all incoming file-sharing protocols, such as those used by Microsoft for peer-to-peer networking, and SUN Microsystems NFS (Network File System). The local network address is 208.213.189.0, and the local Web server's IP address is 208.213.189.55. The mostly open packet filter is shown in Figure 8-14, while the mostly closed packet filter is shown in Figure 8-15.

Figure 8-14 In a mostly open filter, a final accept allows anything that is not specifically denied.

```
SET IP FILTER IN SOURCE=208.213.189.0/24 BLOCK
SET IP FILTER TCP IN DESTINATION=208.213.189.55/32:80 ACCEPT
SET IP FILTER TCP IN DESTINATION=208.213.189.0/24:80 BLOCK
SET IP FILTER TCP IN DESTINATION=208.213.189.0/24:23 BLOCK
SET IP FILTER TCP IN DESTINATION =208.213.189.0/24:137-139 BLOCK
SET IP FILTER UDP IN DESTINATION =208.213.189.0/24:137-138 BLOCK
SET IP FILTER UDP IN DESTINATION =208.213.189.0/24:2049 BLOCK
SET IP FILTER IN SOURCE=0.0.0.0/0 ACCEPT
```

Figure 8-15 In a mostly closed filter, a final block denies anything that is not specifically allowed.

```
SET IP FILTER IN SOURCE=208.213.189.0/24 BLOCK
SET IP FILTER TCP IN DESTINATION=208.213.189.55/32:80 ACCEPT
SET IP FILTER IN SOURCE=0.0.0.0/0 BLOCK
```

Using a Cisco Router as a DHCP Server

DHCP is a client-server protocol that allows devices on an IP network to request configuration information from a DHCP server. Ordinarily, DHCP allocates IP addresses from a central pool on an as-needed basis. DHCP is useful for assigning IP addresses to hosts that are connected to the network temporarily, or for sharing a limited pool of IP addresses among a group of hosts that do not need permanent IP addresses. It can also remove the burden of IP address management for machines that do not need fixed IP addresses.

DHCP increases automation and lessens network administration problems by eliminating the need for the manual configuration of individual computers, printers, and shared file systems. It also prevents the simultaneous use of the same IP address by two clients and allows for configuration from a central site.

A Cisco 700 series router acting as a DHCP server can provide the following information to the DHCP client machines (usually Microsoft Windows 95):

- IP address (example: 199.5.37.248)
- Internet domain name (example: gryphon.com)
- The IP addresses of the primary and secondary Internet Domain Name Service (DNS) servers
- The IP addresses of the primary and secondary IP gateways (i.e., the default route for the clients, usually the IP address of the router's LAN interface)
- NetBIOS Scope (also known as TCP/IP Scope)
- IP Netmask (example: 255.255.255.0)
- The IP addresses of the primary and secondary WINS (Windows Internet Name Service) servers

Limitations

The information configurable in the 700 series DHCP server is the minimum necessary to get a Windows 95 client automatically configured on the network. If you need to send more information to the client machines, you will need to get a more fully functional DHCP server. A DHCP server will run on almost any server operating system. SCO UnixWare and Open

Server, Microsoft NT, Linux, and SUN Solaris all support DHCP servers.

The DHCP server in the 700 series routers is limited to managing a maximum of 254 IP addresses. If your subnet has less than 254 addresses, you'll have no problem. If your subnet has more than 254 addresses, this implementation of DHCP will only serve 254 of them and you do have a problem. If you need to serve more than 254 addresses, you'll need to look to a more fully featured DHCP server.

DHCP is only available on the 760 and 700 series routers. The DHCP code does not exist in the operating system for the older 750 series routers. DHCP is not available for IOS routers. A similar protocol to automatically configure clients dialing into a modem or ISDN line does exist for IOS, but it only supports PPP dial-in clients, not LAN clients. If you need DHCP services for a LAN and have only an IOS-based router, you will not be able to get them from your router.

Configuring DHCP

Configuring the DHCP server on the 700 series routers is actually quite easy. Most of the information used to configure it will already exist in your client PCs. You simply need to extract it from one PC and then set the machine for automatic configuration. The first step is to turn on the DHCP server with the **set dhcp server** command. The next step is to decide on the range of addresses that DHCP will manage. The DHCP server will automatically assign these addresses to clients on the network, and the network administrator will no longer need to manage them. You must pick a starting address, then assign the total number of addresses from that starting point that DHCP will control. If you used an IP address of 204.176.189.100 and a total number of 110, then DHCP will control all IP addresses in the range between 204.176.189.100 and 204.176.189.209. Remember that you count address 204.176.189.100 as the first address, so you are really adding 109 to 100 to get the last IP address controlled by the server.

You should make sure that any machines on the network are not using IP addresses in your chosen range. If they are, you will eventually have multiple machines with the same IP addresses on your network. This will cause problems for the end users, and cause problems in the end for you, too. So, make sure no IP addresses in your range are in use, or pay the price later.

The chosen IP addresses must be part of the same IP network as the router's LAN interface. If they are not, the PCs will never be able to talk to the router after getting an IP address. This is because the PC will be on a different logical network than the router, and therefore unable to see it.

Once you've decided on the range of addresses the DHCP server will control, use the **set dhcp address** command to configure it into the router. From this point on, you've turned over control for these IP addresses to the router's DHCP server. Figure 8-16 shows an example of the command used to configure the DHCP range of addresses on the router.

Figure 8-16 Commands showing the DHCP server is on, and the addresses it controls are 204.176.189.100 through 204.176.189.209.

```
SET DHCP SERVER
SET DHCP ADDRESS 204.176.189.100 110
```

Next, you need to complete the IP address setup by telling the clients their netmask and default gateway. Configure the netmask with the **set dhcp netmask** command. The default gateway is set with the **set dhcp gateway primary** command. Typically, the netmask will be the same as that on the LAN interface of the router. The primary gateway is almost always the IP address of the LAN interface itself. If you have more than one router on the network, you might want to set a secondary default gateway, but this is usually not the case. Examples of these commands can be seen in Figure 8-17.

Figure 8-17 The commands show the netmask and primary gateway configurations for DHCP.

```
SET DHCP NETMASK 255.255.255.0
SET DHCP GATEWAY PRIMARY 204.176.189.1
```

The final commands deal with hostname resolution. Both standard Internet DNS and Microsoft WINS host resolution are supported. You must know the IP addresses of both kinds of servers, if you want to configure them. If used, DNS servers will reside at a corporate site or ISP. WINS servers will always be part of your local or corporate network. In addition to this, you will need to know the Internet domain of your hosts. (If you are the network administrator, you really should know this.) However, if you do not, you can usually find it in the DNS Configuration tab of the TCP/IP properties for a LAN adapter, under Network Neighborhood in Microsoft Windows (see Figure 8-18).

Figure 8-18
The DNS Configuration for Microsoft Windows. The IP addresses for primary and secondary DNS server are listed along with the domain name.

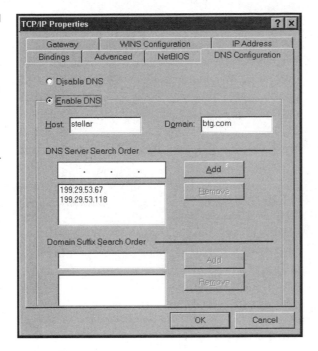

If you are not connected to the Internet and are not using DNS, you might not have an Internet domain; therefore, you will not need to fill in the DNS server or the domain name information. If this is the case, you are probably using WINS, so you will need to add that information instead. Locate it in the WINS Configuration tab of the TCP/IP properties for a LAN adapter, under Network Neighborhood in Microsoft Windows (see Figure 8-19).

Figure 8-19
The WINS configuration information from a Windows PC.

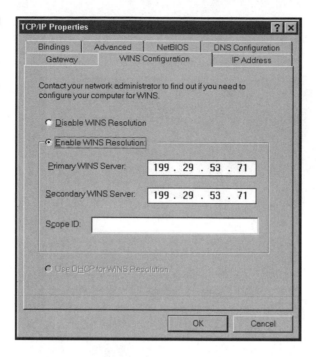

Once you determine this information, you can configure it into the router. Add the DHCP domain with the **set dhcp domain** command. Add the DNS server IP addresses with the **set dhcp dns** command. Finally, add the WINS server IP addresses with the **set dhcp wins** command. You might have noticed that the WINS configuration screen in Figure 8-19 used the same IP address for both the primary and secondary WINS servers. If you only have one WINS server, you might want to use it for both primary and secondary server IDs. Because of the problems involved with remote networks, a WINS server sometimes cannot respond to a client before it times out. By using the WINS server as both primary and secondary server IDs, you double your chances of getting correct information from the server. These configuration commands are shown in Figure 8-20.

Figure 8-20 Final commands to configure DHCP information on router. Both DNS and WINS servers are added along with the Internet domain.

```
SET DHCP DNS PRIMARY 199.29.53.67
SET DHCP DNS SECONDARY 199.29.53.118
SET DHCP DOMAIN btg.com
SET DHCP WINS PRIMARY 199.29.53.71
SET DHCP WINS SECONDARY 199.29.53.71
```

Microsoft Windows Client Configuration

Configuring a Microsoft Windows client to use DHCP is very simple. To do so, remove all information in the WINS and DNS configuration tabs, as well as the default gateway for the LAN adapter. Next, choose "Obtain an IP address automatically" in the IP Address tab (see Figure 8-21). The next time the system reboots, it will ask the DHCP server for an IP address, and all the configuration information you have given the router will be sent to the PC. You can check the accuracy of this information using the **winipcfg** command under Windows 95 (see Figure 8-22) or the **ipconfig / all** command under Windows NT.

Figure 8-21

Configuring a client to use DHCP in Windows.

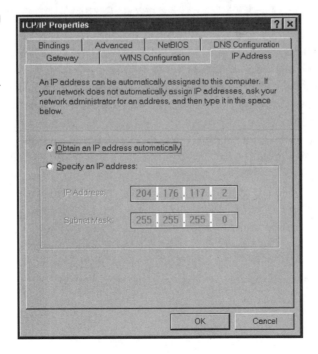

Figure 8-22
The winipcfg window shows the client has received all the information programmed into the router's DHCP server.

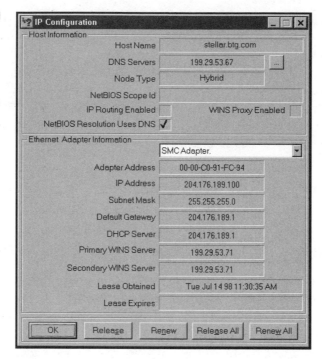

Dial-up Address Pooling in IOS

Address pooling is the PPP equivalent of DHCP in IOS and is also simple to configure. Whether you are on an access server or lower-end routers like a Cisco 2503, address pooling only works on ISDN and low-speed serial line connections. ISDN connections can be both BRI and PRI. Low-speed serial connections can be the modems in access servers or terminal and modem lines on all routers. You can configure the auxiliary port on every IOS router to use a dial-in modem, but certain routers act as small access servers and have many low-speed serial connections available.

For the purposes of this section, we will assume that you have already set up the serial or ISDN lines for dial-in, and are currently using static IP addresses. If your router only has a single dial-in port this is okay, but in the case of multiple ports, routing to dial-in sites becomes extremely difficult. By using address pooling, you can conserve IP address space and make your dial-in configurations easier to maintain.

Limitations

Having the router assign IP addresses to dial-in clients might be easy, but it is limited. Unlike DHCP, which had seven pieces of information to configure remote clients, address pooling only has three. These are the IP address, DNS server IP addresses, and WINS server IP addresses. The client must itself provide information, such as the Internet domain name.

Configuration

Just as with DHCP, you must start by picking a range of addresses for the router to distribute. Set aside one IP address for each low-speed serial port and ISDN B channel on which users will be dialing in. Access servers that use T1s for modems have no B channels, only 24 modem lines per T1. Access servers that use ISDN PRI service will have at least one less dial-in connection per PRI than the total number of channels in their underlying leased line (23 for T1 and 30 for E1). Purely serial access server routers, such as the Cisco 2509, will need one IP address per modem connected to the router.

The IP addresses that you choose should have the same network number as the router's Ethernet interface. If the router has more than one Ethernet address, pick the network to which you want the dial-in users to belong. As with DHCP, these addresses must not be in use anywhere else, or you will get an IP address conflict. An IP address conflict occurs when more than one machine has the same IP address. This confuses the other hosts on the network, because they become unable to distinguish which machine they should talk to. It will also cause much grief for the network administrator, who will have to troubleshoot the problem.

Once you have determined the IP address range, you configure it into the router using the **ip local pool** command. The first option to this command is the name of the address pool. This is an arbitrary name that is used to link asynchronous and ISDN interfaces to the address pool so that they can use its addresses. You can use almost any name, but you should keep it short and concise. If you have only one pool on the router, you could use the name **mypool** for simplicity. The next two options for the command specify the low and high addresses in the pool.

An example of this is shown in Figure 8-23. Here, an access server with 48 modems receives calls through ISDN PRI T1s. Because one channel is lost per PRI for signaling, a maximum of 46 calls are supported, so only 46 IP addresses are needed. Because the low and high numbers are included in the pool, we take the low number and add 45 to it to get the high number.

Figure 8-23 The local IP address pool is defined in global configuration mode.

```
ip local pool default 192.129.3.181 192.129.3.226
```

Next, link this pool into all the Async, Group-Async, and Dialer interfaces on the router that will use it. This is done with the **peer default ip address pool** command, which takes the pool name as its only option. In Figure 8-24, we see this command using the pool name **mypool**.

Figure 8-24 The local pool is linked to all the Dialer, Async, and Group-Async interfaces on the router. This allows them to assign addresses from the pool.

```
interface Group-Async 1
 peer default ip address pool mypool
interface Async 1
 peer default ip address pool mypool
interface Dialer 1
 peer default ip address pool mypool
```

Finally, you can send the IP addresses of the Internet DNS servers and the WINS servers to the dial-in clients using the **async-bootp** command in global configuration mode. This command takes the option **dns-server** to send the primary and secondary DNS server IP addresses and the **nbns-server** option for the primary and secondary WINS servers. As with DHCP above, we will set the primary and secondary WINS server to the same IP address. An example of this is shown in Figure 8-25.

Figure 8-25 The WINS and DNS server addresses are set with the async-bootp command.

```
async-bootp nbns-server 199.29.53.71 199.29.53.71
async-bootp dns-server 199.29.53.67 199.29.53.118
```

Configuring Channelized T1/E1 Cards

Channelized line cards give you the ability to isolate and control each channel of a high-speed serial line (T1 or E1) individually. They do this by providing multiple data paths from the serial line to the interface processor. All of these cards have a built-in DSU, and some also have a built-in

CSU. Those that have only a built-in DSU must have an external CSU to interface between the card and the telco jack (e.g., NP-CT1 and NP-CE1 for Cisco 4000 series). Those that have both a DSU and a CSU built in allow you to plug the telco jack right into the router (e.g., T1 or E1 line card for Cisco AS5200). It's important to note that the existence of a built-in CSU/DSU in a router does *not* allow you to control multiple channels independently.

Routers like the Cisco 2524 can be equipped with a built-in T1 CSU/DSU, but this only provides a single data path to the interface. This means you have the flexibility to select the number of channels to use (1-24), and the speed to use them at (56Kbps or 64Kbps), but only to make one full or fractional data connection. For example, if you purchased a 512Kbps fractional T1 leased line, you would configure the router to use eight 64Kbps channels. The other 16 channels would not be useable by this router.

The channelized line cards come in two specific flavors: T1 or E1. For the rest of this section, we will refer to them as T1 cards, but E1 cards perform the same way. Both varieties will handle a plain T1 or E1, or the same lines with ISDN PRI signaling encoded on them. The ISDN implementation always sacrifices one channel for signaling.

Using a Channelized Card

All channelized cards use the *controller* heading for configuration and management. This is similar to the *interface* heading used for high-speed serial, Ethernet, and Fast Ethernet ports. Configure and maintain the internal DSU under this heading. All *controller* sections of the router configuration will tell you what kind of channelized line card is detected (for example, *controller T1 0*). Multiple cards will be shown as separate *controller* lines (i.e., *controller T1 1, controller T1 2*, and so on). The number of channelized cards supported depends on the type of router you have.

The first thing to do when setting up a channelized card is to configure the framing and the line code. These must match those configured by the telco. If you do not know them, ask your telco installation engineer what they are. Next, you must select a clock source. You only need one primary source per router; all others will be secondary. You must also use the **no shutdown** command to activate the T1 controller. Once you've done this, you should be able to establish basic connectivity with the telco, and they should be able to test the line. A configuration section like this is shown in Figure 8-26.

Figure 8-26 Configuring a controller interface to talk to the telco.

```
as5200#conf t
Enter configuration commands, one per line.  End with CNTL/Z.
as5200(config)#controller t1 0
as5200(config-controller)#no shutdown
as5200(config-controller)#framing esf
as5200(config-controller)#linecode b8zs
as5200(config-controller)#clock source line primary
as5200(config-controller)#^Z
as5200# wr
```

There are three basic ways to configure a channelized card in IOS. The first is a WAN-only T1, which handles multiple fractional T1 connections over a single line. The second is an ISDN PRI, which is useful for ISDN B channel dialup connections or modem connections if there are modems in the router. Finally, there is the T1 line, which routes voice calls to modems.

Assigning Time Slots for Channelized WAN Connections

Use the keyword **channel-group** to create multiple virtual interfaces for WAN-only channelized connections. Each virtual interface uses a unique and contiguous set of T1 channels or time slots for its connection. Despite the appearance of multiplicity, a T1 line is a single line supplied by a single provider (even if only a few channels are in use); all connections on that T1 must come from that provider.

Take the scenario where we have two 384Kbps fractional T1 lines, a 64Kbps line, and a 56Kbps line coming over a single piece of cable. The two 384Kbps lines use six channels each. The 56Kbps and 64Kbps lines each use only one channel. Because we are designing a single line to hold four connections, we can assign each set of channels as we desire, and the telco will configure the line to our specifications. We want to leave room for the 384Kbps connections to grow, especially if the sites they connect to need more bandwidth. Because of this, we will not put the end of one line up against the beginning of the other. Instead, we will leave six unused channels in between. Not wanting to do the same with the connection in the middle, we will put the single channel connections up against the last channels in the T1. The remote side of these connections are fixed and cannot expand, so we have no fears about penning them in.

If we wanted to grow a 384Kbps connection in the future, we would call the telco and arrange for more channels. Next, when they were ready to give us a new larger (or smaller) pipe, we would connect to the remote router and change the number of time slots in its "channel-group" (if it had an internal CSU/DSU). If it used an external CSU/DSU, we would talk the local site administrator through changing the number of time slots assigned to it. Next, we would make the changes in the local router's time slots and have the telco make their changes. If everyone does the same thing, the line should only be down for a short time while the number of channels changes.

Getting back to our example, the first connection uses time slots one through six. The next six are left empty, and time slots 13 through 18 belong to the second connection. The last two connections use time slots 23 and 24. To set these up, we would assign each a "channel-group" number, typically zero through three. See Figure 8-27 to see how the commands would look in the router configuration. Note that the option **speed 64** denotes the use of 64Kbps channels, while its absence denotes the use of 56Kbps channels.

Figure 8-27 The channel group setups for 2 fractional T1 connections and a 56Kbps and 64Kbps leased line.

```
controller T1 0
 framing esf
 linecode b8zs
 clock source line primary
 channel-group 0 timeslots 1-6 speed 64
 channel-group 1 timeslots 13-18 speed 64
 channel-group 2 timeslots 23 speed 64
 channel-group 3 timeslots 24
```

Once you create the channel groups, you'll need to create the interfaces for each. These commands will take the form **interface Serial CTLR:CG**, where *CTRL* is the controller number and *CG* is the channel-group number. In our example, we need to create the interfaces Serial0:0, Serial0:1, Serial0:2, and Serial0:3. Each will get its own description and IP address.

We will also add a bandwidth statement. This has no bearing on how much data passes through the line, but is for reporting statistics on line usage. These interfaces do not exist before we enter them into the global configuration. The act of entering them into the configuration file creates them for our use. These interfaces are initially in a *shutdown* state by default. Before you use them you must enter the **no shutdown** command for each interface. See Figure 8-28 for the layout of the configuration file.

Figure 8-28 *The interface configuration information for the channel groups.*

```
interface Serial0:0
 description 384 Kbps leased line to Norfolk
 ip address 209.135.17.5 255.255.255.252
 bandwidth 384
interface Serial0:1
 description 384 Kbps leased line to Pentagon
 ip address 209.135.17.9 255.255.255.252
 bandwidth 384
interface Serial0:2
 description 64 Kbps leased line to Research Triangle
 ip address 209.135.17.13 255.255.255.252
 bandwidth 64
interface Serial0:3
 description 56 Kbps leased line to Hoboken, NJ
 ip address 209.135.17.17 255.255.255.252
 bandwidth 56
```

Once this is complete, all lines should come up and be operational (assuming the telco has done their part and the remote router and CSU/DSU have been configured). It's important to note that all the remote sites must have their own leased lines, which will be provided by the same telco that is joining them together into one for you. The main reason for doing something like this is to save money.

Although the channelized T1 card costs more than a quad serial board, this is a one-time expense and, as such, is trivial compared to the continuing cost of having four local loops (2 T1, a 64Kbps, and a 56Kbps) brought into your site by a telco provider. These would incur monthly charges totaling a minimum of $1,000. If you combine them into one local loop, the long distance charges stay the same, but the local loop costs drop to around $330 a month. At a savings of $670 a month, the channelized T1 card quickly pays for itself. Also factored into the savings are the one-time charges for four external CSU/DSUs versus a single external CSU. Depending on the level of features and options you prefer to buy, this might make up the cost between the two Cisco cards by itself.

Assigning Time Slots for PRI Connections

Use the **pri-group** keyword to create multiple virtual interfaces for handling dial-in B channel connections for PRI connections. Each PRI usually uses all channels in a T1, although you can order them with fewer channels. The revision of IOS reviewed in this book (11.2) supports only a single ISDN provider. Although you can have multiple PRIs terminating in the same router, under IOS 11.2 they must all come from a single telco provider's ISDN switch.

The first step in setting up the PRI is to assign time slots to the PRI group. Next, create the D channel interface to establish proper ISDN signaling with the telco. To do this, create the interface Serial CTLR:23, where *CTLR* is the number of the T1 controller. It's possible to order multiple PRIs as a group from the telco. In this case, you do not need all the D channels that come with them by default, but you should make sure to have at least two D channels for your PRI groups. This allows you to maintain connectivity with the telco if you lose the PRI with the D channel. If you were purchasing four PRIs for connection to a Cisco AS5300, you could order two with D channels and two without. This would give you two extra B channels on which to receive ISDN or modem dial-in connections.

The D channel interface (Serial0:23) is shown in Figure 8-29. The IP address is usually set to the unnumbered address of the Ethernet port. PPP encapsulation is used here because it is the most universally accepted dialup IP protocol. If you have modems in the router, such as in an AS5200 access server, the command **isdn incoming-voice modem** will send all voice calls to them. If there are no modems, this command is unnecessary and you should order the PRI line without voice capabilities. The exception to this rule depends on how the local telco charges for 56Kbps voice calls.

If the local telco treats 56Kbps ISDN voice calls as a flat rate, you might want to use **voice spoofing** to lower your phone charges. Voice spoofing is an ISDN call placed as 56Kbps voice by a router. When the call is initiated, the telco counts it as a voice call, and in some areas the telco might bill you at voice rates for the entire connection (as little as 10¢ per call, flat rate). Once the voice connection completes, the two routers can still communicate with each other and essentially convert the call to 56Kbps data. This lowers your bandwidth a little, but could potentially lower your phone bill a lot.

Dial-in users receive IP addresses through address pooling. In this case, they get IP addresses out of the pool named **mypool**. The **dialer rotary-group 1** command tells the router that all 23 B channels handled by this D channel interface are part of the group interface Dialer 1. The **dialer-group 1** command tells the router that **dialer-list 1** (defined further in the global configuration) lists all packets considered interesting enough to make the router dial out to a site. In this case, all IP packets are considered interesting. Finally, STAC compression is enabled for all B channel connections.

Figure 8-29 The configuration information for a PRI connected to a router.

```
controller T1 0
 framing esf
 clock source line primary
 linecode b8zs
 pri-group timeslots 1-24
interface Serial0:23
 ip unnumbered Ethernet0
 encapsulation ppp
 isdn incoming-voice modem
 peer default ip address pool mypool
 dialer rotary-group 1
 dialer-group 1
 compress stac
!
dialer-list 1 protocol ip permit
```

While the D channel interface (Serial0:23) handles the physical layer of the PRI, interface Dialer 1 handles the B channels as synchronous interfaces. It uses the same unnumbered IP address, encapsulation, and address pool as the D channel interface. The command **dialer in-band** tells the router that DDR (Dial-on-Demand Routing) is configured for dial-in calls only. Dial-out DDR requires many different configurations. The **dialer idle-timeout 600** sets the idle time-out to 600 seconds. If this interface is idle for ten minutes, the router will hang up on it. The **dialer-group 1** command tells the router that the dialer-list command in Figure 8-30 determines what packets will reset the idle timer. This command can save you money if dial-in users walk away from their machines while connected, especially if the company pays for the dial-in line or has a toll-free (800 or 888) number.

Figure 8-30 also turns on STAC compression which helps increase throughput. The PPP protocol uses PAP and then CHAP for authentication. Microsoft Windows clients use PAP; routers and UNIX systems can use either PAP or CHAP. Finally, multilink PPP negotiation is allowed.

Figure 8-30 *The configuration information for the B channels of the PRI.*

```
interface Dialer1
 ip unnumbered Ethernet0
 encapsulation ppp
 peer default ip address pool mypool
 dialer in-band
 dialer idle-timeout 600
 dialer-group 1
 compress stac
 ppp authentication pap chap
 ppp multilink
```

Assigning Time Slots for T1 Modems

There's not much difference between setting up T1 controllers for WAN connections and for modems, except that the T1 you are connecting to will be a voice T1 and all calls will be routed to the modems. Slightly different signaling is used to support a voice T1, and the keyword **cas-group** is used to tell the router to send all calls to the modems. You also need to select the T1 voice call signaling method. This will be **e&m-fgb** for modem pooling. You must also specify the type of dialing to use. Typically, this is DTMF (Dual Tone Multi-Frequency), although you can also choose to use DNIS (Dialed Number Identification Service).

With DNIS configured as part of the **cas-group** command, the system collects DNIS digits for incoming calls, which it then redirects to specific modem pools. You must be running MICA modems in the system and have at least 10 percent of your total modems in the default modem pool. There must be free modems in the default pool to detect the incoming called number (or DNIS) before handing the call off to the appropriate modem in the pool. Therefore, two modems are necessary to handle each incoming call.

WARNING

Make sure your switch provides in-band address information for incoming analog calls before you enable this feature. These options can be seen in Figure 8-31.

Figure 8-31 *Controller configuration for a voice T1 to support modems on an access server.*

```
controller T1 0
 framing sf
 clock source line primary
 linecode ami
 cas-group 1 timeslots 1-24 e&m-fgb dtmf dnis
```

Once you've configured DNIS, you will have the physical interfaces for 24 modems available. You should consolidate these into one or more "Group-Async" interfaces for ease of configuration. See the next section for setting up modems.

Configuring Modems

To set up modems, you need to configure both their physical and data layer interfaces. It makes no difference if they are built into an access server or connected to a serial port. Some access servers have many serial ports, but almost every router has an auxiliary port to which you can attach a modem. The physical interfaces are set up using the **line X Y** command, where *X* is the first serial line or built-in modem, and *Y* is the last. You will need to set **login local,** which will read individual user names and passwords set with the **username** command. The **modem dial-in** command sets the modem to dial-in only mode. The **modem inout** command sets the modem for dial-in and dial-out. (There is no command to set the modem to dial-out only.) The command **autocommand ppp** tells the modem to go into PPP mode as soon as a modem connection is established. Finally, **transport input all** tells the router to use all protocols when a connection is made. These commands can be seen in Figure 8-32.

Figure 8-32 *The configuration information for modem lines.*

```
line 1 48
 login local
 modem Dialin
 autocommand ppp
 transport input all
```

Grouping ports together into "Group-Async" interfaces helps make the data interface layer setup easier. Otherwise, you would have to enter the same information repeatedly for all modems configured alike. It is in the "Group-Async" interface that you will assign IP addresses to modem users, enable compression, and list which asynchronous ports belong to the group interface.

In Figure 8-33, we begin **interface Group-Async1** by choosing to use the unnumbered IP address of the Ethernet port. Next, we select passive TCP header compression. This allows incoming systems to request Van Jacobson header compression, but the router will not block systems that do not support it. To select header compression under Windows 95, open the My Computer icon, and then pick Dialup Networking. Right-click on the dialup connection you want to edit and select Properties, then go to the Server Types tab and select TCP/IP Settings. You should see a window just like Figure 8-34. Make sure that Use IP header compression is selected.

The selected encapsulation mode is PPP. The command **async mode dedicated** tells the router to put the modem connection directly into PPP mode when the connection is made. This mode stops normal text-based logins and forces all users to use PPP. To return to a configuration that will support text logins, use the command **async mode interactive**. Next, define the ip address pool to use **mypool**. Then, set the compression algorithm to STAC. Next, set the PPP authentication to PAP first and then CHAP. Finally, add modems number one through 48 to this "Group-Async" interface by using the **group-range** command.

Figure 8-33 The data layer configuration information for modem lines.

```
interface Group-Async1
 ip unnumbered Ethernet0
 ip tcp header-compression passive
 encapsulation ppp
 async mode dedicated
 peer default ip address pool mypool
 compress stac
 ppp authentication pap chap
 group-range 1 48
```

Figure 8-34
The TCP/IP settings box in Windows 95, where you can turn on header compression.

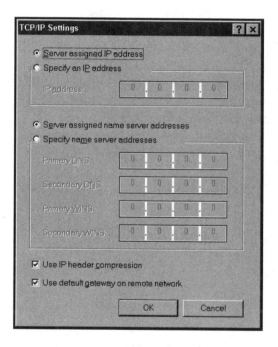

Configuring IPX Routing

IPX is the protocol used by Novell NetWare servers and clients. If you are running NetWare and you want to route IPX over LAN, WAN, and dialup lines, you need to assign an IPX network number to each individual segment of the network. IPX network numbers are arbitrary hexadecimal numbers up to eight characters long. All NetWare servers on a segment must have the same network number, as must all routers. Clients, whether

PCs or printers, automatically learn their IPX network number from a server or a router on their network segment. If you change an IPX network number on a LAN segment, you must ensure that all servers also change network numbers and all clients reboot.

You must make sure that all segments of the network have duplicate IPX network numbers. The best way to do this is to draw a diagram of your network and assign IPX network numbers to each router interface. All router interfaces on the same network share the same IPX network number. A sample diagram is shown in Figure 8-35. As you can see, all ISDN and modem dial-in users share the same IPX network number **ABC123**. The LAN side of the access server, the router connection to LAN 2, and all the clients off that hub will be on IPX number **DEF456**. LAN segment 1 off the router's second Ethernet port uses IPX number 10101010. The leased-line connection between routers uses IPX number B1, and the Ethernet on the remote site is all on IPX network DEF623.

Figure 8-35

Each network segment, LAN, WAN, and dial-in, gets its own IPX network number.

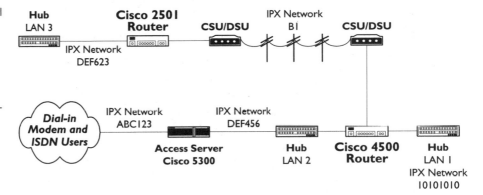

Configuring IPX Routing in IOS

The first step in configuring IPX routing in IOS is to turn it on. This is done by entering the **ipx routing** command into the global configuration. After entering the command, you will notice that it acquires another keyword. This is the router's MAC (Media Access Layer) address, sometimes called the Ethernet address. This is shown in Figure 8-36.

Figure 8-36 IPX routing is turned on globally in the router with the ipx routing command.

```
wan4500#conf t
Enter configuration commands, one per line.  End with CNTL/Z.
wan4500(config)#ipx routing
wan4500(config)#^Z
wan4500#wr
Building configuration...
[OK]
wan4500#show config
Using 2686 out of 129016 bytes
!
version 11.2
...
ipx routing 0060.471f.51c1
...

wan4500#
```

Once you've turned on IPX routing, you can start adding IPX network numbers to the interfaces. LAN and WAN interfaces are easy. Enter the configuration for that interface and add the IPX network number with the **ipx network** command. Figure 8-37 shows the Cisco 4500 router from Figure 8-34 being set up with the proper IPX network numbers. That is all it takes to route IPX on LAN and WAN interfaces.

Figure 8-37 Set IPX network numbers, one per interface.

```
wan4500#conf t
Enter configuration commands, one per line.  End with CNTL/Z.
wan4500(config)#int e0
wan4500(config-if)#ipx network 10101010
wan4500(config-if)#interface e1
wan4500(config-if)#ipx network def456
wan4500(config-if)#int s0
wan4500(config-if)#ipx network b1
wan4500(config-if)#^Z
wan4500#wr
Building configuration...
[OK]
wan4500#
```

Configuring IPX Routing for Dial-in Users

IPX routing for dial-in users is only slightly more complicated. Because each remote machine is, in effect, its own WAN segment, you might think you have to assign each one its own IPX network number. This would be a bear to configure and maintain, as well as a waste of a large amount of IPX network numbers. Be glad that Cisco has tamed the bear for you.

To set up IPX networking on an access server, you must first activate IPX routing and then configure the Ethernet port to match the IPX network number of all other routers and servers on that LAN segment. Next, create a new interface called "Loopback0". This interface will not have an IP address, but it will contain the IPX network number for all dial-in connections. Finally, go to the "Group-Async" and "Dialer" interfaces and add the command **ipx ppp-client Loopback0**. This will bind the IPX network number in interface "Loopback0" to all dial-in connections. This is shown in Figure 8-38.

Figure 8-38 IPX networking for dial-in users adds one network number to the "loopback0" interface and pointers to "loopback0" from the "Group-Async" and "Dialer" interfaces.

```
wan4500#conf t
Enter configuration commands, one per line.   End with CNTL/Z.
wan4500(config)#int e0
wan4500(config-if)#ipx network def456
wan4500(config-if)#interface Loopback0
wan4500(config-if)#no ip address
wan4500(config-if)#ipx network abc123
wan4500(config-if)#interface Group-Async1
wan4500(config-if)#ipx ppp-client Loopback0
wan4500(config-if)#interface Dialer1
wan4500(config-if)#ipx ppp-client Loopback0
wan4500(config-if)#^Z
wan4500#wr
Building configuration...
[OK]
wan4500#
```

Configuring IPX for Cisco 700 Series Routers

Configuring IPX routing for 700 series routers is a bit more complex. You must know how IPX networking is set up, and you must configure IPX routing for both the LAN and WAN profiles. The first step is to turn IPX routing on. This is done with the **set ipx routing on** command. Next, you need to set the IPX network number with the **set ipx network NNN** command, where *NNN* is the IPX network number. Next, you must decide whether to use IPX spoofing.

IPX spoofing leads NetWare servers to believe that a session is still active, even though the ISDN connection is down. It does this by having the router respond to a server's Watchdog requests on behalf of a remote client. If there is a NetWare server on your end, you might want to turn it on. Benefits of IPX spoofing include:

- Local acknowledgment of queries
- No link responses
- Efficient use of the link
- Minimal operator intervention

When the number of IPX or SPX sessions is limited, this can cause connectivity problems by denying logins to legitimate users, so be careful about using it. The default command for IPX spoofing is **set ipx spoofing off**. If you want to activate it, replace the keyword **off** with the number of minutes (between 1 and 32,000) you want to spoof an idle connection.

To specify the forwarding of NetBIOS (Type 20) packets to a profile, use the **set ipx netbios accept** command. If you are using a NetBIOS protocol (such as Windows for Workgroups over IPX), you must use this to pass the packets through the router. If you are not using this, you can replace the keyword **accept** with **block**.

The dynamic routing protocol for IPX is IPX RIP. If there is only one router on the network, there is no need to enable IPX RIP in your LAN profile. This is done with the **set ipx rip update off** and **set ipx rip receive off** commands. If you want to pass IPX routing information, replace the keyword **off** with the keyword **periodic** in the **update** command and **on** in the **receive** command.

Finally, you need to set the IPX frame type information. This will be located on your IPX servers and clients. If you do not know it, try stepping through all four choices until it works, but you will never know if other problems are causing IPX routing failures if you do. Your choices for frames are SNAP, 802.2, 802.3, and Ethernet_II. The command to set the frame type is **set ipx framing TYPE**. All these commands are listed in Figure 8-39.

Figure 8-39 IPX configuration settings for the LAN profile.

```
SET USER LAN
SET IPX ROUTING ON
SET IPX NETWORK  15D0004
SET IPX SPOOFING OFF
SET IPX NETBIOS ACCEPT
SET IPX RIP UPDATE OFF
SET IPX RIP RECEIVE OFF
SET IPX FRAMING 802.3
```

The WAN profile configuration for IPX over the ISDN line is essentially the same as for the LAN profile. The basic difference is the IPX framing type. For router-to-router connections over ISDN, set the IPX frame type to **none**. This is shown in Figure 8-40.

Figure 8-40 IPX configuration settings for a WAN profile.

```
SET USER WAN4500
SET IPX ROUTING ON
SET IPX NETWORK  3B61A8
SET IPX SPOOFING OFF
SET IPX NETBIOS ACCEPT
SET IPX RIP UPDATE OFF
SET IPX RIP RECEIVE OFF
SET IPX FRAMING NONE
```

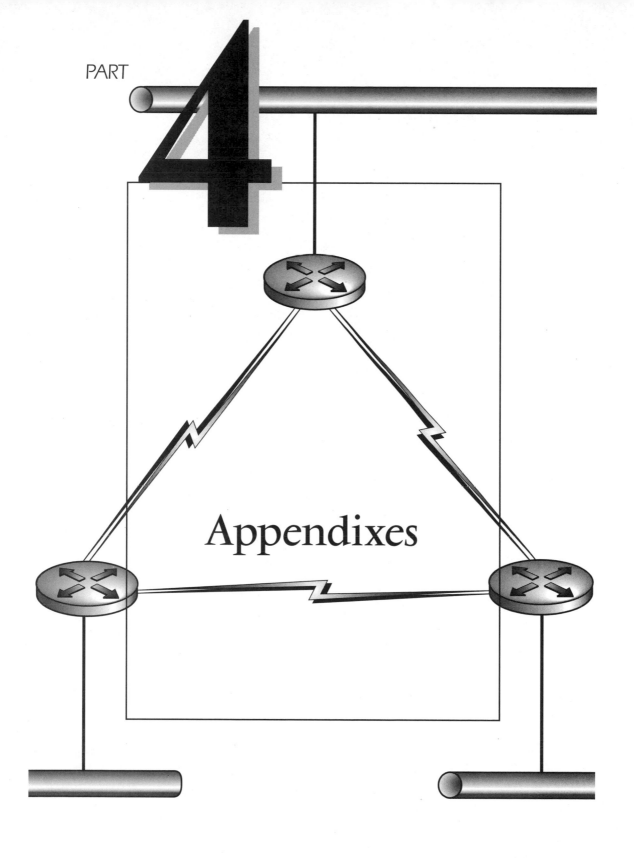

4

Appendixes

APPENDIX A

 ## Tables

700 Series Router Part Numbers and Descriptions

Table A-1

Part number and description list for 760 and 770 series routers

Description	Product Number
Cisco 760-M Series	
ISDN BRI Router without NT-1, without POTS	CISCO761M
ISDN BRI Router with NT-1, without POTS	CISCO762M
ISDN BRI Router without NT-1, with 2 POTS	CISCO765M
ISDN BRI Router with NT-1, with 2 POTS	CISCO766M
Cisco 770 Series	
ISDN BRI Router with 4-port Hub, without NT-1, without POTS	CISCO771M
ISDN BRI Router with 4-port Hub, with NT-1, without POTS	CISCO772M
ISDN BRI Router with 4-port Hub, without NT-1, 2 POTS	CISCO775M
ISDN BRI Router with 4-port Hub, with NT-1, with 2 POTS	CISCO776M

1000 Series Router Part Numbers and Descriptions

Table A-2

Variations in the Cisco 1000 series

Product Number	WAN Connections	LAN Connections	Console Port	PCMCIA Slot	North America/ International
Cisco 1003	ISDN BRI	Ethernet 10BaseT	RJ-45	Flash ROM	International
Cisco 1004	ISDN BRI with NT-1	Ethernet 10BaseT	RJ-45	Flash ROM	North America
Cisco 1005	EIA/TIA-232, EIA/TIA-449, V.35, X.21, EIA-530	Ethernet 10BaseT	RJ-45	Flash ROM	Both

1600 Series Router Part Numbers and Descriptions

Table A-3

Comparison of the 1600 series models

Model	Cisco 1601	Cisco 1602	Cisco 1603	Cisco 1604	Cisco 1605-R
Base Configuration	1 Ethernet 1 serial sync/async	1 Ethernet 1 56Kbps 4-wire DSU/CSU	1 Ethernet 1 ISDN BRI S/T	1 Ethernet 1 ISDN BRI U (with NT-1)	2 Ethernet
WAN Interface Slot	1	1	1	1	1
Supported Optional WAN Interface Card	Serial sync/async T1/FT1 DSU/CSU 56/64K DSU/CSU ISDN BRI S/T ISDN BRI U	Serial sync/async T1/FT1 DSU/CSU 56/64K DSU/CSU ISDN BRI S/T ISDN BRI U	Serial sync/async T1/FT1 DSU/CSU 56/64K DSU/CSU ISDN BRI Leased Line S/T	Serial sync/async T1/FT1 DSU/CSU 56/64K DSU/CSU ISDN BRI Leased Line S/T	Serial sync/async T1/FT1 DSU/CSU 56/64K DSU/CSU ISDN BRI S/T ISDN BRI U

2500 Series Router Part Numbers and Descriptions

Table A-4

Comparison of different features in the 2500 series

Model	Ethernet	Token Ring	Low-Speed Serial	High-Speed Serial	ISDN BRI	Hub Ports
2501	1	0	0	2	0	0
2501CF	Software disabled	0	2	0	0	0
2501LF	1	0	2	0	0	0
2502CF	0	Software disabled	2	0	0	0
2502LF	0	1	2	0	0	0
2502	0	1	0	2	0	0
2503	1	0	0	2	1	0
2503I	1	0	Software disabled	0	1	0
2504	0	1	0	2	1	0
2504I	0	1	Software disabled	0	1	0
2505	0	0	0	0	0	8 Ethernet
2507	0	0	0	0	0	16 Ethernet
2509	1	0	8	2	0	0
2510	0	1	8	2	0	0
2511	1	0	16	2	0	0
2512	0	1	16	2	0	0
2513	1	1	0	2	0	0
2514	2	0	0	2	0	0
2515	0	2	0	2	0	0
2516	0	0	0	2	1	14 Ethernet
2517	0	0	0	2	1	14 Token Ring
2518	0	0	0	2	1	23 Ethernet
2519	0	0	0	2	1	23 Token Ring

Table A-4 continued

Model	Ethernet	Token Ring	Low-Speed Serial	High-Speed Serial	ISDN BRI	Hub Ports
2520	1	0	2	2	1	0
2520CF	Software disabled	0	2	2	Software disabled	0
2520LF	1	0	2	2	Software disabled	0
2521	0	1	2	2	1	0
2521CF	0	Software disabled	2	2	Software disabled	0
2521LF	0	1	2	2	Software disabled	0
2522	1	0	8	2	1	0
2522CF	Software disabled	0	8	8	Software disabled	0
2522LF	1	0	8	8	Software disabled	0
2523	0	1	8	2	1	0
2523CF	0	Software disabled	8	8	Software disabled	0
2523LF	0	1	8	8	Software disabled	0
2524	1	0	0	0	0	0
2525	0	1	0	0	0	0

2600 Series Router Tables

Table A-5

WAN and voice interface card listings with part numbers

Part Number	Listing
WIC-1DSU-T1	T1/fractional T1 CSU/DSU
WIC-1DSU-56K4	One-port four-wire 56Kbps CSU/DSU
WIC-1T	One-port high-speed serial
WIC 2T	Dual high-speed serial
WIC-2A/S	Two-port async/sync serial
WIC-1B-S/T	One-port ISDN BRI
WIC-1B-U	One-port ISDN BRI with NT-1
VIC-2FXS	Two-port FXS voice/fax interface card for voice/fax network module. Used to connect directly to phones and fax machines.
VIC-2FXO	Two-port FXO voice/fax interface card for voice/fax network module. Used to connect to PBX or key system and to provide off-premise connections.
VIC-2E/M	Two-port E&M voice/fax interface card for voice/fax network module. Used to connect to PBX or key system trunk lines.

Table A-6

Network module listing with part numbers

Part Number	Listing
NM-1V	One-slot voice/fax network module
NM-2V	Two-slot voice/fax network module
NM-4A/S	4-port async/sync serial network module
NM-8A/S	8-port async/sync serial network module
NM-16A	High-density 16-port async network module
NM-32A	High-density 32-port async network module

3600 Series Router Tables

Table A-7

This table lists the minimum software versions necessary to use a network module, as well as the maximum number of modules allowed in a single chassis

Part Number	Description	Max per 3640	Max per 3620	Minimum IOS version
NM-1E	1-Port Ethernet	4	2	11.2(4)XA
NM-1FE-FX	1-Port Fast Ethernet, FX only	3	2	11.2(10)P
NM-1FE-TX	1-Port Fast Ethernet, TX only	3	2	11.2(6)P
NM-1E2W	1 Ethernet 2 WAN card slot	4	2	11.1(7+)AA
NM-1E1R2W	1 Ethernet 1 Token Ring 2 WAN card slot	4	2	11.1(8+)AA
NM-2E2W	2 Ethernet 2 WAN card slot	4	2	11.1(7+)AA
NM-4A/S	4-Port async/sync serial	3	1	11.1(7+)AA
NM-4B-S/T	4-Port ISDN-BRI	3	1	11.1(7+)AA
NM-4B-U	4-Port ISDN-BRI with NT-1	3	1	11.1(7+)AA
NM-8A/S	8-Port async/sync serial	3	1	11.1(7+)AA
NM-8B-S/T	8-Port ISDN-BRI	3	1	11.1(7+)AA
NM-8B-U	8-Port ISDN-BRI with NT-1	3	1	11.1(7+)AA
NM-1CT1	1-Port Channelized T1/ISDN-PRI	3	1	11.1(7+)AA
NM-1CT1-CSU	1-Port Channelized T1/ISDN-PRI with CSU	3	1	11.1(7+)AA
NM-2CT1	2-Port Channelized T1/ISDN-PRI	3	1	11.1(7+)AA
NM-2CT1-CSU	2-Port Channelized T1/ISDN-PRI with CSU	3	1	11.1(7+)AA
NM-1CE1B	1-Port Channelized E1/ISDN-PRI balanced	3	1	11.1(7+)AA
NM-1CE1U	1-port Channelized E1/ISDN-PRI unbalanced	3	1	11.1(7+)AA
NM-2CE1B	2-port Channelized E1/ISDN-PRI balanced	3	1	11.1(7+)AA
NM-2CE1U	2-port Channelized E1/ISDN-PRI unbalanced	3	1	11.1(7+)AA
NM-4E	4-port Ethernet	3	2	11.2(6)P
NM-4T	4-port serial	4	2	11.2(4)XA
NM-16A	16-port asynchronous module	3	1	11.2(7)P
NM-32A	32-port asynchronous module	3	1	11.2(7)P
NM-6DM	6-port digital modem	2	0	11.2(9)XA

(cont.)

Table A-7 continued

Part Number	Description	Max per 3640	Max per 3620	Minimum IOS version
NM-12DM	12-port digital modem	2	0	11.2(9)XA
NM-18DM	18-port digital modem	2	0	11.2(9)XA
NM-24DM	24-port digital modem	2	0	11.2(9)XA
NM-30DM	30-port digital modem	2	0	11.2(9)XA
NM-COMPR	Compression module	1	1	11.2(7)P

NOTE

Neither configuration of two NM-1FE and two NM-4E nor one NM-1FE and three NM-4E is supported.

Table A-8

This table lists the minimum software versions necessary to use a WAN interface card, as well as the maximum number of modules allowed in a single chassis

WAN Interface Card	Max per Combo (NM-1E2W, 2E2W, 1E1R)	Minimum IOS Version
WIC-1T	2	11.1(7+)AA
WIC36-1B-U	1	11.1(7+)AA
WIC36-1B-S/T	1	11.1(7+)AA
WIC-1B-U	2	11.2(4)XA
WIC-1B-S/T	2	11.2(4)XA
WIC-1B-U	2	11.2(4)XA
WIC-1DSU-56K4	2	11.2(4)XA

Table A-9

Memory allocation chart for the Cisco 3600 series router

Total DRAM	Processor Memory	IO Memory
16 MB	12 MB	4 MB
20 MB	15 MB	5 MB
24 MB	18 MB	6 MB
32 MB	24 MB	8 MB
40 MB	30 MB	10 MB
48 MB	36 MB	12 MB
64 MB	48 MB	16 MB
96 MB	72 MB	24 MB
128 MB	96 MB	32 MB

4000 Series Router Tables

Table A-10

The maximum supported network processor modules configurable in 4000 series routers

Maximum Supported Network Processor Modules	Cisco 4000-M	Cisco 4500-M	Cisco 4700-M
1-port Ethernet	3	-	-
2-port Ethernet	3	3	3
6-port Ethernet	-	3	3
1-port Token Ring	3	3	3
2-port Token Ring	3	3	3
1-port single-attachment multimode FDDI	1	2	2
1-port dual-attachment multimode FDDI	1	2	2
1-port dual-attachment single-mode FDDI	1	2	2
2-port synchronous serial	3	3	3
4-port synchronous serial	3	3	3
4-port ISDN BRI	2	2	2
8-port ISDN BRI	1	2	2
1-port Channelized T1/ISDN PRI	1	2	2

(cont.)

Table A-10 continued

Maximum Supported Network Processor Modules	Cisco 4000-M	Cisco 4500-M	Cisco 4700-M
1-port Channelized E1/ISDN PRI (balanced)	1	2	2
1-port Channelized E1/ISDN PRI (unbalanced)	1	2	2
4-port serial E1/G.703 (balanced)	3	3	3
4-port serial E1/G.703 (unbalanced)	3	3	3
1-port single-mode ATM OC-3c	—	1	1
1-port multimode ATM OC-3c	—	1	1
1-port ATM DS-3	—	2	2
1-port ATM E3	—	2	2
1-port Fast Ethernet	—	2	2
1-Port HSSI	—	2	2
2T16S (2 high-speed serial & 16 low-speed sync/async)	—	2	2

Table A-11

Incompatible network processor module configurations

NPM Type	Product Number
1 ATM OC-3c, 1 FDDI, 1 ATM DS-3, or ATM E3	1 NP-1A-MM or SM + 1 NP-1F-D-MM/S-M/D-SS + 1 NP-1A-DS3 or E3
1 ATM OC-3c, 1 Fast Ethernet, 1 ATM DS-3 or E3	1 NP-1A-MM or SM + 1 NP-1FE + 1 NP-1A-DS3 or E3
2 Fast Ethernet and 1 FDDI	2 NP-1FE + 1 NP-1F-D-MM/S-M/D-SS
2 Fast Ethernet and 1 ATM DS-3 or E3	2 NP-1FE + 1 NP-1A-DS3 or E3
2 Fast Ethernet and 1 ATM OC-3c	2 NP-1FE + 1 NP-1A-MM or SM
2 ATM OC-3c	2 NP-1A-MM or SM
3 FDDI	3 NP-1F-D-MM/S-M/D-SS
1 ATM OC-3c and 2 FDDI	1 NP-1A-MM or SM + 2 NP-1F-D-MM/S-M/D-SS

APPENDIX B

Webliography

Book Specific Site

http://paul.tibex.com	The author's personal Web site.
http://paul.tibex.com/Router-Book/newsyslog	Location of the "newsyslog" UNIX shell script.

Cisco

http://www.cisco.com	Cisco's main Web site.
http://www.cisco.com/pcgi-bin/tablebuild.pl/tftp	Free TFTP server for Microsoft Windows from Cisco.
http://www.cisco.com/wwl/export/encrypt.html	Web page that has information about export restrictions on DES encryption enable versions of IOS.
http://www.cisco.com/pcgi-bin/tablebuild.pl/faststep	The location where you can download the latest version of FastStep free of charge.
http://www.cisco.com/pcgi-bin/tablebuild.pl/configmaker	The location where you can download Cisco Config Maker free of charge.
http://www.cisco.com/cgi-bin/tablebuild.pl/dial-out	The location where you can download free dial-out software if you have a CCO account.
http://www.cisco.com/public/serv_doc.shtml	Free Cisco documentation site.
http://www.cisco.com/kobayashi/serv_doc.shtml	Cisco documentation site for CCO registered users.
http://www.cisco.com/public/registration.shtml	Application to obtain a CCO account.
http://www.cisco.com/warp/public/701/64.html	Cisco official stance on password encryption.
http://www.cisco.com/univercd/cc/td/doc/product/access/acs_mod/cis4000/4000cn/1000npm.htm	Installation guide for a Channelized T1/PRI card for Cisco 400 series routers.

NTP Information

http://www.eecis.udel.edu/~ntp/	An introduction to NTP.
http://www.eecis.udel.edu/~ntp/software.html	Platform-specific NTP clients.
ftp://ftp.udel.edu/pub/ntp	Archive of NTP software and related utilities.
http://ds.internic.net/rfc/rfc1305.txt	NTP Version 3 Specification (RFC 1305).
comp.protocols.time.ntp	Usenet newsgroup.

Manufacturer Information

http://www.livingston.com	Livingston Enterprises, recently acquired by Lucent Technologies. Inventors of RADIUS. Source code for RADIUS freely available at this site.
http://www.kentrox.com	Manufacturer of digital conversion devices.
http://www.adrtan.com	Manufacturer of digital conversion devices.
http://www.adtran.com/cpe/t1/t1.csu/t1csuace/ t1csuace.html	Product information on the Adtran T1 CSU ACE, a CSU-only device.
http://www.adtran.com/cpe/isdn/netterm/ index.html#nt1ace	Product information on the Adtran NT-1 ACE device.
http://www.adtran.com/cpe/isdn/netterm/t400/t400.html	Product information on the Adtran NT-1 T400 rack-mounted NT-1 system.

Freeware/Shareware Info

http://www.tucows.com	The ultimate collection of Winsock software.
http://starbase.neosoft.com/~zkrr01	The home of Netterm, an excellent WIN95 Telnet program.
http://wombat.doc.ic.ac.uk/foldoc/foldoc.cgi	The free online dictionary of computing. Has many useful pieces of information, including the proper name of the # symbol. Just enter "octothorpe" and see for yourself.
http://www.cert.org	
ftp://ftp.cert.org/pub/tools/tcp_wrappers	CERT/CC, the home of TCP Wrappers and other security-related information.
http://www.ee.ethz.ch/~oetiker/webtools/mrtg	MRTG, the Multi-Router Traffic Grapher.

Internet Standard Info

http://www.iana.org/numbers.html	Protocol numbers and assignment services by type.
http://www.isi.edu/in-notes/iana/assignments/protocol-numbers	The official list of protocol TCP/IP numbers.
http://www.isi.edu/in-notes/iana/assignments/icmp-parameters	ICMP parameter information.
http://info.internet.isi.edu:80/7c/in-notes/rfc/.cache	RFC finder. Search RFCs by number, title, and author.
http://info.internet.isi.edu:80/in-notes/rfc/files/rfc950.txt	RFC 950

Miscellaneous Internet Info

http://www.mtnds.com/af	Acronym finder. Helps you divine the meanings of all those obnoxious acronyms.
http://www.eff.org/descracker.html	EFF builds DES Cracker, which proves that Data Encryption Standard is unsecure.
ftp://ftp.isi.edu/in-notes/iana/assignments/ethernet-numbers	List of MAC addresses and which manufacturers own them.
http://sunsite.informatik.rwth-aachen.de/jargon300/main.html	The Jargon Lexicon.
http://www.coolsig.com/pun.htm	Humorous puns.

APPENDIX C

Telecommunications Background for ISDN*

Before discussing any details of ISDN or B-ISDN technology, standards, protocols, or implementations, it's necessary for the reader to have some baseline understanding of certain aspects of telecommunications. This appendix will review some of the data and telecommunications background topics relevant to this understanding and is intended to provide a broad overview rather than in-depth analyses or motivation. In this way, the appendix will provide review for some readers and a first introduction for others. The topics presented in this appendix include:

- *Communications basics*. Introduces terms and concepts such as analog and digital signaling, amplifiers and repeaters, and passband and bandwidth, as well as the structure of the U.S. telephone network, the telephone local loop, and multiplexing.

- *Digital telephony.* Discusses why the telephone network has migrated from an analog network to a digital one and describes how human voice is digitized, how digital signals are carried on the local loop, and how full-duplex communication is accomplished on a digital local loop. The digital carrier hierarchies are also introduced.

- *Types of switched networks.* Defines, compares, and differentiates among circuit switching, packet switching, and fast packet switching technologies.

- *Open Systems Interconnection (OSI) Reference Model.* The OSI model describes a framework for network communications protocols. The OSI model will be introduced and defined, as will be the protocol architecture for packet switching and X.25.

---

*This appendix appeared in chapter 2 of *ISDN: Concepts, Facilities, and Services,* signature edition, by Gary C. Kessler and Peter Southwick, published by McGraw-Hill, New York, 1998.

Communications Basics

Analog and Digital Signals

One of the most important concepts for our discussion of telecommunications is that of a *signal*. Signals are the representation of information. In today's communications systems, signals are usually an electrical current or voltage, where the current or voltage level is used to represent data. Communications systems can employ either analog or digital signals (Figure C-1).

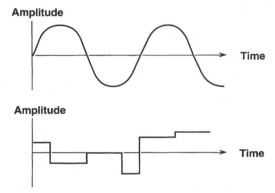

Figure C-1
Analog signals (top) and digital signals (bottom).

An *analog signal* is one that can take on a continuous set of values within some given range, to directly represent information. Examples of analog signals are human voice, video, and music. Analog signals are also sometimes referred to as modulated signals.

A *digital signal* is one that may take on only a discrete set of values within a given range, such as a battery that can supply either 13 or 23 volts (V). Binary signals, in particular, are digital signals that may take on only two values, 0 or 1. Digital signals are sometimes referred to as unmodulated signals.

The distinction between analog and digital signals is important. Sound is produced when air is set in motion by a vibrating source, such as the vocal cords or the strings of a guitar. When the vibrating source pushes out, the air particles around it are compressed; when the source pulls back, the air particles are pulled apart. This compression and expansion of air particles causes a chain reaction through the air away from the original source, generating a sound wave. Sound waves are analog signals, where each in-and-out vibration is called a *cycle*. The frequency of the signal is measured in cycles per second, or hertz (Hz). A sound wave with a frequency of 261.63Hz, for example, is the musical note middle C.

An analog signal can be transported over an electrical circuit if the sound waves can be made to alter the characteristics (voltage, frequency, or amperage) of the electrical circuit in a manner that represent the analog signal. This function is performed by a microphone, similar to the one found in your telephone.

Human voice comprises a particular type of analog signal, namely, a mixture of sinusoidal (sine) waves. The telephone network has been designed specifically to handle analog, human voice signals. An ISDN will only carry digital signals, although we will still want to send human voice through the network. Later discussion in this appendix will describe how human voice is carried in a digital network.

Amplifiers and Repeaters

The analog telephone network contains amplifiers to boost the signals so that they can be carried over long distances. Unfortunately, all copper media (e.g., twisted pair and coaxial cable) act as an antenna to pick up electrical signals from the surrounding environment. This noise can come from many sources, such as fluorescent lights, electric motors, and power lines. An amplifier, by the nature of its function, boosts the signal (e.g., the human voice) and background noise equally. The effects of noise, then, are additive in an analog network; the noise boosted by one amplifier becomes input to the next amplifier.

Amplifiers in the analog network are poorly suited for digital signals. Digital signals are represented as square waves, although they leave the transmitter in a rounded-off form, looking much like an analog signal. An amplifier, then, would accept a poorly formed digital signal plus any noise on the line and output a louder, degraded signal.

Digital networks use signal regenerators (or repeaters) instead of amplifiers. A signal regenerator accepts the incoming digital signal and then creates a new outgoing signal. Repeaters are typically placed every 6000 feet or so in the long distance digital network. Since the signal is regenerated, the effects of noise are not additive from repeater to repeater.

Structure of the Telephone Network

The telephone network structure in the United States has an interesting history that is beyond the scope of this book. Nevertheless, the evolution of the network over the last 15 years is worth examining because of its impact on user services during the 1980s and beyond.

The Predivestiture Network

Figure C-2a shows the major components of the public switched telephone network (PSTN) in North America prior to 1984. The implementation of this hierarchical network was started in the 1930s and essentially completed in the 1950s; it has undergone continual modifications as technology and population demographics have changed and the effects of divestiture have been felt. The 10-digit telephone numbers commonly used in North America expedite call routing within this switching hierarchy; in the simplest of implementations the first three digits identify the area code, the next three digits identify the end office, and the last four digits identify the end user.

Figure C-2a
Telephone network switching hierarchy in the United States (predivestiture).

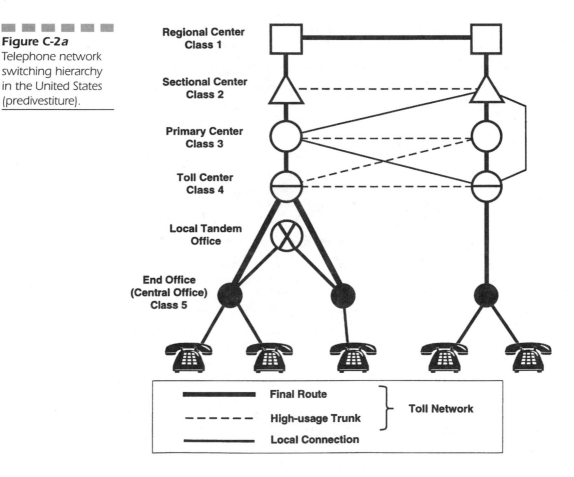

An end user, such as a residential or business customer, is directly connected to a telephone network end office, also called a class 5 or C.O. Users are typically connected to the C.O. over a single twisted wire pair called the *local loop*. In today's telephone networks, the number of customers requesting service has often outnumbered the capacity of the end offices. Rather than invest in larger and larger switching systems, network providers often install multiple switches in a single C.O. or wire center. This has led to some confusing terminology. For the purpose of this book, the building that houses the switching equipment is called the *C.O.* and the equipment providing the switching service is called the *local exchange* (LE). For large networks, a single C.O. can contain multiple LEs.

Class 4 offices served two functions. As a toll switch, a class 4 office was part of the long distance (toll) network. Alternatively, a class 4 office could act as a tandem switch, to interconnect those class 5 offices not having sufficient interoffice traffic to justify direct trunks. Local tandem office switches also handled overflow traffic on direct trunks between end offices. The distinction between toll and tandem became particularly important in the United States after the 1984 divestiture of AT&T resulted in the separation of communications resources within the network.

Routing between C.O.s uses the fewest number of intermediate switching offices to minimize the cost of carrying the traffic. The actual route selected depends on such factors as the distance between the two C.O.s, the current network traffic level, and time of day.

A connection between two users who are physically connected to the same C.O. requires only the involvement of that single switching office. Where two subscribers were connected to different C.O.s and the two class 5 offices were attached to the same class 4 office, that toll center would make the connection. When the C.O.s were further apart, other switching offices were used, although it was not necessary that class 5, 4, or 3 offices always connected through the next higher level of switch. A higher-class switch could perform lower-class switching functions; a class 5 office, for example, could be served by a class 4, 3, 2, or 1 office.

The final (primary) route structure shown in Figure C-2a was supplemented by an alternate routing structure. To minimize heavy traffic loads at the higher levels and signal degradation when the route involved many trunks and switching offices, high-usage trunks were used between any switching offices where economically justified.

By 1980, there were over 19,000 class 5 offices and 200 million local loops in the Bell System in the United States. There were also about 900 class 4 offices, 204 class 3 offices, 63 class 2 offices, and 10 class 1 offices.

The Modification of Final Judgment (MFJ), signed by Judge Harold H. Greene in August 1982, represented the settlement of the U.S. Government's 1974 antitrust suit against AT&T. The MFJ was the basis of the breakup of AT&T and the Bell operating telephone companies.

AT&T's Plan of Reorganization, filed in December 1982, provided the new structure and organization of the U.S. telephone industry after January 1, 1984. According to the plan, AT&T would retain long distance communication services and communications equipment manufacturing businesses, as well as other assets such as Bell Laboratories. Local telephone service, provided by 22 Bell operating companies (BOCs), were organized into seven regional Bell holding companies (RBHCs), or regional BOCs (RBOCs). All Bell System assets were assigned to either AT&T or an RBOC, since the MFJ disallowed joint ownership of switching equipment. As a result, AT&T kept the toll network switches (class 1 to 4 offices and some tandem switches) and the RBOCs kept local switching equipment (class 5 and some tandem offices).

The Postdivestiture Network

Figure C-2*b* shows the telephone switching hierarchy that resulted from divestiture. Local telephone service areas were redrawn by divestiture into approximately 250 local access and transport areas (LATAs). The RBOCs, of course, are not the only local telephone companies. There are several hundred independent telephone companies (ITCs) in the United States, which are non-Bell-system providers such as Cincinnati Bell, Frontier Telephone,[1] General Telephone (GTE), Southern New England Telephone (SNET),[2] and others. The LATAs were defined ostensibly to ensure a fair and equal market to the RBOCs and ITCs. Since the BOCs and ITCs are limited to transporting traffic only within a LATA (intraLATA), they are called local exchange carriers (LECs). The LECs maintain C.O.s and tandem offices for high-volume inter-C.O. traffic.

Transport of traffic between LATAs (interLATA) is carried by the interexchange carriers (IECs), such as AT&T, MCI, Sprint, and WorldCom.[3] There are a few exceptions to this rule; several high-traffic corridors have been defined, such as in the New York City area, where the LEC provides some interLATA service. The interLATA toll network is owned by the IECs. The IECs maintain point-of-presence (POP) switches to carry interLATA traffic. C.O.s may connect directly to the POP or via an access tandem (AT) switch.

[1]Formed after the purchase of Rochester Telephone by Long Distance North.
[2]Now affiliated with SBC.
[3]Formed by the merger of LDDS and WilTel.

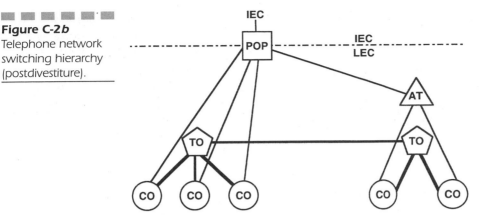

Figure C-2*b*
Telephone network
switching hierarchy
(postdivestiture).

IntraLATA traffic has typically been carried by the LEC. This market has been opened for competition, so now a customer will be served by the LEC and can choose an IEC for interLATA traffic and another carrier for intraLATA toll calls. This environment has created a very large number of service providers and complicates the orderly network structure of the old Bell system.

The Telecommunications Act of 1996 is again changing the structure described above. Where LECs were once limited to providing local service only (and limited to a given geographic region) and IECs to long distance service, we will soon find LECs and IECs competing equally for both local and long-haul service. In addition, we will see an increasing number of competitors in the local access market (once a monopolistic haven for the LEC). These competitive local exchange carriers (CLECs) will offer local dial tone and other voice and data services.

Passband and Bandwidth

Before analyzing the requirements for transmitting human voice in a digital form, we must first define the bandwidth associated with voice and the telephone local loop.

Recall that the frequency of an analog signal is the number of complete sine waves (or vibrations) sent every second and is measured in cycles per second, or hertz. The *passband* of a channel is the range of frequencies that can be carried by that channel; the *bandwidth* is the width of the passband. For example, while one television channel may use the 470.5- to 476.5-megahertz (millions of hertz, MHz) passband and another channel uses the 800- to 806-MHz passband, both channels have a bandwidth of 6MHz.

Human voice can produce sounds in the approximate frequency range of 30 to 10,000Hz (10 kilohertz, or kHz), for a bandwidth of 9.97kHz. The ear can hear sounds in the 20- to 20,000-Hz frequency range (19.98-kHz bandwidth).

The Telephone Local Loop

The telephone local loop has a 4-kHz-band channel with the frequency range from 0 to 4000Hz. This channel actually carries human voice in the frequency range of roughly 300Hz to 3400Hz. This may be surprising considering that the human voice produces sounds between 30Hz and 10,000Hz. How can a channel with a bandwidth of 3.1kHz carry the information content of a source with a 9.97-kHz bandwidth?

In fact, the local loop is not meant to carry just any analog signal but is optimized for human voice. Figure C-3 shows that the major portion of the relative energy of the human voice signal is in the passband from about 200Hz to 3500Hz. This is the frequency range where the bulk of the power, intelligibility, and recognizability of the voice signal occurs. Thus, the 300- to 3400-Hz passband is adequate for acceptable-quality human voice transmissions.

Figure C-3

Average speech signal energy.

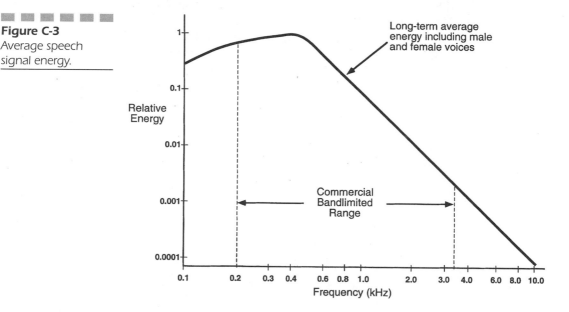

Note that a channel with a bandwidth of 3.1kHz cannot carry all of the information in the voice's frequency range. Voice can be limited to a 3.1-kHz band because the ear can obtain most of the necessary information for conversation (namely, intelligibility and recognition) from that narrow band.

Consider the case of music, however, which is intended to be pleasing over a larger frequency spectrum than is required in normal voice conversation. A transmission facility carrying music must use a larger bandwidth than voice. Think about what happens when someone plays a musical instrument over the telephone; it sounds flat and tinny because it is missing all frequency components below 300Hz and above 3400Hz.

The primary reason that the telephone network uses the narrow 3.1-kHz band rather than the entire 10kHz of voice is that the narrow band allows more telephone conversations to be multiplexed over a single physical facility. This is particularly important for the facilities connecting telephone switching offices.

Multiplexing

Multiplexing in a network allows a single resource to be shared by many users. In particular, multiplexers in the telephone network allow many voice conversations to be carried over a single physical communications line.

Analog communications facilities typically use frequency division multiplexing (FDM) to carry multiple conversations. FDM divides the available frequency among all users and each user has an assigned channel for as much time as necessary (see Figure C-4). In the case of voice, each conversation is shifted to a different passband with a bandwidth of approximately 4kHz (3.1kHz for the voice signal and 900Hz for guard bands to prohibit interchannel interference). Since the bandwidth is held constant, the integrity of the user's information is maintained even though the passband has been altered.

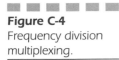
Figure C-4
Frequency division multiplexing.

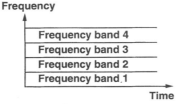

Frequency

| Frequency band 4 |
| Frequency band 3 |
| Frequency band 2 |
| Frequency band 1 |

Time

FDM is a scheme with which we are all familiar. Television stations, for example, each require a 6-MHz passband and all TV channels simultaneously share the available bandwidth of the air. The TV set in our house, then, acts as a demultiplexer to tune in only the passband (i.e., the channel) that we want to watch. This is also the same principle used for cable TV and radio channels.

Digital signals are typically multiplexed on a communications facility using time division multiplexing (TDM). Whereas FDM provides each user with part of the frequency spectrum for all of the time that the user requires, a TDM scheme provides each user with the entire frequency spectrum for a small burst of time (Figure C-5). In the figure, time slots are granted on a round-robin basis to the five users who share the channel.

Figure C-5
Time division
multiplexing.

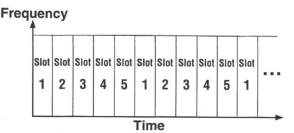

Digital Telephony

The Move to a Digital Telephone Network

Prior to the early 1960s, the United States telephone network was an integrated analog network, meaning that all devices, facilities, and services were analog in nature. In fact, plain old telephone service (POTS) was all that was offered; the telephone network merely carried analog utterances from one point to another.

While the telephone local loop today is still predominately analog, the rest of the network has been migrating toward using digital facilities for over 30 years. In the United States, AT&T started investigating the use of digital transmission facilities and switches in the 1950s. The first digital lines used in North America were T1 carriers, introduced into the network in 1962 for traffic between telephone switching offices. T1 carriers use two wire pairs to separate the transmit and receive function, as opposed to the local loop's single pair.

The first digital switch, AT&T's Number 4*ESS* (Electronic Switching System), was introduced into the toll network in 1976 and Nortel[4] introduced their digital toll switch, the DMS-200, in early 1980. Throughout the 1980s, digital switches were introduced into C.O.s as well, notably Nortel's DMS-100 and AT&T's No. 5*ESS* switch, introduced in 1981 and 1982, respectively. The majority of C.O.s in the United States now use digital switches.

The introduction of digital switches and digital carrier facilities allowed portions of the telephone network to operate more efficiently and meant that new types of communications services could be offered to some customers. Even if all switching offices and interoffice trunks in the network were digital today, the network still contains analog local loops. The "analog" local loop, then, is the weakest link in the "end-to-end digital" chain, and POTS continues to be the primary service available to most end users.

The ultimate goal is to build an IDN, which is a network where all switches, interoffice trunks, local loops, and telephones are digital.

There are a number of reasons for converting network facilities from analog to digital, but the overriding one is economy. Digital facilities and digital devices are less expensive to design, build, and maintain than comparable analog devices. Indeed, the microprocessor revolution of the last 25 years has caused digital devices to propagate to all facets of life and to plummet in price, while the cost of analog devices has remained relatively stable. Another reason for this conversion is that the digital equipment results in less noise being transmitted along with the information signals. This means that a digital facility will provide "cleaner" communications paths. Finally digital devices are less prone to mechanical failure.

Digital C.O.s are easier to design because the computer *is* the switch. Since most digital C.O.s use some form of TDM, the speed of a *digital switch* can be increased by defining more time slots. The limiting factor is the speed at which signals can be turned on and off within the digital devices. As computer processors become faster and relatively less expensive, it becomes easier to build faster and larger digital switches.

Once the network has been completely converted to digital, it's a natural conceptual step to observe that many types of different services may be carried by this network if all these services are delivered in a digital form.

Digitizing Voice and Pulse Code Modulation

To carry human voice in a digital form, the voice signal is sampled 8000 times per second. This sampling rate is based upon Harry Nyquist's Sampling Theorem, which shows that to be able to accurately reproduce an

[4]Formerly Northern Telecom International (NTI).

analog signal from a series of samples, sampling must occur at twice the highest frequency of the signal. The local loop passband is taken to be between 0 and 4000Hz (the total bandwidth of an FDM voice channel including both the voice signal and guard bands). The maximum frequency, 4kHz, requires a sample rate of 8000 times per second, corresponding to a sample interval of 125 microseconds (ms).

Each sample of the voice signal is converted to a digital bit stream. The process of converting the analog sample to a bit stream is pulse code modulation (PCM) and is performed by a device called a CODEC (COder-DECoder). The CODEC may be located in a digital switch, in which case the local loop between the telephone and switch carries analog signals. Alternatively, the CODEC may be placed in the telephone set, in which case the local loop carries digital signals.

Figure C-6 shows the voice digitization scheme. The voice signal is sampled once every 125 ms, or once every 1/8000 s. This sampling, called pulse amplitude modulation (PAM), results in an analog level corresponding to the signal at that moment. The amplitude of the PAM sample is mapped to a discrete value on the amplitude axis; this digital encoding is the PCM step.

Figure C-6
Pulse code
modulation.

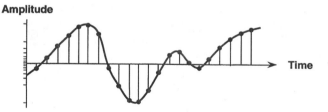

Amplitude

Time

Note the nonlinearity of the PCM amplitude scale. The amplitude levels are defined to be closer together at lower volumes and farther apart at higher volumes; this is called *companding* (compression expanding). There are two main companding algorithms used in digital telephony; the m-law is used primarily in the United States, Canada, and Japan, while the A-law is used throughout most of the rest of the world.

The PCM companding rules define 255 (m-law) or 256 (A-law) amplitude levels; therefore, each voice sample is coded as an 8-bit word. Since 8000 samples are taken each second, the bit rate of a single voice channel is 64,000bps. This is sometimes referred to as digital signaling level 0, or DS-0.

It should be noted that the analog voice signal cannot be mapped exactly onto the digital amplitude scale. Thus, the digitized signal is not an exact replica of the original signal; the difference is called the *quantization error*. The quantization error has an additive effect, so the error becomes greater each time the signal undergoes an analog-to-digital (A/D) or digi-tal-to-analog (D/A) conversion (which was the case when switches were analog and trunks were digital). Due to the large number of amplitude levels and the use of companding, the quantization error is minimized, and what little remains is easily compensated for by the listener.

Companding reduces the effect of the quantization error by utilizing a nonlinear scale on the amplitude axis. By concentrating on the lower-amplitude (volume) signals as shown in Figure C-6, PCM is able to achieve 9-bit (512 levels) accuracy while only actually employing an 8-bit code. For the comfort of most humans, PCM is designed to catch the subtleties and nuances when people are talking softly rather than when they are yelling. PCM with companding (A-law or m-law) meets the quality standards of the analog telephone network and is considered "toll quality."

The Digital TDM Hierarchy

T1 carriers were the first digital carriers employed in the United States. A T1 carrier multiplexes 24 voice channels over a single transmission line using TDM. The basic unit of transmission is a *frame*, which contains one PCM sample from each of the 24 channels. Since a sample is represented by 8 bits, a single frame contains 192 bits of user data. Each frame is pre-ceded by a single framing bit; thus, a single T1 frame contains 193 bits (Figure C-7). Since each frame contains one sample from each voice chan-nel, there must be 8000 frames per second on the T1 channel. This yields a bit rate of 1.544Mbps, which is also known as digital signaling level 1 (DS-1). Since 8000bps are for framing, the actual user data rate is 1.536Mbps.

Figure C-7
T1 frame format.

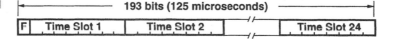

The T1 carrier multiplexes 24 voice channels using TDM. Several T1 carriers, in turn, can be multiplexed using TDM to form even higher-speed carrier channels. The number of channels multiplexed together is defined by the digital TDM hierarchy. The T-carrier system in the United States, with its associated digital signal (DS) level designator, follows the AT&T digital TDM hierarchy (Table C-1). A portion of this hierarchy is also used in Canada, Japan, Taiwan, and South Korea.

Table C-1

TDM Hierarchy Used in North America, Europe, and Japan

Digital Multiplexing Level	Number of Equivalent Voice Channels	Bit Rate (Mbps) N. America	Europe	Japan
DS-0/E0/J0	1	0.064	0.064	0.064
DS-1/J1	24	1.544		1.544
E1	30		2.048	
DS-1C/J1C	48*	3.152		3.152
DS-2/J2	96	6.312		6.312
E2	120		8.448	
E3/J3	480		34.368	32.064
DS-3	672	44.736		
DS-3C	1344*	91.053		
J3C	1440*			97.728
E4	1920		139.264	
DS-4	4032	274.176		
J4	5760			397.200
E5	7680		565.148	

*Intermediate multiplexing rates.

The other widely used TDM hierarchy is based upon the Conference of European Postal and Telecommunications (CEPT) administrations standard (Table C-1). The first level of the CEPT digital hierarchy multiplexes 32 time slots (each with 8 bits, yielding 64-Kbps channels), yielding a frame with 256 bits (Figure C-8) and a bit rate of 2.048 Mbps. One of the 32 time slots is used for signaling, one is used for frame alignment, and the remaining 30 are used for actual user data, resulting in a user data rate of 1.920Mbps. This is referred to as the CEPT level 1, or E1, frame format.

Figure C-8

E1 frame format.

Time Slot 0	Time Slot 1	//	Time Slot 31

256 bits (125 microseconds)

"T" and "E" carriers predate digital switching. Therefore, in the early days of digital carriers, the switches were still analog. That meant that a CODEC had to be placed on both ends of every digital carrier between every pair of offices. Thus, one telephone connection might be routed through several switches, requiring that the coding/decoding process be performed several times. In a fully digital network, there will be a single coding and single decoding step, since the CODEC will be part of the end-user equipment. Even if the local loop is analog, the CODEC will be placed in the C.O., which would still only require a single coding and decoding operation.

The telecommunications industry realized many years ago that higher speeds could be economically achieved by using an optical fiber medium. To ensure international compatibility at higher speeds, work began in the mid-1980s to define a single digital hierarchy based on fiber and able to incorporate the "low-speed" copper-based digital hierarchies. The digital hierarchy for optical fiber is known in North America as the Synchronous Optical Network (SONET).

The SONET optical hierarchy is based upon building blocks in increments of 51.84Mbps, roughly corresponding to the DS-3 line rate. The 51.84Mbps rate is called the Synchronous Transport Signal level 1 (STS-1) when referring to an electrical signal or Optical Carrier level 1 (OC-1) when referring to an optical signal. Standards already define the format for rates from 51.84Mbps (OC-1) to 9953.28Mbps (OC-192), as shown in Table C-2.

SONET not only defines high-speed communications over fiber but also defines a consistent multiplexing scheme. With SONET, an OC-n line rate is exactly n times 51.84Mbps, so an OC-n transmission is formed by byte-multiplexing n OC-1 frames. This results in the very straightforward design of SONET multiplexers. It is also very different from the T1 and CEPT hierarchies where different levels use different multiplexing and framing schemes.

The SONET standard is specified for North America; its international counterpart is known as the Synchronous Digital Hierarchy (SDH). The main format difference between the two is that the basic SDH rate is 155.52 Mbps, designated Synchronous Transport Module level 1 (STM-1), which is equivalent to SONET's OC-3/STS-3. SDH rates are also shown in Table C-2.

Table C-2

SONET Optical Carrier (OC) and SDH Synchronous Transport Module (STM) Levels

Line Rate (Mbps)	SONET Level	SDH Level
51.840	OC-1	
155.520	OC-3	STM-1
466.560	OC-9	
622.080	OC-12	STM-4
933.120	OC-18	
1244.160	OC-24	STM-8
1866.240	OC-36	STM-12
2488.320	OC-48	STM-16
4976.640	OC-96	STM-32
9953.280	OC-192	STM-64

Digital Signals on the Local Loop

A major stumbling block to sending digital signals between the C.O. and customer site is today's local loop. The local loop comprises a twisted pair of 22-26 gauge copper wire. The twisting of the wire pair reduces the crosstalk and interference from multiple pairs within the same bundle of wires within a cable. The average length of a local loop in the United States is about 18,000 ft (18 kft, or 5.5 km).

Load coils, which are induction loops, counteract the buildup of capacitance created by long runs of twisted pair. Load coils are placed on the local loop to reduce the distortion of voice frequencies in the wire pair. While the load coils ensure that the voice signal is recognizable after traveling the distance between the customer site and the C.O., they effectively limit the voiceband to frequencies below 4000Hz. *Bridged taps* are also present on the local loop; they reduce installation time for new customer connections but also negatively affect digital transmission on the loop by attenuating the transmitted signals. In the United States, loops longer than 18,000 ft (5.4 km) have load coils on the loop every 6000 ft (1.8 km), starting 3000 ft (900 m) from the central office.

In the United States today, the composition of local loops is:

- Nonloaded loops no more than 18 kft in length (70 percent).
- Loaded loops greater than 18 kft in length (15 percent).
- So-called *derived loops,* comprising nonloaded loops up to 12,000 ft in length connected to remote wiring distribution equipment connected to the central office via a fiber or digital carrier (15 percent).

The problem with the analog local loop is that while 3.1kHz is sufficient for carrying human voice signals, it is not sufficient for carrying the frequencies required to represent high-speed digital data. Square waves are composed by combining sine waves of different frequencies. Stable, recognizable square waves require frequency components much higher than 4000Hz, making the loaded local loop inadequate for digital communication.[5]

The 4000Hz bandwidth limitation of the local loop is imposed by the network architecture and not by the physical medium itself. In fact, a twisted pair may be used in analog telephony applications with a bandwidth up to 250kHz, which requires amplifiers every 16.5 to 19.8 kft (5 to 6 km), and in digital applications with bit rates over 6Mbps, which requires repeaters approximately every 9 kft (3 km). Therefore, digital communication over twisted pairs is possible once load coils are removed and bridged taps are accounted for on the line. This unloaded local loop, if used for digital applications, is called a *digital subscriber line* (DSL). The text covers the family of DSL standards and protocols.

It should be noted that some current LAN products and standards utilize unshielded twisted pair media at data rates above 100Mbps; SONET/SDH speeds (155Mbps) can also be achieved. The length of the wire, however, is limited to a hundred or so meters, well short of the local loop requirements of several miles. This distance limitation is due to the attenuation of frequencies of the signal. As data transfer rates increase, the usable distances decrease, if all other factors remain the same. As an example, a 20kHz signal will travel, and be recognized, twice as far as a 40kHz signal.

Full-Duplex Communication on the Local Loop

A nonloaded local loop can carry digital transmissions. The next step is to accomplish simultaneous, two-way (full-duplex) communication over a digital loop.

---

[5]Fourier's theorem states that any repeating, periodic waveform can be approximated by the sum of a (possibly infinite) set of sine waves. A 1000Hz square wave, for example, would require sine wave components with frequencies 500, 1500, 2500, 3500, ... Hz. Even this relatively low-speed square wave would be severely degraded in the local loop's 300- to 3400Hz passband.

Today's analog local loops carry sounds in both directions at the same time. The voice signals from both parties are on the local loop simultaneously; in addition, bridged taps, wire gauge changes, and splices can cause echo of the signal back to the transmitter. Full-duplex communication over the local loop is not a problem in analog applications. When people talk over the telephone, the brain filters out their words when they are echoed back. For data applications, modems typically split the bandwidth of the local loop in half to achieve full-duplex communication; the originating modem will usually transmit in the lower half of the passband, and the answering modem will usually transmit in the upper half.

Splitting the bandwidth in half is not possible in a digital environment, since digital signals cannot be confined to a given passband. Alternatively, the T1 approach could be adopted; two pairs of wire could be used, one for transmit and one for receive. This solution, however, is not a viable one for the local loop since hundreds of millions of miles of new cable would have to be installed in the United States alone. Instead, two other approaches are used to achieve full-duplex digital communication over a two-wire DSL.

The first method is called *time-compression multiplexing* (TCM). TCM works as follows: If we wish a facility to operate at *x*-bps full-duplex, we can simulate that by operating the facility at 2*x*-bps half-duplex, where each data stream travels in opposite directions over the shared facility at different times. TCM requires facilities at both ends of the communications channel to constantly and quickly turn the line around, an operation called *ping-ponging*.

The half-duplex facility, in fact, really has to operate at a rate somewhat above 2*x* bps to accommodate facility turnaround time and propagation delay. In those systems employing TCM, most 56 and 64Kbps full-duplex signals are carried on a 144Kbps half-duplex channel, a ratio of 2.57:1 and 2.25:1, respectively. TCM was developed in the early 1980s for AT&T's Circuit Switched Digital Capability service and is used today over two-wire facilities in AT&T's Switched 56 and Nortel's Datapath services. It was proposed for ISDN local loops but is not used due to the restrictions in cable length (9000 ft).

The second approach to achieving full-duplex communication over the DSL is to use a device called a *hybrid with echo canceler*. The hybrid circuit mixes and separates the transmit and receive signals onto a single twisted pair. An echo canceler does exactly what its name implies; the transmitter remembers what it is sending and "subtracts" the appropriate signal from the incoming transmission, thus eliminating the returning echo. This requires complex algorithms but, in fact, is the method of choice for use in high-speed modems and on ISDN local loops.

Types of Switched Networks

To fully understand and appreciate ISDN services, it's necessary to understand circuit, frame, and packet switching (*circuit-, frame-,* and *packet mode,* respectively, in the ISDN vernacular). These switching techniques are in common use today and are supported by an ISDN. Before discussing these types of switching, it's useful to examine the characteristics of voice and data calls.

Voice calls typically have the following characteristics:

- *Delay sensitive.* Silence in human conversation conveys information, so the voice network cannot add (or remove) periods of silence.
- *Long hold time.* Telephone calls usually last for a relatively long time compared to the time necessary to set up the call; while it may take 3 to 11 s to set up a telephone call, the average call lasts for 5 to 7 minutes (min).
- *Narrow passband requirement.* As we have already seen, a 3.1kHz passband is sufficient for human voice. Furthermore, increasing the bandwidth available for the voice call does not affect the duration of the call.

Data calls have different characteristics, including:

- *Delay insensitive.* Most user data does not alter in meaning because of being delayed in the network for a few seconds; a packet containing temperature information from the bottom of Lake Champlain, for example, will not change in meaning due to a short delay in the network.
- *Short hold time.* Most data traffic is bursty (i.e., the bulk of the data is transmitted in a short period of time, such as in interactive applications). A 90/10 rule is often cited to demonstrate this: 90 percent of the data is transmitted in 10 percent of the time. Since data transmission will tend to be very fast, long call setup times yield inefficient networks.[6]
- *Wide passband utilization.* Data can use all of a channel's available bandwidth; if additional bandwidth is made available for a data call, the duration of the call can decrease.

Figure C-9 shows the general structure of a switched network. Hosts (end users) are connected to a network to gain communications pathways to each other. Nodes are switches within the network. In a switched network, the path between a pair of hosts is usually not fixed. Therefore, host 1 might connect to host 3 via nodes A, C, E, D or via nodes A, B, D.

---

[6]For the purpose of this discussion, a data call is defined as a single interatctive session between hosts. This is not to be confused with the amount of time spent on line by a person (i.e., surfing the net).

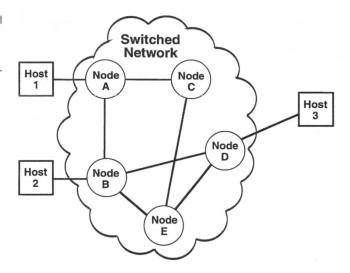

Figure C-9
Components of a
switched network.

In the telephone network, telephones could be considered hosts while LEs are nodes. The network is switched because two end users do not have a permanent, dedicated path between them. Instead, a path is established on request and released at the end of the call. One primary difference between types of switching networks is whether the communications channel allocated between nodes for a given call is shared with other calls or not.

Circuit Switching

Circuit switching is the most familiar type of switching to most people; the telephone network provides an excellent example of this type of network. In a circuit switched network, the communications pathway between two users is fixed for the duration of the call and is not shared by other users. During the call, the circuit is equivalent to a physical pair of wires connecting the two users. Although several users may share one physical line by use of FDM or TDM, only one user is assigned to a single channel at any given time.

In circuit switching, a connection is obtained between two users by establishing a fixed pathway through the network. The route is established after the calling party initiates the call setup procedure by telling the network the address of the called party (i.e., after the user dials the telephone number).

Circuit-switched connections are well suited for voice traffic. The dedicated pathway is required due to the delay-sensitive nature of voice calls. Also, the long call setup time is compensated for by the relatively long call hold time.

For similar reasons, circuit-mode connections are not as well suited for data calls. The bursty nature of data means that a long call setup procedure wastes time for a short transmission of data. Since the circuit switched network is optimized for human voice, all channels have a narrowband passband (4kHz or 64Kbps); again, this means that data calls will have a longer duration. If the connection is maintained between sessions, dedicating the channel means that the channel is idle much of the time. While data may be (and is) carried over circuit switched facilities, it is an inefficient use of those facilities and not optimal for data transmission.

It should be noted that a new set of digital circuit-mode services have entered the market. These services offer wideband circuit-switched channels at rates to 45Mbps. These dial-up wideband services are typically employed as backup facilities for disaster recovery operations where the value of the connection more than compensates for the data's inefficiencies.

Packet Switching

Packet switching was first described for data communications in the early 1960s. With packet switching, there is no dedicated end-to-end physical connection between two users during information exchange; instead, users submit their messages to the network for delivery to another user. The end-to-end connection between users, then, is logical rather than physical. Since internode channels are not dedicated to a specific end-to-end connection, they may be shared by many end-to-end logical connections. In this way, packet switching optimizes use of network resources by allowing several applications to share transmission facilities so that physical channels are never idle except in the total absence of traffic. Packet switching is suitable only for delay-insensitive traffic because variations in traffic loads can cause queuing delays.

In packet switched networks (PSNs), user messages are subdivided into units for transmission called *packets*. While packets may vary in size, they have a fixed maximum, such as 128 or 4096 octets. The receiver has the responsibility to reassemble the original message from the incoming packets.

A packet switched connection defines a logical pathway between two hosts through the packet network but does not dedicate any physical facilities to that connection. In this way, several packet switched connections can share the physical resources, optimizing use of the network resources. When packets are received by a node, they are placed in buffers and sent on to the next node in the path at the next available opportunity. Having multiple users share a physical resource on an as-needed basis is a type of *statistical TDM.*

A potential problem with statistical TDM is that some transmissions will be delayed. For example, if two packets are ready for transmission on the same physical line at the same time, the node will send one of them and buffer (store) the other one. The short delay is not a problem for many data applications, however, since the most common data applications are delay-insensitive. Delay-sensitive applications,[7] however, cannot use this scheme.

Packets are sent to a network node by the user (host) and are forwarded through the network from node to node until delivered to the destination host. As we observed above, the transmitting node must store the packet until it can forward it to the next node. For this reason, packet switching is called a *store-and-forward* strategy.

Packet networks can operate in one of two connection modes, namely *connection-oriented* or *connectionless.* In a connection-oriented, or *virtual circuit (VC)* network, an end-to-end logical connection must be established between two hosts before data exchange can take place. Connection-oriented networks are somewhat analogous to the telephone network: before people can talk to each other, a call must be established. The route of the connection is set up exactly once; and the network can handle error and flow control since the route is usually fixed for the duration of a connection. With connectionless, or *datagram* network, no logical connection is needed prior to the exchange of data. These networks are analogous to the postal system: a datagram is transmitted whenever there is data to send; each datagram is individually routed (and, therefore, may arrive at the destination out of sequence); and neither error nor flow control can efficiently be provided by the network.

Two other terms are used to describe the services of a packet network. *Reliable service* means that the network guarantees sequential delivery of packets and can notify senders when packets have been lost. An *unreliable service* refers to one where the network does not guarantee packet delivery and does not notify the sender when packets are lost or discarded.

Traditional packet switched public data networks (PSPDNs), offer a reliable, VC service. When two hosts wish to communicate, they establish a VC between them defining the logical host-to-host connection. A reliable VC connection means that while packets are guaranteed to be delivered to the destination and to be delivered in sequence, no physical lines are dedicated

---

[7]Some data applications, such as stock market information and real-time monitoring systems, are, in fact, delay-sensitive and cannot tolerate excessive network delays.

to the connection between the two hosts. Even though all packets associated with a VC probably follow the same route through the network, no user "owns" a physical line. For example, in Figure C-9, a VC between host 1 and host 3 and a VC between host 2 and host 3 will certainly share the physical path between nodes B and D and the physical path between node D and host 3.

The Internet, as a particular example of a packet network, offers an unreliable datagram service for its users. Datagram packets are sent into the network, each having its own address and each finding the "best" route to the destination. The network does not guarantee delivery of packets, much less sequential delivery. The Internet depends on protocols at the end-communicating hosts for a "reliable" end-to-end connection. This networking strategy might seem to be the weaker of the packet networking alternatives, but datagram systems are very popular because of the simplicity of the underlying network and the relative reliability of the facilities. Datagram networks also display a better recovery in the face of mode outages because each packet is routed independently.

Fast Packet Technologies

The concepts behind packet switching have yielded new high-performance packet-mode services called *fast packet switching*. Fast packet services and technologies are characterized by an assumption that the network infrastructure is a low-error-rate, high-speed digital network and depends on end-user systems for error correction (and some error detection). Today's fast packet services are, in fact, unreliable; data units with errors are discarded by the network and end users are not notified of such data loss. Fast packet services, described more in the text, have two forms, *Frame Relay* and *cell relay*.

Frame Relay is conceptually similar to VC packet switching. Frames can be of varying size, much like packets in a PSN. Hosts on a Frame Relay network establish a VC prior to exchanging frames, and the network discards frames with errors. The difference is that the hosts are responsible for end-to-end reliable communication. Frame Relay is an additional packet-mode service for ISDN and is described in more detail in the text.

Cell relay, unlike Frame Relay and packet switching, uses a fixed-size transmission entity called a *cell*. Utilization of a fixed-size cell allows many optimizations to be made in network switches and has better statistical multiplexing capabilities, allowing the concurrent transport of many traffic types, including voice, video, graphics, and data. Cell relay is currently being offered in both connection-based (VC) and connectionless (datagram) forms. A connection-oriented cell relay technology is the basis of asynchronous transfer mode (ATM) and is discussed more in the text. Connectionless cell relay technology is the basis of SMDS and is also discussed in the text.

Open Systems Interconnection Reference Model

During the 1960s and 1970s, companies such as Burroughs, Digital Equipment Corporation (DEC), Honeywell, and IBM defined network communications protocols for their computer products. Because of the proprietary nature of the protocols, however, the interconnection of computers from different manufacturers, or even between different product lines from the same manufacturer, was very difficult.

In the late 1970s, the International Organization for Standardization (ISO) developed the Reference Model for Open Systems Interconnection. The OSI model comprises a seven-layer architecture that is the basis for open network systems, allowing computers from any vendor to communicate with each other.

The goals of the OSI model are to expedite communication between equipment built by different manufacturers. The layering of the OSI model provides transparency; that is, the operation of a single layer of the model is independent of the other layers.

The OSI model is described here because it provides an excellent reference with which to compare and contrast different protocols and functionality. Implementations of OSI are few and far between, however, and it could be argued that the Transmission Control Protocol/Internet Protocol (TCP/IP) is the best implementation so far of an open systems protocol suite.

OSI Layers

The OSI model specifies seven functional protocol layers (Figure C-10). Peer layers across the network communicate according to *protocols*; adjacent layers in the same system communicate across an *interface*. Network architectures (such as ISDN and B-ISDN) specify the function of the layers, the protocol procedures for peer-to-peer communication, and the communication across the interface between adjacent protocol layers. Actual implementations and algorithms are not typically specified.

Figure C-10
Reference model for
OSI.

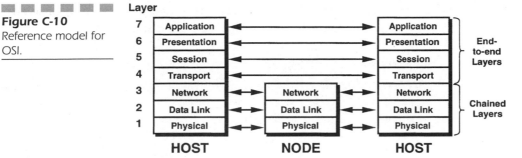

The lower three layers of the OSI model are:

- *Physical Layer* (*layer 1*). Specifies the electrical and mechanical characteristics of the protocol used to transfer bits between two adjacent devices in the network; common examples include EIA-232-E (formerly RS-232-C), EIA-530, High-Speed Serial Interface (HSSI), V.24, V.28, and V.35.

- *Data Link Layer* (*layer 2*). Specifies the protocol for error-free communication between adjacent devices across the physical link; common examples include IBM's Binary Synchronous Communications (BISYNC) and Synchronous Data Link Control (SDLC) protocols, DEC's Digital Data Communication Message Protocol (DDCMP), ISO's High-level Data Link Control (HDLC), and ITU-T's Link Access Procedures Balanced (LAPB), Link Access Procedures on the D-channel (LAPD), and Link Access Procedures to Frame Mode Bearer Services (LAPF).

- *Network Layer* (*layer 3*). Specifies protocols for such functions as routing, congestion control, accounting, call setup and termination, and user-network communications. Examples include IP, ISO's Connectionless Network Protocol (CLNP), and ISDN's call control procedures (Q931 and Q2931).

These three layers are called the *chained layers* and comprise procedures for host-to-node and node-to-node communication. End users (hosts), as well as all switching devices (nodes) along the route between the hosts, must implement these protocol layers.[8]

The upper four layers of the OSI model are:

- *Transport Layer* (*layer 4*). Specifies the functions and classes of service for error-free communication between hosts across the subnetwork. Examples include TCP and ISO's Transport Protocol (TP).

---

[8]Exceptions are the switches in fast packet networks. These devices, while using three layers for VC establishment (Frame Relay and ATM), use only a two layer stack for normal data transfers.

- *Session Layer (layer 5).* Specifies process-to-process communication, error recovery, and session synchronization.
- *Presentation Layer (layer 6).* A set of general, non-application-specific user services, such as encryption, authentication, and text compression.
- *Application Layer (layer 7).* Specifies the user interface to the network and a set of specific user applications. Sample applications and protocols include TCP/IP's Simple Mail Transfer Protocol (SMTP) and ITU-T X.400 for e-mail, X.500 for directory services, TCP/IP's Telnet and ISO's VT protocol for remote login and virtual terminals, TCP/IP's File Transfer Protocol (FTP) and ISO's File Transfer Access Method (FTAM) for file transfers, TCP/IP's Simple Network Management Protocol (SNMP) and ISO's Common Management Information Protocol (CMIP) for network management, and the Hypertext Transfer Protocol (HTTP) for the World Wide Web.

These four layers are called the *end-to-end layers* since they are implemented only in hosts. End-to-end information is transparent to the chained layers. The network nodes that deal with the chained layers generate higher-layer protocol traffic specific to their applications; a switching node, for example, could generate network management traffic using the SNMP protocol, but this would not affect the operation of the chained layers or the network nodes.

The ITU-T standard ISDN protocols define a user-network interface that comprises only the chained layers. While an ISDN itself can provide many types of services using many types of protocols, the ISDN user-network interface is designed to be a common set of protocols for user access to the network, regardless of the required service.

Packet Switching and X.25

ITU-T Recommendation X.25 defines the interface between a user and a PSPDN. User hosts are called *data terminal equipment* (DTE) and the network nodes are called *data circuit-terminating equipment* (DCE). X.25 is very important to ISDNs; packet switching will be supported by ISDNs, and X.25 is the most widely used packet switching protocol today. Recommendation X.25 defines three protocol layers corresponding to a user-network interface:

- *Layer 1.* Exchanges bits between the DTE and DCE; the Physical Layer specified by X.25 is based on Recommendations X.21 and X.21 *bis*.[9]

---

[9]X.21 is not implemented in public X.25 networks in North America; the common customer premises interface is EIA-232, EIA-530, or V.35, which are options under X.21 *bis*.

- *Layer 2.* Ensures error-free communication between the DTE and DCE; the X.25 Data Link Layer protocol is LAPB.
- *Layer 3.* Provides rules for the establishment of virtual calls and the ability to have several simultaneous virtual calls on a single physical channel between the DTE and DCE; this protocol is called the Packet Layer Protocol (PLP).

ITU-T Recommendation X.75 is similar to X.25. Originally written for internetworking between PSPDNs, it has taken on a more general role for internetworking many types of packet networks, including PSPDNs and ISDNs.

Protocol Architectures

This book will not specifically discuss OSI, packet switching, or details of Recommendation X.25. A basic understanding of the OSI model, however, will enhance understanding of the discussion of ISDN and B-ISDN protocol suites. In addition, an understanding of the X.25 protocol architecture and packet switching will enhance understanding of ISDN packet-mode operations and fast packet services.

APPENDIX D

ISDN Terms, Definitions, and Standards*

An ISDN is a digital network that can provide many types of services to a user. The real thrust of the ISDN standards is not how the network operates but how the user communicates with the network and accesses network services. ISDN standards, then, define the interface between the user and the network. This interface is in the form of a set of protocols, including a message set used to request services.

Most people have heard many of the terms commonly associated with ISDN, such as D-channel, B-channel, 2B1D, 23B1D, basic rate, primary rate, NT1, TA, bearer services, ITU-T, ANSI. This appendix will introduce and define many of the terms used in the standards, literature, and vendor's ISDN product and service descriptions.

The use of these terms in this book is not intended to confuse or intimidate the reader. On the contrary, the terms have rather precise meanings and facilitate discussion about the network, its components, and its services. The concepts of ISDN are actually quite straightforward except for the new language that has been introduced to discuss them.

ISDN cannot succeed as a global telecommunications strategy without international standards. This appendix will conclude with an introduction to the organizations responsible for creating the ISDN standards. It is impossible to understand any of the ISDN compatibility issues without some knowledge of the players in the ISDN standards game.

The international standards provide a common framework for all national service providers. In the United States, we do not have a single service or equipment provider. Because of this environment, an additional set of standards is necessary for consistent implementation of an ISDN. These definitions are described in the National ISDN (NI) standards, a set of implementation documents that define the services and signaling for the United States.

---

*This appendix appeared in chapter 2 of *ISDN: Concepts, Facilities, and Services,* signature edition, by Gary C. Kesslar and Peter Southwick, published by McGraw-Hill, New York, 1998.

ISDN Channels

In data communications, a *channel* is a unidirectional conduit through which information flows. A channel can carry digital or analog signals comprising user data or network signaling information. In ISDN and other digital TDM environments, a channel generally refers to a time slot on a transmission facility and is full-duplex (bidirectional).

In today's telephone network, the local loop connection between the user and C.O. provides a single analog channel, used for different types of information. First, the loop is used to carry signals between the user's equipment and the network. The telephone, for example, places a short circuit on the line to indicate that the handset has been taken off-hook. A dial tone from the network signals the user to enter the telephone number. Pulses or tones representing the dialed digits, busy signals, and ringing signals also appear over the local loop. Second, after the call is established, the loop carries user information, which may be voice, audio, video, or data, depending upon the application. These two types of usage could be said to represent two logical channels, one for signaling and one for user services.

In an ISDN, the local loop carries only digital signals and comprises several channels used for signaling and user data. The different channels coexist on the local loop using TDM. There are three basic types of channels defined for user communications in an ISDN, differentiated by their function and bit rate (Table D-1):

Table D-1

ISDN Channel
Types

Channel	Function	Bit Rate
B	Bearer services	64Kbps
D	Signaling and	16Kbps (BRI) packet-mode data 64Kbps (PRI)
H_0	Wideband bearer service	384Kbps
H_1	Wideband bearer services	
H_{10} (23B)*	1.472Mbps	
H_{11} (24B)	1.536Mbps	
H_{12} (30B)	1.920Mbps	
N364	Variable bandwidth bearer services	64Kbps to 1.536Mbps in 64-kbps increments

*An H_{10}-channel is defined by ANSI, but not by the ITU-T.

- *D-channel.* Carries signaling information between the user and the network; may also carry user data packets
- *B-channel.* Carries information for user services, including voice, audio, video, and digital data; operates at the DS-0 rate (64 Kbps)
- *H-channel.* Same function as B-channels but operates at bit rates above DS-0

The sections below describe these channels in more detail.

The D-Channel

All ISDN devices attach to the network using a standard physical connector and exchange a standard set of messages with the network to request service. The contents of the service-request messages will vary with the different services requested; an ISDN telephone, for example, will request different services from the network than will an ISDN television. All ISDN equipment, however, will use the same protocol and same set of messages. The network and user equipment exchange all service requests and other signaling messages over the ISDN D-channel. Typically a single D-channel will provide the signaling services for a single ISDN interface (access point). It is possible for a single ISDN device (e.g., a PBX) to be connected to the network with more than one ISDN interface. In this scenario, it is possible for the D-channel to provide signaling information for many ISDN interfaces. This capability saves channel and equipment resources by consolidating all signaling information on one channel; it is only available on the T-carrier ISDN interface, as discussed below.

Although the D-channel's primary function is for user-network signaling, the exchange of these signaling messages is unlikely to use all of the available bandwidth. Excess time on the D-channel is available for user's packet data and, indeed, the transport of packet-mode data is the secondary function of the D-channel. The excess time is deemed to be great enough to allow service providers to offer user data services at rates up to 9.6Kbps on the D-channel. This is a bargain for users because the full 16Kbps of the D-channel is typically available. User-network signaling messages always have priority over data packets.

The D-channel operates at either 16 or 64Kbps, depending upon the user's access interface, which is discussed later.

The B-Channel

Signals exchanged on the D-channel describe the characteristics of the service that the user is requesting. For example, an ISDN telephone may request a circuit-mode connection operating at 64Kbps for the support of a speech application. This profile of characteristics describes what is called a *bearer service*. Bearer services are granted by the network, allocating a circuit-mode channel between the requesting device and the destination. At the local loop, the B-channels are designated to provide this type of service.

The primary purpose of the B-channel, then, is to carry the user's voice, audio, image, data, and video signals. No service requests from the user are sent on the B-channel. B-channels always operate at 64Kbps, the bit rate required for digital voice applications.

The B-channel can be used for both circuit-mode and packet-mode applications. A circuit-mode connection provides a transparent user-to-user connection, allowing the connection to be specifically suited to one type of service (e.g., television or music). In the circuit mode, no protocols above the physical layer (64Kbps) are defined by the ITU-T for the B-channels; each user of a B-channel is responsible for defining the protocols to be used over the connection. It is also the responsibility of the users to assure compatibility between devices connected by B-channels. Packet-mode connections support packet switching equipment using protocols such as X.25 or Frame Relay. The ISDN can provide either an internal packet-mode service or provide access to an existing PSPDN for packet service. In either case, the protocols and procedures of the PSPDN must be adhered to when requesting packet-mode service.

B-channels can be used on an on-demand basis, as described above, or on a permanent basis. If a B-channel is provisioned for permanent service, no D-channel signaling is required for the operation of the B-channel. A sample application might be the provisioning of a permanent B-channel for high-speed (64-kbps) PSPDN access or Frame Relay access.

The most important point to remember is the relationship between B- and D-channels. The D-channel is used to exchange the signaling messages necessary to request services on the B-channel.

H-Channels

A user application requiring a bit rate higher than 64Kbps may be obtained by using wideband channels, or H-channels, which provide the bandwidth equivalent of a group of B-channels. Applications requiring bit rates above 64Kbps include LAN interconnection, high-speed data, high-quality audio, teleconferencing, and video services.

The first designated wideband channel is an H_0-channel, which has a data rate of 384Kbps. This is equivalent to logically grouping six B-channels together.

An H_1-channel comprises all available time slots at a single-user interface employing a T1 or E1 carrier. An H_{11}-channel operates at 1.536Mbps and is equivalent to 24 time slots (24 B-channels) for compatibility with the T1 carrier. An H_{12}-channel operates at 1.920Mbps and is equivalent to 30 time slots (30 B-channels) for compatibility with the E1 carrier.

ANSI has designated an H_{10}-channel, operating at 1.472Mbps and equivalent to 23 time slots on a T1 interface. This channel was defined by ANSI to support a single wideband channel and a D-channel on the same T1 access facility; with an H_{11}-channel, a D-channel and wideband channel cannot coexist on the same T1 interface.

Another set of ISDN channels has been defined for variable bit rate applications, called an Nx64 channel. This channel is similar in structure to the H-channels except it offers a range of bandwidth options from 64Kbps to 1.536Mbps in increments of 64Kbps. When a user requests an Nx64 channel for a given call, the service request contains the type of channel (Nx64) and the value of N (1 to 24). A benefit to users of an Nx64 channel is that they do not require inverse multiplexing equipment on the premises since the network maintains time slot sequence integrity between the N 64-kbps time slots. Another advantage of the Nx64 channel is the ability to customize the bandwidth requirements to the application.

Access Interfaces

An *access interface* is the physical connection between the user and the ISDN that allows the user to request and obtain services. The concept of an access interface is a familiar one to users of today's networks. Most residences, for example, have a single-line telephone and, accordingly, a single connection to the local C.O. This single local loop can be said to comprise two logical channels, as described earlier, one for user-network signals (on- and off-hook) and one for user data (voice and tones).

As the number of simultaneous users increases at a customer location, so does the requirement for the number of physical resources to handle those users. A second local loop, for example, can provide a second telephone line, while multiple trunk circuits can provide multiple lines between a customer's PBX and the C.O. Access to other networks and/or network services (e.g., a packet network or the Internet) can be provided by bringing additional lines to the customer's premises. It is not uncommon for a business location to have many individual lines connecting it to the C.O. for such services as telephony, fax, a point-of-sale terminal, and remote security.

ISDN access interfaces differ somewhat from today's telephone network access interfaces. First, one goal of ISDN is to provide all services over a single network access connection (physical resource), independent of the equipment or service type. Second, ISDN access interfaces comprise a D-channel for signaling multiplexed with some number of B-channels for user data. This design allows multiple information flows simultaneously on a single physical interface.

ISDN recommendations from the ITU-T currently define two different access interfaces, called the *basic rate interface* (BRI) and *primary rate interface* (PRI). These access interfaces specify the rate at which the physical medium will operate and the number of available B-, D-, and H-channels (Table D-2).

Table D-2

ISDN Access
Interface Structures

Interface	Structure*	Total Bit Rate	User Data Rate
Basic rate interface (BRI)	$2B1D_{16}$	192Kbps	144Kbps
Primary rate T1	$23B1D_{64}$†	1.544Mbps	1.536Mbps
interface (PRI) E1	$30B1D_{64}$	2.048Mbps	1.984Mbps

*The D-channel operates at 16Kbps in the BRI and at 64Kbps in the PRI.

†This is one possible PRI configuration, and the most common today. Other configurations are also possible, such as 24B.

Bellcore documents use a slightly different set of terms, namely, *basic rate access* (BRA) and *primary rate access* (PRA). The use of this terminology stems from the separation of the service access from the physical interface; a BRA, for example, could be physically delivered to a location in a form other than a single two-wire interface.

Basic Rate Interface

The BRI comprises two B-channels and one D-channel and is designated 2B1D. The BRI D-channel always operates at 16Kbps.

The BRI will typically be used in one of two ways. First, it can provide ISDN access between a residential or business customer and the ISDN LE. Alternatively, it can provide ISDN access between user equipment and an ISDN-compatible PBX in a business environment. As a tariffed offering, the BRI can be ordered in configurations other than 2B1D, and other no-menclature may be encountered. If the BRI is to be used only for telephony and no data will be sent on the D-channel, the configuration is sometimes called *2B1S* (the D-channel is for signaling only). If only a single B-channel is required, a *1B1D* or *1B1S* arrangement may be ordered; packet data is allowed on the D-channel in the former and not in the latter.

Finally, if only low-speed (9.6-kbps) packet data is required, a *0B1D* configuration can be ordered. These configurations allow ISDN to be customized for customer applications and are priced differently based on the number of active channels. It should be noted that in all of these configurations, the interface's physical characteristics are the same; the only difference is in which channels have been activated by the LE and what type of traffic is allowed on the D-channel.

The user data rate on the BRI is 144Kbps (2x64Kbps+16Kbps), although additional signaling for the physical connection requires that the BRI operate at a higher bit rate. The specific rates of the interface and the overhead associated with those rates are discussed in the text.

Primary Rate Interface

The PRI also has a number of possible configurations. The most common configuration in North America and Japan is designated 23B1D, meaning that the interface comprises 23 B-channels plus a single D-channel operating at 64Kbps. Optionally, the D-channel on a given PRI may not be activated, allowing that time slot to be used as another B-channel; this configuration is designated 24B.[1] This PRI description is based on the T1 digital carrier. It operates at a bit rate of 1.544Mbps, of which 1.536Mbps are user data.

A 30B1D PRI is also defined that comprises 30 B-channels and 1 D-channel. Based on the E1 digital carrier, it operates at 2.048Mbps, of which 1.984Mbps are user data.

The PRI contains more channels than a typical end-user device will use. The PRI is, in fact, primarily intended to provide access to the network by some sort of customer premises switching equipment, such as a remote access server PBX, multiplexer, or host computer.

---

[1]The presence of a D-channel at the user-network interface is essential in ISDN for the exchange of signaling information to control services. Therefore, at least one PRI at a customer interface must be configured as 23B1D. Since the D-channel on one PRI may control other physical interfaces, subsequent PRIs may be configured as 24B. In these cases, a second PRI is often configured with a backup D-channel.

When a wideband application requires more throughput than that provided by a B-channel, the PRI can be configured to provide H-channel access. When this configuration is used, the number of available B-channels will decrease by the number of time slots used by the H-channel(s). An example would be a videoconferencing system needing 384Kbps (an H_0-channel) for a call. The supporting PRI would have extra bandwidth available for a D-channel and 17 B-channels. If the video system needed an H_{11}-channel, no B- or D-channel time slots would be available. This flexibility allows the PRI to act as a wideband access system and a narrowband access system, depending on the application active at any time. The same bandwidth (time slots) can be configured for different types of channels on demand.

Functional Devices and Reference Points

Several different devices may be present in the connection between CPE and the network to which the CPE is attached. Consider the relatively simple example of a customer's connection to the telephone network. All of the subscriber's telephones are connected with inside wiring to a junction box in the customer's building; the local loop provides the physical connection between the junction box and the LE. As far as the customer is concerned, the CPE is communicating directly with the exchange; the junction box is transparent.

Other equipment may also be present. If a PC is attached to the telephone network, for example, a modem will replace the telephone. In a PBX environment, the telephones and modems are attached to the PBX, which will provide on-site switching; the PBX is, in turn, connected to the LE.

Protocols describe the rules governing the communication between devices in a network. With all of the devices mentioned here, questions might arise as to which protocols are to be used where and who is responsible for defining the protocols. The telephone, for example, uses a familiar protocol that is specified by the network; certain current represents the off-hook signal, special pulses or tones represent the dialed digits, and so on.

A modem follows the same protocol as a telephone on the side that connects to the telephone network. It uses a different protocol, however, on the side that connects to a PC; EIA-232-E and the Hayes AT-command set, for example, are commonly used between a PC and external modem. The modem acts as a signal converter so that digital signals output from the PC will be suitable for the analog telephone network.

The presence of a PBX adds another layer of complexity. A telephone connected to a PBX follows protocols specified by the PBX manufacturer, which is why many PBX-specific telephones are not usable on the public telephone network. The PBX, in turn, must use network-specified protocols for the PBX-to-network communication.

In today's communications environment it is often difficult to separate the devices from the functions they perform. The case of the PC communicating over the telephone network is an example. Above we described three devices, a PC, a modem, and a network; each has a specific function and is governed by a set of protocols. What would happen if the PC had an internal modem? The number of functional devices would remain the same, but the number of physical devices would be reduced to two, the PC and the network. In this example the number of functional devices and the number of actual physical devices differ due to the packaging of the devices.

These same ideas are extended to ISDN. The ISDN standards define several different types of devices. Each device type has certain functions and responsibilities but may not represent an actual physical piece of equipment. For that reason, the standards call them *functional devices.*

Since the ISDN recommendations describe several functional device types, there are several device-to-device interfaces, each requiring a communications protocol. Each of these functional device interfaces is called a *reference point.*

The paragraphs below describe the different functional devices and reference points, which are shown in Figure D-1.

Figure D-1
ISDN functional devices and reference points.

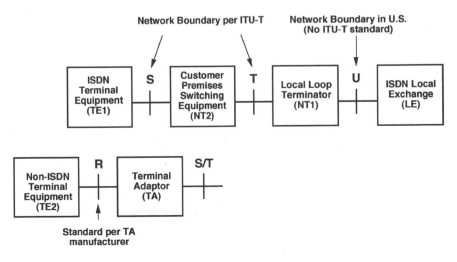

ISDN Functional Devices

The network device that provides ISDN services is the *LE.* ISDN protocols are implemented in the LE, which is also the network side of the ISDN local loop. Other LE responsibilities include maintenance, physical interface operation, timing, and providing requested user services.

Some ISDN exchange manufacturers further break down the functions of the LE into two subgroups called *local termination* (LT) and *exchange termination* (ET). The LT handles those functions associated with the termination of the local loop, while the ET handles switching functions. For simplicity and generality, this book will usually refer only to the LE and avoid specific references to LT or ET except where necessary. Also included in the LE is equipment specialized to support the ISDN services. These have to do with the signaling used in ISDN and the incorporation of packet-mode or frame-mode data in the ISDN list of services. The first is a packet handler (PH). This device is responsible for the decoding of all ISDN signaling packets passed between the LE and the ISDN subscriber. It is also used to distinguish user X.25 data on the D-channel from signaling data and routes the user data toward its destination on the associated PSPDN. The second device (or devices) is the network signaling system employed for the ISDN. In today's environment this signaling system is Signaling System No. 7 (SS7) and is described in this book. The SS7 device is responsible for the creation and interpretation of the signaling messages used between LEs in the ISDN. The final device is a frame handler (FH), which has a function similar to the PH but supports Frame Relay user traffic rather than ISDN signaling and X.25 traffic. The FH, like the PH, can be an integral part of the LE or an adjunct processor attached to the LE.

Network termination type 1 (NT1), or local loop terminator equipment, represents the termination of the physical connection between the customer site and the LE. The NT1's responsibilities include line performance monitoring, timing, physical signaling protocol conversion, electrical conversion, and power transfer.

Network termination type 2 (NT2) equipment are those devices providing customer site switching, multiplexing, and/or concentration. This includes PBXs, multiplexers, routers, host computers, terminal controllers, and other CPE for voice and data switching. An NT2 will be absent in some ISDN environments, such as residential or Centrex ISDN service. NT2s distribute ISDN services to other devices that are attached to it. In this role, the NT2 might perform some protocol conversion functions as well as distribution functions. One of the primary distribution functions is the network signaling on behalf of the attached terminals. The NT2 is responsible for all signaling to the network. As an example, a PBX might terminate an analog telephone and allow access to an ISDN PRI for a connection to other subscribers. In this case the PBX is providing protocol conversion from the analog voice to the ISDN digital voice and is collecting the dialed digits from the telephone and creating a signaling message for the LE.

Terminal equipment (TE) refers to end-user devices, such as an analog or digital telephone, X.25 data terminal equipment, ISDN workstation, or integrated voice/data terminal (IVDT). *Terminal equipment type 1* (TE1) are those devices that utilize the ISDN protocols and support ISDN services, such as an ISDN telephone or workstation. *Terminal equipment type 2* (TE2) are non-ISDN-compatible devices, such as the analog telephones in use on today's telephone network.

A *terminal adapter* (TA) allows a non-ISDN device (TE2) to communicate with the network. TAs have particular importance in today's ISDN marketplace; nearly every device in use in today's data and telecommunications environment is TE2. TAs allow analog telephones, X.25 DTEs, PCs, and other non-ISDN devices to use the network by providing any necessary protocol conversion.

The reader should note that a single physical piece of equipment can take on the responsibilities of two or more of the functional devices defined here. For example, a PBX might actually perform NT1 (local loop termination) and NT2 (customer site switching) functions; this combination is sometimes referred to as NT12. In the same theme, an ISDN telephone can be purchased that has a TA and an NT1 built-in; this combination is referred to as a bargain.

ISDN Reference Points

The ISDN reference points define the communication protocols between the different ISDN functional devices. The importance of the different reference points is that different protocols may be used at each reference point. Four protocol reference points are commonly defined for ISDN, called R, S, T, and U.

The R reference point is between non-ISDN terminal equipment (TE2) and a TA. The TA will allow the TE2 to appear to the network as an ISDN device, just like a modem allows a terminal or PC to communicate over today's telephone network. There are no specific ISDN standards for the R reference point; the TA manufacturer will determine and specify how the TE2 and TA communicate with each other. Examples of R reference point specifications include EIA-232-E, V.35, and the Industry Standard Architecture (ISA) bus.

The S reference point is between ISDN user equipment (i.e., TE1 or TA) and network termination equipment (NT2 or NT1). The T reference point is between customer site switching equipment (NT2) and the local loop termination (NT1). ISDN recommendations from the ITU-T, the primary international standards body for ISDN, specifically address protocols for the S and T reference points. In the absence of the NT2, the user-network interface is usually called the S/T reference point.[2]

One of the more controversial and pivotal aspects of ISDN, at least in the United States, was the transmission standard across the local loop between the NT1 and the LE, called the U reference point. The ITU-T considers the physical NT1 device to be owned by the network administration; that makes the local loop part of the network. Therefore, the ITU-T views the S or T reference points as the user-network boundary. ITU-T recommendations do not address internal network operations, so they have no standard for transmission across the local loop (U reference point).[3]

The U.S. Federal Communications Commission (FCC), however, does not adopt this same view. Since the NT1 is on the customer's site, the FCC considers it to be customer owned. Since network equipment (the LE) is on one side of the U reference point and user equipment (the NT1) is on the other, it is clearly the local loop that represents the user-network boundary according to the FCC. Furthermore, operation across the user-network boundary in the United States must be described by a public standard and, in fact, is the subject of a U.S. national standard from the American National Standards Institute.

Although not shown in Figure D-1 or described further in this appendix, some manufacturers define a V reference point between LEs in an ISDN. This reference point identifies the network node interface and is transparent to the user.

B-ISDN Channels, Functional Devices, and Reference Points

For reference, it should be noted that ITU-T B-ISDN standards use the same functional device and reference point designations as defined above. The notation for devices and protocols with broadband capability, however, includes the letter *B*. A B-ISDN terminal, for example, will be designated B-TE1, and the B-ISDN T reference point will be designated T_B.

---

[2]The ambivalence of what to call this bus results in different providers referring to the user-network interface as the S, T, or S/T interface in the absence of the NT2. We will use the term S/T because it is somewhat more "complete." It is an S interface from the viewpoint of the TE and a T interface from the viewpoint of the NT1.

[3]In fact, the ITU-T standards do not actually refer to the U reference point; they mention the R, S, and T reference points and the *transmission line.*

Standards Organizations

The ITU-T

The organization primarily responsible for producing international ISDN standards is the International Telecommunication Union Telecommunication Standardization Sector (ITU-T), formerly known as the International Telegraph and Telephone Consultative Committee (CCITT, or Comité Consultatif International Télégraphique et Téléphonique). Although the ITU has been an agency of the United Nations (U.N.) since 1948, the ITU's formal beginning dates back to 1865, and it is the world's oldest intergovernmental agency.

The ITU-T produces standards describing access to public telecommunications networks and the services to be offered by those networks but does not specify the internal operation of the networks. It is for this reason that the ITU-T does not define the U reference point; the ITU-T views the local loop as part of the network and, therefore, an internal matter.

Since the 1960s, CCITT standards, called *recommendations*, were formally adopted at plenary sessions held every 4 years. The recommendations were published in a set of books referred to by the color of their cover; 1988 recommendations are contained in the Blue Book, 1984 in the Red Book, 1980 in the Yellow Book, and 1976 in the Orange Book, for example.

This schedule and publishing scheme fell out of favor during the 1980s due to the time lost waiting for the next plenary and the tremendous amount of paper that was required to publish recommendations, including republishing those recommendations that had not changed; the Red Book, for example, was 9900 pages in length and the Blue Book, just 4 years later, was about 20,000 pages. At the 1988 Plenary Session, the CCITT passed a resolution that each new or revised recommendation would be published as soon as it was finalized. This not only responded to environmental concerns but also expedited availability of completed works.

The CCITT's sister standards organization is the International Radio Consultative Committee (CCIR). The CCIR concentrates on specifications for radio communications, including radio- and satellite-based ISDN. In March 1993, the ITU underwent a significant reorganization and reassignment of responsibilities. One result was that both the CCITT and CCIR were renamed to the ITU-T and ITU Radiocommunication Standardization Sector (ITU-R), respectively. The quadrennial CCITT Plenary Assembly is now known as the World Telecommunication Standardization Conference.

There are five classes of membership within the ITU-T:

1. *Administration members* represent a country's telecommunications administration and act as the official voting representative. The Postal, Telephone, and Telegraph (PTT) administration is typically a country's Class A member; since the United States does not have a PTT, the State Department is the U.S. Class A member.

2. *Recognized Private Operating Agencies* (RPOA) are private or government organizations that provide a public telecommunications service, such as Lucent, MCI, Sprint, and BT Tymnet.

3. *Scientific and industrial organization members* are any other commercial organization with an interest in the ITU-T's work, such as Alcatel, Lucent, DEC, IBM, Nortel, and Siemens.

4. *International organization members* include other international organizations with an interest in the ITU-T's work, such as ISO.

5. *Specialized treaty agencies* are agencies organized by treaty whose work is related to the ITU-T's work, such as the World Health Organization and World Meteorological Organization.

Although only Class A members can officially vote at the sessions, all members can participate at the study group (SG) and working group level. As the official U.S. representative, the State Department coordinates all U.S. participation with the ITU-T.

The work of the ITU-T is performed by 15 SGs and other committees (Table D-3). ITU-T recommendations are identified by a letter followed by a number, where the letter indicates the general topic of the recommendation series. Notable topics include:

- *E-series.*   Telephone network and ISDN
- *G-series.*   International telephone connections and circuits
- *I-series.*   ISDN
- *Q-series.*   Telephone switching and signaling networks
- *V-series.*   Digital communication over the telephone network
- *X-series.*   Public data communication networks

Table D-3

Study and Advisory Groups of the ITU Telecommunication Standardization Sector (1993–1996)

SG 1—Service Definition

SG 2—Network Operation

SG 3—Tariff and Accounting Principles

SG 4—Network Maintenance

SG 5—Protection Against Electromagnetic Environment Effects

SG 6—Outside Plant

SG 7—Data Networks and Open System Communications

SG 8—Terminals for Telematic Services

SG 9—Television and Sound Transmission

SG 10—Languages for Telecommunication Applications

SG 11—Switching and Signaling

SG 12—End-to-End Transmission Performance of Networks and Terminals

SG 13—General Network Aspects

SG 14—Modems and Transmission Techniques for Data, Telegraph, and Telematic Services

SG 15—Transmission Systems and Equipment

Telecommunication Standardization Advisory Group (TSAG)

ITU involvement with ISDN dates back over 20 years. In 1968, a CCITT SG meeting convened to discuss the integration of switching and transmission. The meeting resulted in the formation of a special SG devoted to this topic (Study Group Special D), which later became SG XVIII. ITU-T SG 11 (formerly CCITT SG XVIII) has responsibility for digital networks including ISDN. Among other things, they are responsible for writing the I-series recommendations defining ISDN and specifying appropriate services and protocols. Figure D-2 shows the general organization of the I-series recommendations.

Figure D-2
Organization of ITU-T
I-series (ISDN)
recommendations.
(*From ITU-T Recom-
mendation I.110*)

ITU-T I-SERIES RECOMMENDATIONS

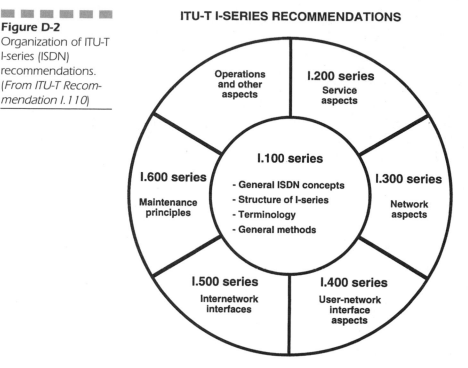

Study Group D dealt with IDNs and integrated services networks (ISNs); the former is a network that contains digital switches and transmission facilities from end to end, and the latter is a network that offers many types of services from a single network. In 1971, another CCITT meeting was convened to discuss these terms. Several countries wanted the word *digital* added to the ISN term since integrated services can, conceivably, be offered by an analog network, which was not the subject of SG XVIII's work. Other countries felt that integration of services was only feasible in a digital environment, thus adding the word was redundant. The compromise was to coin the term *integrated services (digital) network*. Eventually the parentheses were dropped, yielding the term that we have today. Note that this activity was occurring well before digital switches were widely introduced into the telecommunications network.

Under the direction of SG XVIII, CCITT leadership in organizing and developing ISDN standards grew. The first set of ISDN recommendations were formally published in 1984 (Red Book), followed by updated specifications in 1988 (Blue Book) and almost continuously since then.

Other SGs participate in the ISDN standards process by virtue of the recommendations that they prepare, which often overlap. Recommendations for public data networks (X-series), ISDN and telephone network switching and signaling (Q-series), and addressing and numbering plans

(E-series), for example, can all pertain to ISDN. For this reason, several I-series recommendations are also assigned Q-, X-, or other series' recommendation numbers. Support of X.25 terminals on an ISDN, for example, is described in Recommendations I.462 and X.31; these two standards are identical. Similarly, ISDN signaling procedures on the D-channel are listed as both Recommendation I.451 and Q.931. In the Red Book, dual-listed recommendations were often published in both locations; this changed in the Blue Book so that recommendations were published in only one location and referenced in the others. In this book, ITU-T recommendations will be referred to by the series and number where they are actually published. An I-series or other alternate designation, if any, will be given in parentheses.

The American National Standards Institute

ANSI is the primary standards-setting body in the United States. Formed in 1918, ANSI is a nonprofit, nongovernmental organization supported today by more than a thousand trade organizations, professional societies, and corporations. ANSI itself does not create standards per se, but rather coordinates and sanctions the activities of appropriate organizations that do write standards.

ANSI Standards Committee T1 is responsible for producing U.S. national telecommunications standards. T1-series standards include T1 and other digital carrier specifications,[4] ISDN, the U.S. version of SS7, SONET, and Frame Relay.

The secretariat for the T1 Committee is the Alliance for Telecommunications Industry Solutions (ATIS). ATIS was originally incorporated as a not-for-profit association in 1983 and called the Exchange Carriers' Standards Association (ECSA). Renamed in 1993, ATIS comprises members of the telecommunications industry to address exchange access, interconnection, and other technical issues that have resulted from divestiture. ATIS supports a number of industry forums on topics such as ordering and billing, network operations, bar code specifications, electronic data interchange, open network architecture, network reliability, and electrical protection.[5]

The work of the T1 committee, formed in 1984, is handled by six subcommittees, each dealing with different aspects of telecommunications. The various T1 subcommittees and working groups are listed in Table D-4, and T1 standards related to ISDN and B-ISDN are listed in the text.

---

[4]The designation of the T1 carrier and the T1 committee is coincidental. The *T-carrier* designation for digital carriers was made by AT&T in the 1960s, and the *T1* assignment for telecommunications was made by ANSI in the 1980s.

[5]ATIS also sponsors the ANSI O5 Committee, developing standards for wood poles and wood products for utility structures.

Table D-4

Subcommittees and Working Groups of the ANSI T1 Committee (July 1995)

T1A1—Performance and Signal Processing

T1A1.2—Network Survivability Performance

T1A1.3—Performance of Digital Networks and Services

T1A1.5—Multimedia Communications Coding and Performance

T1A1.7—Signal Processing and Network Performance for Voiceband Services

T1E1—Interfaces, Power and Protection of Networks

T1E1.1—Analog Access

T1E1.2—Wideband Access

T1E1.4—Digital Subscriber Loop (DSL) Access

T1E1.5—Power Systems—Power Interfaces

T1E1.6—Power Systems—Human and Machine Interfaces

T1E1.7—Electrical Protection

T1E1.8—Physical Protection

T1M1—Internetwork Operations, Administration, Maintenance and Provisioning

T1M1.1—Internetwork Planning and Engineering

T1M1.3—Testing and Operations Support Systems and Equipment

T1M1.4—Administrative Systems (inactive)

T1M1.5—OAM&P Architectures, Interfaces and Protocols

T1P1—Systems Engineering, Standards Planning and Program Management

T1P1.1—Program Management and Standards Planning

T1P1.2—Systems Engineering for Personal Communications Networks and Service Aspects

T1P1.3—Systems Engineering for Wireless Access and Terminal Mobility

T1P1.4—Wireless Interfaces

T1S1—Services, Architectures and Signaling

T1S1.1—ISDN Architecture and Services

T1S1.3—Common Channel Signaling

T1S1.5—Broadband ISDN

T1X1—Digital Hierarchy and Synchronization

T1X1.3—Synchronization and Tributary Analysis Interfaces

T1X1.4—Metallic Hierarchical Interfaces

T1X1.5—Optical Hierarchical Interfaces

Recognizing the hierarchical organization of ANSI will help in understanding and appreciating the standards-making process. Each committee and working group meets approximately three to six times each year, and sometimes more. Each group comprises individuals representing companies that have an interest in the progression of the standard, including vendors, manufacturers, users, and service providers.

Suppose, for example, that the T1S1.1 task group produces a new ISDN specification for adoption as a standard. All members of the task group must reach a consensus before the specification advances to the draft standard phase. When the group is ready to forward the standard, it goes to the T1S1 subcommittee. That level, too, must approve the document before it is forwarded; any negative comments are referred to the task group. After the subcommittee approves the document, it is forwarded to the T1 committee, where the document enters a public comment period during which time *anyone* can make a comment on the draft standard. Again, negative comments must be resolved by the task group. Subsequent drafts again go out for public comment. Only after all of these stages are passed can a standard be formally adopted. Due to the schedule of meetings and the required time period for comments, even a relatively noncontroversial draft standard can take a year or more for formal adoption.

ANSI is playing a significant role in the development of ISDN standards. In particular, the local loop operation (U reference point) for the BRI is standardized in the United States only by ANSI, since it is not the topic of any ITU-T recommendation. ANSI is also actively creating other ISDN, B-ISDN, and related standards for the United States.

ANSI maintains a liaison to the ITU-T and ISO. ANSI standards are often forwarded to the international standards community for adoption worldwide or to form the basis of an international standard.

Bellcore

After the breakup of AT&T, Bellcore was formed as the research and development arm of the seven RBOCs in the United States. Bellcore is an active participant in the national and international standards process.

Bellcore is responsible for defining implementation standards and service requirements for the RBOCs. Historically, Bellcore produced a series of documents. Technical Advisories (TAs) were draft specifications that, after industry review, become Technical References (TRs) for implementation; Framework Advisories (FAs) provided general technology guidance and overview; and Special Reports (SRs) provided general information that was outside the scope of implementation or technology specifications. In 1994, Bellcore adopted a new scheme whereby most technical specifications are called Generic Requirements (GRs).

In 1996, Bellcore was sold to Science Applications International Corporation (SAIC). Prior to that time, Bellcore was funded by the RBOCs. Bellcore has taken a lead role within the United States for defining many aspects of services to be offered by local telephone companies, including ISDN, B-ISDN, Frame Relay, SONET, metropolitan area networks (MANs), switching technology, operations technology, network management, and billing systems. In addition to producing a large number of ISDN-related reports and specifications, they have developed National ISDN, a family of implementation specifications providing guidance to the industry to ensure compatibility between ISDN switches, services, and CPE from multiple vendors.

The European Telecommunications Standards Institute

Anticipating the approach of a single-market economy in the late 1980s, the European Commission published a report that argued that the harmonization of Europe required a pan-European telecommunications network infrastructure based upon standard equipment and services. From this, the European Telecommunications Standards Institute (ETSI) was founded in 1988 to accelerate the development of such standards for the European Union (then called the European Community). ETSI is an independent, self-funded organization, headquartered in France.

ETSI's membership composes over 400 equipment manufacturers, public network service providers, users, and research organizations from over two dozen European countries. About a dozen non-European countries, such as Australia, Canada, Israel, Japan, and the United States, have observer status in ETSI, while the Commission of the European Communities and the European Free Trade Association Secretariat each has a special Counselor status.

ETSI's technical work is performed under the auspices of a Technical Assembly comprised of 11 technical committees (Table D-5) and over 60 subtechnical committees, project teams, and working groups. Like most standards organizations, ETSI works on a consensus basis. Subcommittee's draft documents require technical committee approval before going out for public comment. Technical committees review the document after the public inquiry phase, followed by voting by the national standards organizations of ETSI member countries. Once forwarded by a subtechnical committee, a standard may take nearly a year before it is finally adopted, unless accelerated procedures are adopted. In addition, absolute consensus is not required for adoption of a standard; a document can be approved by a 71 percent weighted vote of the members. Formally approved ETSI specifications are called a European Telecommunications Standard (ETS), while an Interim ETS (I-ETS) is an approved specification that must be discarded or converted to an ETS within 2 to 5 years. Compliance with ETSI standards is voluntary.

Table D-5

ETSI Technical
Committees (1995)

Business TeleCommunications (BTC)*

Equipment Engineering (EE)

Human Factors (HF)

Methods for Testing and Specification (MTS)†

Network Aspects (NA)

Radio Equipment and Systems (RES)‡

Satellite Earth Stations and Systems (SES)

Signaling Protocols and Switching (SPS)

Special Mobile Group (SMG)

Terminal Equipment (TE)

Transmission and Multiplexing (TM)

*Formerly BT.

†Formerly called Advanced Testing Methods (ATM).

‡Includes work of the former Paging Systems (PS) committee.

Other Standards Organizations

There are many other standards organizations that affect computer networking and telecommunications, representing government agencies, professional organizations, and industry. Among these other organizations creating ISDN-related standards are:

■ *ISO.* Formed in 1947, ISO is a nongovernmental organization with a charter to promote the development of worldwide standards to facilitate international cooperation, communication, and commerce. ISO's networking standards include the OSI Reference Model, the

HDLC bit-oriented protocol, international LAN standards, and OSI protocols. ISO has over 100 members, each representing a national standards organization; ANSI is the U.S. representative to ISO.[6]

■ *International Electrotechnical Commission (IEC).*   Created in 1906, the IEC is one of the world's oldest international standards organizations. Focusing on the areas of electronics and electricity, the IEC and ISO closely coordinate their activities and many of their standards are jointly adopted.

■ *National Institute for Standards and Technology (NIST).*   Formerly known as the National Bureau of Standards (NBS), NIST has taken a lead role in defining ISDN applications. In particular, NIST has formed the North American ISDN Users' Forum (NIUF) to identify ISDN applications and to guide and encourage manufacturers in developing those applications that are of most interest to users. The NIUF will be discussed later in this book.

■ *United States Telephone Association (USTA).*   Formerly the U.S. Independent Telephone Association (USITA), the USTA is a national trade association representing local exchange carriers in the United States. Originally founded in 1897, at the time when Alexander Graham Bell's original patents were expiring, the USITA represented the non-Bell, or ITCs. After the breakup of AT&T in 1984, their charter changed to represent all LECs, so the word *independent* was dropped from the name. The USTA provides a broad range of services, including representing the industry before governmental and legislative bodies, hosting an annual trade show, providing training, and producing specifications to enhance network and vendor interoperability.

Other standards bodies focusing on other types of networks affect ISDN as well. The Institute of Electrical and Electronics Engineers (IEEE), an international professional society headquartered in the United States, is accredited by ANSI to produce standards in several areas; in particular, the IEEE 802 Project creates LAN and MAN standards. The Internet Engineering Task Force (IETF) is responsible for producing standards related to the Internet, the international network interconnecting thousands of subnetworks around the world using the TCP/IP protocol suite. Both the IEEE and IETF have generated ISDN-related internetworking specifications.

In the United States, AT&T has long published standards for manufacturers wishing to attach their equipment to the public telephone network. Although local telephone service is not currently offered by AT&T, they manufactured the majority of C.O. switches used by the local telephone

---

[6]The term *ISO* is not an acronym, but comes from the Greek term *isos* meaning *equal.*

companies in the United States today. AT&T technical bulletins and other publications remain industry standards for both local telephone service from the C.O. and long distance services via AT&T's toll network. AT&T continues to play an important role in ANSI and ITU-T standards development. In 1995, the manufacturing portion of AT&T was divested and was incorporated under the name Lucent Technologies. Lucent carries on AT&T's role in standards and equipment advancements.

Industry Consortia

The major standards organizations mentioned above—including ITU, ANSI, and ISO—create *de jure* (by law) standards, meaning that their specifications are mandated by some form of legislation or treaty and provide certain guarantees and/or protections to those who adhere to the standards. Unfortunately, the de jure standards process, as described above, can be very slow. This sometimes leads to standards being adopted that are incomplete or out of date upon publication, leading to a confused marketplace rather than a cohesive one.

In the last several years, a number of important *de facto* (by fact) "standards" organizations have evolved, particularly in the areas of fast packet switching technologies and B-ISDN. These groups were formed as industry consortia to promote and accelerate development of a single technology. All of the consortia involve service providers, equipment vendors, and users and are international in their scope. All include committees working on technical aspects of the technology, as well as public education and awareness. These groups form *implementation agreements* rather than standards; these agreements specify the way in which member companies have agreed to implement these technologies and services but do not provide de jure standards, although the implementation agreements are invariably based on existing de jure standards or are forwarded to appropriate standards organizations.

The most important of the industry consortia for our study of ISDN and related technologies are:

- The ADSL Forum, formed in 1994 to help telephone service providers and equipment vendors realize ADSL's market potential. The ADSL Forum focuses on network, protocol, architectural, and marketing issues related to ADSL, VDSL, and other xDSL technologies.
- The ATM Forum (ATMF), formed in 1991 to address specific implementation issues for ATM services that were not covered in ITU recommendations.

- The Frame Relay Forum (FRF), formed in 1991 to address technical Frame Relay issues that were beyond the scope of the existing ANSI and ITU Frame Relay standards.

- The SMDS Interest Group (SIG), formed in 1991 to promote Bellcore's SMDS specifications. It was started specifically to address technical issues that were beyond the scope of the SMDS user-network interface and to promote awareness of the service. The SIG was disbanded in 1997, ostensibly because it had fulfilled its charter and the service was stable from a technical perspective.

Summary

ISDN terminology is different from today's telecommunications terminology and is, therefore, sometimes cumbersome. Nevertheless, the terms have precise meaning and provide a common language platform with which to discuss ISDN issues.

Similarly, there appear to be an overabundance of standards and organizations that produce them. Each, however, has its own charter and responsibilities. Increasingly, when charters overlap, standards groups cooperate to eliminate redundant standards. However, national and international standards will continue to exist; the international standards bodies will focus on basic operations, procedures, and internetworking while the national standards bodies will focus on issues specific to their country's networks (and which, in some cases, would never be addressed or resolved by an international body).

This appendix has introduced the important ISDN terms and standards organizations. Armed with these, we now look at ISDN services and protocols.

GLOSSARY

AA   Accidental Administrator. A person responsible for their network whose primary duties and training are in other fields.

ADSL   *See* xDSL.

AIM   Advanced Integration Module. New series of add-on boards available for certain routers like the 2600 series.

AMI   Alternate Mark Inversion.

AppleTalk   Apple Computers LAN protocol.

APPN   Advanced Peer-to-Peer Networking. Part of IBM's LAN protocols.

ATM   Asynchronous Transfer Mode. Relatively new scalable WAN and LAN networking technology.

B8ZS   Bipolar 8 Zero Substitution.

B Channel or Bearer Channel   A 64Kbps ISDN channel used to carry voice and data calls.

BGP   Border Gateway Protocol. The dynamic routing protocol used between ISPs to manage extremely large routing tables.

BOD   Bandwidth on Demand. A protocol used with MPPP to add additional dial-up connections, as necessary, to increase bandwidth.

Boot Flash   Flash memory used to store an emergency copy of IOS. If installed, it will take the place of a Boot ROM.

BRI   Basic Rate Interface. Low-speed ISDN connection providing up to 128Kbps of data, two phone lines, or both. It consists of two B (Bearer) channels and one D (Data) channel.

CCO   Cisco Connection Online. Cisco's Web site.

CCP   Console Command Processor. Part of the PPP protocol negotiation.

CDDI   Copper Distributed Data Interface. FDDI LAN technology over copper wire instead of fiber optic cable. 100Mbps.

CDP   Cisco Discovery Protocol. A proprietary Cisco network protocol used by Cisco routers to discover other Cisco routers on the network.

CERT/CC   The Computer Emergency Response Team/Coordination Center. A publicly accessible group dedicated to network security.

CHAP   Challenge Handshake Authentication Protocol. High-security method of authenticating dial-in users in PPP.

CLI   Command Line Interface. The text-based interface common to all IOS-based routers.

CO   Central Office. Any place where the phone company has located telephone switching equipment.

CSU   Channel Service Unit. A device that manages a digital connection to a digital phone line.

CSU/DSU   Channel Service Unit/Data Service Unit. A type of digital modem used for switched and leased data lines.

D Channel or Data Channel   A channel in ISDN lines used to set up calls and carry out-of-band information about the calls. In PRI lines the D channel is 64Kbps. In BRI lines the D channel is 16Kbps.

Data Encryption   A means of implementing security whereby data is encrypted and decrypted on the fly over WAN lines.

DCE   Data Circuit-terminating Equipment or Data Communications Equipment. A type of serial device connection (for example, a modem).

DDR   Dial-on-Demand Routing. Protocol for creating dial-up WAN connections, which are automatically initiated on an as-needed basis.

DEC Net   Digital Equipment Corporation's LAN protocol.

DES   Data Encryption Standard. Available in 40-bit and 56-bit. Method of providing secure connections through data encryption until it was broken in July 1998.

Demarc or Demarcation Point   The physical location where the phone company's responsibility for voice and data lines ends within a given building.

DHCP   Dynamic Host Configuration Protocol. A network protocol used to automatically configure client machines on a network.

DLCI   Data Link Connection Identifier. Identification number for Frame Relay circuits.

DLSW+   Data Link Switching Plus. A legacy networking protocol. A type of serial device connection (for example, a dumb terminal).

DNIS   Dialed Number Identification Service. A telephony standard that can be set on high-speed data lines.

DNS   Domain Name Service. Internet protocol that resolves host names to Internet protocol addresses (i.e., www.btg.com resolves to 204.176.115.69).

DRAM   Dynamic Random Access Memory. *See* Main Memory.

DS0   A data circuit carrying 56Kbps or 64Kbps of information. It may be its own line, or one channel in a DS1 (T1/E1). Can also be referred to as a 56 or 64Kbps leased line.

DS1   A high-capacity data line. Also referred to as a T1 or E1 line.

DSU   Data Service Unit. A device that manages a digital connection to a router.

DTE   Data Terminal Equipment.

DTMF   Dual Tone Multi-Frequency. The standard used by all touch tone dial phones. Each generates two tones, one for the row and one for the column on the keyboard.

E1   Digital leased line that has 2.048Mbps of throughput available. Consists of thirty-two 64Kbps channels. Channels can be ordered as needed from the phone company.

ED   Early Deployment. IOS releases, which deliver support for new features and platforms in their regular maintenance updates.

EIA   Electronic Industries Association. Specifies the serial connector standards, such as EIA-232 (formerly RS-232).

EGP   Exterior Gateway Protocol. A dynamic routing protocol.

EIGRP   Enhanced Interior Gateway Routing Protocol. A Cisco proprietary dynamic routing protocol.

EMI   Electromagnetic Interference.

EPROM   Electronically Programmable ROM. ROM used to hold programs that cannot be changed once they have been loaded into the ROM chip. On Cisco routers, EPROM memory is used to store a scaled-down copy of IOS for emergency boot-up and to allow access to Flash to change IOS code.

ESF   Extended Superframe Format.

Ethernet   Most prevalent LAN technology. 10Mbps.

Ethernet Hub   *See* Hub.

Frame Relay   Wide-area network technology that can provide redundancy of data path and cheaper long haul connections. It does this by creating private paths through a large packet-switched network.

Fast Ethernet   New faster replacement for Ethernet. 100Mbps.

FCS   First Customer Ship. An initial release of any product to the general public.

FDDI   Fiber Distributed Data Interface. Digital fiber optic LAN technology. 100Mbps.

Firewall   A network security device that governs and logs network access between different public and private networks.

Flash Memory   Memory that does not lose its information when powered off. Used like a small hard disk to store router OS. Available as a SIMM or a PCMCIA card, depending on the router using it.

FRAD   Frame Relay Access Device. A network device specifically designed to work on a Frame Relay network.

GD   General Deployment. IOS releases considered stable.

GNU   GNU's Not Unix. The Free Software Foundation's GNU project.

HDLC   High-Level Data Link Control. A method of WAN data encapsulation.

Hexadecimal or Hex   It is a number system with a base of 16 (e.g., 0, 1, 2, 3, 4, 5, 6, 7, 8, 9, A, B, C, D, E, F).

HP   Hewlett Packard. Manufacturer of computer and network hardware and software.

HSSI   High-Speed Serial Interface. High-speed WAN connection supporting speed up to 54Mbps.

HTTP   Hypertext Transport Protocol. Internet standard protocol for WWW connections.

Hub   An active hardware device that connects multiple Ethernet devices together onto the same physical network.

IBM   International Business Machines. A very large multi-national computer company.

ICMP   Internet Control Message Protocol. A higher level protocol, such as TCP, that rides on top of IP, the Internet Protocol. ICMP is used to control aspects of network connections and to debug them. The **ping** and **traceroute** programs send ICMP packets.

IGRP   Interior Gateway Routing Protocol. A dynamic routing protocol proprietary to Cisco.

In-Band   Call information sent through the same channel as the call itself. When a voice call is placed on a POTS line, the tones or clicks used to indicate the number you are dialing are carried on the same line as the call itself.

Inter-LATA   Any phone service that occurs between LATAs.

Intra-LATA   Any phone service that happens within a LATA.

IOS   Internetworking Operating System. The Operating System of most Cisco routers.

IP   Internet Protocol. The main low-level networking protocol that is used on the Internet.

IPCP   Internet Protocol Control Protocol. Part of the PPP protocol negotiation.

IPX/SPX   Internetwork Packet Exchange/Sequenced Packet Exchange. Network protocol used by Novell Netware.

ISDN   Integrated Services Digital Network. Digital phone and data service available to businesses and homes.

ISO   International Organization for Standardization. An international body that works to standardize network protocols and many other things.

ISP   Internet Service Provider. Any company providing Internet access to dial-in or leased-line users.

IXC   Inter-Exchange Carrier. Phone company providing services between LATAs.

L2F   Layer 2 Forwarding Protocol. The underlying link-level technology for both Multichassis MP and Virtual Private Networks.

LAPB   Link Access Procedure Balanced. A method of WAN data encapsulation.

LAN   Local Area Network. A data network contained within a small area, such as a home or a building.

LAT   Local Area Transport. DEC Net remote terminal protocol.

LATA   Local Access and Transport Area. Geographical areas created by the breakup of Bell Telephone.

LCP   Link Control Protocol. Part of the PPP protocol negotiation.

LED   Light Emitting Diode.

MAC Address   Media Access Layer Address, also known as an Ethernet Address. A set of six two-digit hexadecimal numbers burned into an Ethernet product by its manufacturer.

MAC Layer   Media Access Layer.

Main Memory   The memory in the router used to load the OS and perform many generic functions.

MAN   Metropolitan Area Network. A data network spanning multiple sites within a given metropolitan area.

MIB Management Information Base (not Men in Black). SNMP configuration files specific to individual pieces of equipment. Often used by network management software, such as HP OpenView.

MICA Modem ISDN Channel Aggregation. Cisco Trademarked modem/ISDN integration technology.

MMP Multichassis Multilink Point-to-Point Protocol. Cisco protocol that allows multiple connections from a single site to terminate in multiple access servers while still looking like one single larger connection.

MOP Maintenance Operation Protocol. A network file transfer protocol.

MPPP Multi-link PPP. Method of extending PPP so that multiple connections can be added together for higher bandwidth and lower latency. Must be supported at both ends of the connection.

MRTG Multi-Router Traffic Grapher. A free program that graphs statistics taken from routers. Available at http://www.ee.ethz.ch/~oetiker/webtools/mrtg.

NASDAQ National Association of Security/Securities Dealers Automated Quotations. A U.S. stock market that is home for many high-tech companies.

NAT Network Address Translation. A technology used to hide multiple machines behind a single IP address. Can also be used as a firewall.

NFS Network File System. A method of sharing files over a network standardized by SUN Microsystems.

NM Network Module. Type of plug-in module used in 2600 and 3600 routers.

NMS Network Management System. Any product that helps you manage your network (for example, HP OpenView).

NPA/NXX Numbering Plan Area/Network Numbering Exchange. The first six digits of a ten-digit phone number.

NPM Network Processor Module. Type of plug-in module used in 4000 series routers.

NT-1 Network Terminal One. A type of digital modem for ISDN service. The telephone company supplies this everywhere in the world except North America. It is the physical box on-site that converts U-loop into S/T-loop.

NTP Network Time Protocol. A protocol used for synchronizing date and time for computers and routers.

NVRAM Nonvolatile RAM. RAM that, like flash RAM, keeps its information after power is cycled. On Cisco routers, NVRAM is used to store configuration information.

Octothorpe The proper name for the symbol "#".

OS Operating System. The software that tells the router how to work.

OSI Reference Model for Networking A seven-layer network design promoted by ISO.

OSPF Open Shortest Path First. A dynamic routing protocol.

Out-Of-Band Call detail information that is not sent through the same channel as the call itself (i.e., a voice call is carried on an ISDN B channel, but the call setup information—the number to dial, type of call, duration, etc.—is carried on the D channel).

PAP Password Authentication Protocol. Low-security method of dial-in user authentication in PPP.

PCMCIA Personal Computer Memory Card International Association. A standard for PC cards for notebook and laptop computers as well as certain routers. Also, People Can't Memorize Computer Industry Acronyms.

POTS Plain Old Telephone Service. Analog phone lines found in homes and small offices.

PPP Point-to-Point Protocol. Networking protocol used primarily in dial-up modem and ISDN connections. Can also be used over WAN lines.

PPS Packets Per Second. A measure of router speed.

PRI Primary Rate Interface. High-speed ISDN line riding on a T1 or E1 digital leased line. All channels are 64Kbps bearer channels except for one, which is a data channel reserved for call setup and other things.

PROM Programmable Read Only Memory. Usually refers to a chip in hardware that contains software that cannot change unless reprogrammed by special equipment.

PSTN Public Switched Telephone Network. The collection of all the telephone companies and their networks.

Q921 Very low-level ISDN control protocol.

Q931 Higher level ISDN control protocol.

QoS Quality of Service. A method of guaranteeing bandwidth to latency-critical network applications, such as voice over IP.

RADIUS   Remote Authentication Dial-In User Service. A protocol invented by Livingston Enterprises (recently acquired by Lucent) for authenticating dial-in users across multiple dial-in servers.

RAM   Random Access Memory.

RCP   Remote Copy Protocol. The Berkeley network file transfer protocol.

RFI   Radio Frequency Interference.

RFQ   Request for Quotation. A document created by an end user and sent to a vendor asking for a price quote on specific products or services.

RIP   Routing Information Protocol. A dynamic routing protocol often used because WIN NT and UNIX systems can understand it.

RISC   Reduced Instruction Set Computing. A type of computer chip design that is fast for processing certain tasks.

RMON   Remote Network Monitoring. Network monitoring suite of protocols.

RO   Remote Office. Medium-sized office that has a WAN or MAN connection back to a larger corporate network.

ROM   Read Only Memory. Usually refers to a chip in hardware that contains software that cannot be changed. Can also refer to memory that is write protected.

RPS   Redundant Power Supply. The ability to add additional power supplies to a router, making it more resilient with regard to power problems.

RSVP   Resource Reservation Protocol. Part of a suite of protocols used to deliver QoS.

SCO   The Santa Cruz Operations. Manufacturer of UNIX for Intel platforms.

SCSI   Small Computer Systems Interface. A computer peripheral bus, usually used for hard disk drives and CD-ROM readers.

SDSL   *See* xDSL.

SF   Superframe Format.

Shared Memory   Specialized memory available in some routers to keep transient information, such as packet data.

SIMM   Single In-line Memory Module.

SLIP   Serial Line Internet Protocol. A dial-in protocol, such as PPP.

SMDS   Switched Multimegabit Data Service. A type of WAN connection. Usually higher speed than a T1.

SMTP Simple Mail Transfer Protocol. The Internet standard for the exchange of electronic mail.

SNAP Standard Network Access Protocol. Type of Ethernet framing.

SNMP Simple Network Management Protocol. Network protocol used to monitor and manage devices on a network.

SOHO Small Office/Home Office. Small office that has a WAN or MAN connection back to a larger corporate network or the Internet.

SPID System Profile ID. An extremely long phone number for ISDN lines.

STAC Method of on-the-fly data compression.

S/T Loop ISDN service in the home; made to run short distances from an NT-1.

SYN IP packets used to initiate (or synchronize) a network connection.

T1 Digital leased line that has 1.544Mbps of throughput available. Consists of 24 64Kbps channels. Channels can be ordered as needed from the phone company.

TAC Technical Assistance Center. Cisco's technical support center.

TCP Transmission Control Protocol—The main higher level networking protocol used on the Internet to manage data connections.

Telco Abbreviation for Telephone Company.

TIA Telecommunication Industry Association. *See* EIA.

Token Ring Network topology invented and standardized by IBM.

TCP/IP Transmission Control Protocol/Internet Protocol. The combined main protocol for the Internet.

TFTP Trivial File Transfer Protocol. A method of file transfer that does not require passwords. Usually used to back up router configuration information and IOS images.

U Loop ISDN service brought to the home by the phone company. Made to run long distances from the phone company CO to the end-user location.

UDP User Datagram Protocol. A higher level protocol, such as TCP, that sits above IP, the Internet Protocol.

VIC Voice Interface Card. Plug-in cards used in 2600, 3600, and AS5300 series routers to route voice over IP.

VIP Versatile Interface Processors. Network interface modules for high-end routers; not covered in this book.

VPDN   Virtual Private Dial-Up Networking. Encrypted dial-up connections.

VPN   Virtual Private Networks. Encrypted network connections.

WAN   Wide-Area Network. A data network that spans a large geographical area.

WFQ   Weighted Fair Queuing. . Part of a suite of protocols used to deliver QoS.

WIC   WAN Interface Card. WAN modules for certain Cisco routers.

WINS   Windows Internet Name Service. Hostname to IP address resolution protocol used by Microsoft file-sharing.

X.25   A packet-switched WAN technology.

xDSL   Digital Subscriber Line. A new high-speed data service just becoming available to homes and businesses. Can be synchronous or asynchronous.

INDEX

A